Pennsylvania Native Plants

PERENNIALS: HABITAT AND CULTURE

GEOFFREY MEHL

THE PENNYSTONE PROJECT

www.pennystone.com

ABOUT THE PENNYSTONE PROJECT

The Pennystone Project explores landscape applications of plants indigenous to Pennsylvania and encourages stewardship of the varied and complex ecosystems found in the northern Appalachians.

The case for sustainable landscape practices and the merits of broad conservation issues are widely discussed elsewhere. Our focus is on detailed and comprehensive information as a resource to gardeners in the development of personal landscapes.

Visit the project website at http://www.pennystone.com

Pennsylvania Native Plants / Perennials: Habitat and Culture
ISBN-13: 978-0615606415

Published by Pennystone Books, Henryville, Pennsylvania

CONTENTS

Contents

INTRODUCTION

Success with native plants in home landscapes begins with a different perspective. Instead of adapting a site to a design, the site drives the design. Instead of controlling appearance, we collaborate with nature. Instead of standardized artistic expression, we celebrate serendipity. We are not the master, but the steward, and with our stewardship we participate, rather than dominate.

Everyone wants a "simple" garden: easy, quick, affordable, low-maintenance, pest-free, constantly blooming, perfectly groomed, durable for the kids and dog, plus loaded with curb appeal. It adds up to anything but simple.

It's very easy to venture forth on the first balmy days of spring to the local garden center and browse the aisles for impulse purchases that might, say, add a nice touch of color to that forlorn area near the forsythia, along with the chemicals to enforce it. It's easy to be enchanted by the colorful array of landscaping books lurking near the checkout counters of the local home center. And it's really easy to hire a landscape contractor to bring in heavy equipment, truckloads of material, make all the decisions and depart with a check that has too many zeroes.

But ours is a different path. We're thinking green in the context of the environment, not money. We're anxious about the state of the planet and want to make a difference. We're discarding artificial and embracing natural. We rather like butterflies (and spiders, too). In a complicated world, we crave a little patch of serenity.

While there are many gorgeous coffee-table books to inspire us and many exciting conservation areas to intrigue us, native plants in the home landscape can be an uncertain territory of trial and error.

So let's simplify a few things and have some fun. The goal of The Pennystone Project is to sift through all the data and gather information useful to gardeners in Pennsylvania and perhaps avoid frustration and disappointment. With nearly 1,000 native perennials available from reputable vendors, the first step is to do some kitchen table detective work. What matters most with native plants is matching them up with the appropriate habitat.

We have several options:

> To include some natives with an existing landscape, we need to find those that fit in nicely with our old favorites.

> To represent a variety of ecosystems in a landscape, we need to group plants appropriately for the types of microhabitats we plan to create – rain gardens, woody slopes, rock gardens, meadows, even water and streams.

> To landscape specifically for the type of site we have, we need to develop a list of plants that match the local habitat.

If we know the sort of circumstances each plant prefers in the wild, and if we have a sense of garden conditions that work, we have a good start. As we continue to browse, we assemble a workable list, and from height and bloom information we can organize a design. After that, we need to know where to shop.

WHAT'S NATIVE, WHAT MATTERS

All native plants are wildflowers, but not all wildflowers are native plants. By virtually all standards, a native plant is a species that was comfortably ensconced on the North American continent when the Europeans stepped off the boat... with a sack of seeds and some potted plants. They farmed. They timbered. They brought in more plants, not all of them very nice (some have gone on to fame as invasives). They built cities and towns and factories and roads to connect them. They did not do vegetation mapping.

Like all scientists, botanists like stuff neat and orderly. Over time, they separated natives from non-natives and began to map *range* – the areas on the continent where a given species grows. As they progressed, they began to chart *distribution* within states. This led to the temptation of parochial thinking. Is this plant native to our state ... our county? And if it isn't, should we put it in our garden?

This leads to some disconcerting dilemmas. Several species of plants – all native to North America – are considered "introduced" to Pennsylvania. Many splendid landscape species are rare and found in narrowly defined geographic regions within the state – but may well flourish in our garden.

But consider that range maps are based on historical records and contemporary observations and accordingly draw a fluid line on a national map. Distribution reflects field observations within the past 75 years or so, usually on public land, and rather than setting up arbitrary rules should prompt questions: what sort of habitat does it prefer? Is there a pattern? Is it only here because it's fussy, or because this is the last refuge in a fully-developed state? Does it depend on the presence of other species? Is the ecotype genetically appropriate?

These are the nagging issues that keep conservationists and restoration ecologists awake at night, but they should not concern home landscapers. After all, a garden is an artistic expression, a compression of nature, a recreational endeavor. So gardeners have the luxury of accepting the definition of "native" as indigenous to the continent, of recognizing that plants within a range are fair game for the landscape, and that distribution patterns provide clues that help whittle the palette down to manageable size. We can even keep old introduced favorites and add natives useful to existing landscapes.

Among natives, there is much to work with. For the record, 1,925 species of native plants reside in Pennsylvania. Of these, 281 are annuals (50 of which are commercially available, always as seed). Among perennials, 662 do not appear to be commercially available, and so our list is whittled down to a convenient 982 species, a decent number for starters.

These numbers do not include *bryophytes* – mosses, lichens, liverworts – which are non-vascular plants, many in number, and have limited range and cultivation information.

Among the perennial species we'll investigate:

Trees and shrubs: 241 commercially available species, a list of 19 that do not appear to be available. Trees and shrubs are lumped together because in many cases, one man's shrub is another man's tree, an issue that involves many of the understory layers of forests and woodlands. In all cases, height ranges are listed to help us decide for ourselves. All trees flower, but most are relatively inconspicuous. Many shrubs and some small trees are cultivated for floral displays, however, so flower color and bloom time is included.

Ferns (pteridophytes), including fern allies, are herbaceous vascular plants that reproduce by spores rather than flowers. Of 93 species found in Pennsylvania, 50 are commercially available (although fern enthusiasts often exchange spores, so many more are possible). There are two general types of ferns: those with an upright, non-spreading rhizome and those with spreading, or creeping rhizomes that form colonies from expanding root systems. Fern allies include club mosses and horsetails. Size is expressed in frond length.

Grasses, sedges and rushes (graminoids): 201 commercially available species, many as seed, and 212 species that do not appear to be commercially available. Sizes are described in terms of total height. These plants are generally ignored by deer and with good selection and management can create dramatic landscapes. Some species are short enough to be considered as lawn alternatives, but rarely can be cut lower than 3 inches. Some vendors sell seed mixes for various types of habitats and purposes.

Vines (woody and herbaceous) – 25 commercially available species, 23 not available. Size is generally described in terms of how many feet the plant can extend from a single base, and flower color/season when of interest to landscapers. Although vines in the wild can be troublesome to trees and shrubs, they offer interesting landscape opportunities for arbors and privacy fences.

Forbs (all other flowering plants) – 465 commercially available species and 365 listed that do not appear in the commercial marketplace. Listings include size ranges, flower color/season and some landscape suggestions. Light requirements and soils are critical factors in choosing species for our individual landscapes.

DODGING PAROCHIALISM

In this discussion, we have quite deliberately avoided describing distribution on the basis of counties except when a species is so rare that the only observed sites are very narrowly reported. Instead, our discussion leads us to more regional thinking (south or north, east or west, perhaps general quadrants – southeast, southwest, northeast, northwest) to give us a general sense of distribution patterns.

Additionally, specific area concentrations are identified by U.S. Forest Service (USFS) *ecoregions* (see map). All these extend beyond Pennsylvania's borders and are identified by numbers and names as *sections* of three larger *provinces*:

Laurentian Mixed Forest
212F – Northern Glaciated Allegheny Plateau
212G – Northern Unglaciated Allegheny Plateau

Eastern Broadleaf Forest
221A – Lower New England
221B – Hudson Valley
221C – Upper Atlantic Coastal Plain
221D – Northern Appalachian Piedmont

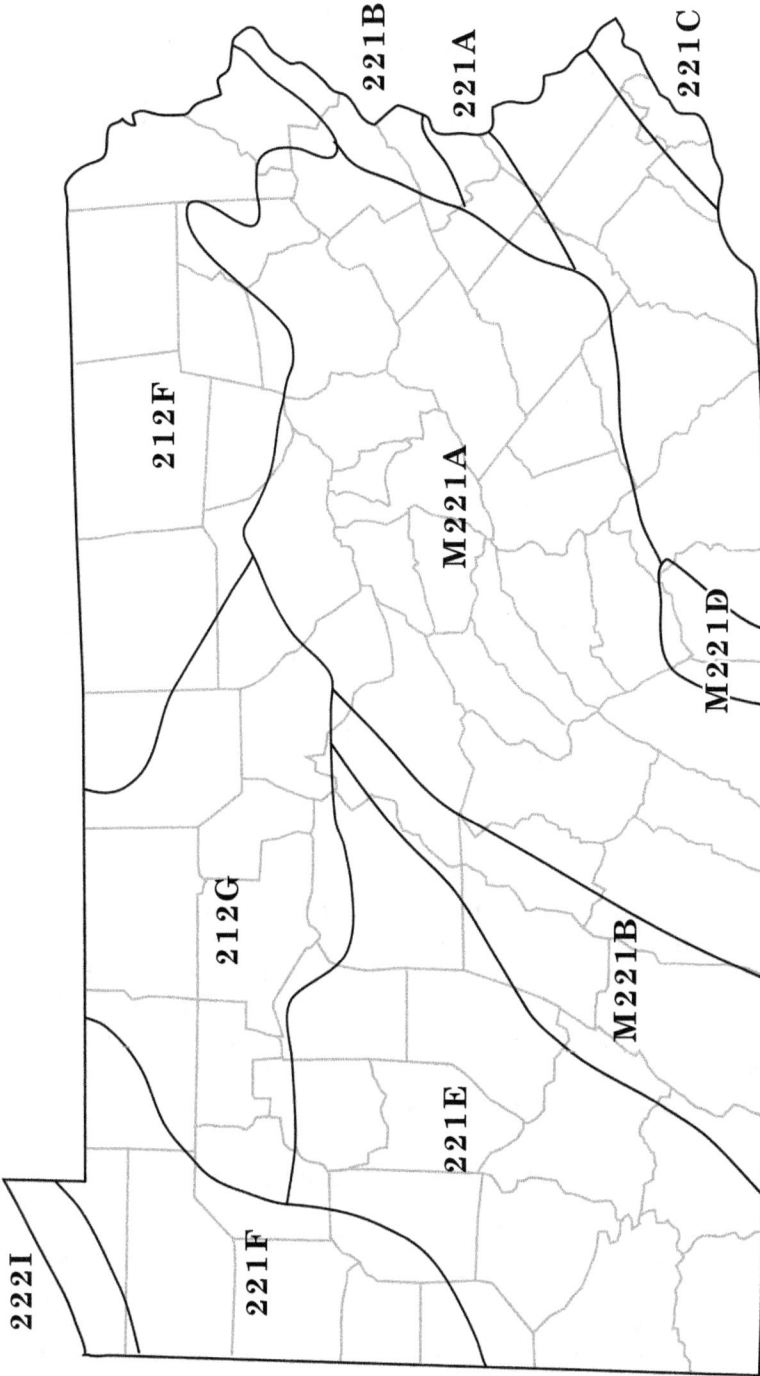

Legend: 212F - Northern Glaciated Allegheny Plateau; 212G - Northern Unglaciated Allegheny Plateau; 221B - Hudson Valley Section, Eastern Broadleaf Forest; 221A - Lower New England Section, Eastern Broadleaf Forest; 221C - Atlantic Coastal Plain; 221D - Northern Piedmont Section, Eastern Broadleaf Forest; M221A - Northern Ridge and Valley Section, Central Appalachians; M221D - Blue Ridge Mountains; M221B - Allegheny Mountains; 221E - Southern Unglaciated Allegheny Plateau; 221F - Western Glaciated Allegheny Plateau; 222I - Erie and Ontario Lake Plain

221E – Southern Unglaciated Allegheny Plateau
221F – Western Glaciated Allegheny Plateau
222I – Erie and Ontario Lake Plain

Central Appalachian Broadleaf Forest – Coniferous Forest – Meadow
M221A – Northern Ridge and Valley
M221B – Allegheny Mountains
M221D – Blue Ridge Mountains

For the sake of simplicity in our lists, we refer to:

"The northern Allegheny plateaus" as including Northern Glaciated, Northern Unglaciated and Western Glaciated plateaus

"Central Appalachians" as including Northern Ridge and Valley, Allegheny Mountains and Blue Ridge Mountains.

"Piedmont" as including the Northern Appalachian Piedmont and the Lower New England

"Southern Allegheny Plateau" as including the Southern Unglaciated Allegheny Plateau

"The western Allegheny plateaus" as including Western Glaciated and Southern Unglaciated Allegheny plateaus and the Allegheny Mountains.

"The Allegheny front" – the very eastern edge of the Allegheny Mountains and very western edge of the Northern Ridge and Valley section.

They are not the only maps; the U.S. Environmental Protection Agency has one, and the National Resource Conservation Service of the U.S. Department of Agriculture has another. They are slightly different in boundaries, substantially different in names, and defined in different ways. But USFS ecoregions are especially helpful because they are used in ongoing research of *ecological communities*, which identify the composition of *plant associations* – i.e., what trees, shrubs and herbaceous plants often grow together. (The Pennystone Project discusses them all, with maps, on its website at www.pennstone.com.)

HABITAT DESCRIPTIONS MATTER

Many field guides and botanical research sources provide brief notes on habitat preferences, from which we can fashion a richly detailed mosaic. Some, for example, describe *Actaea racemosa* (black cohosh) habitat as "rich woods," and many field guides might simply say "found in woods." But data from several create greater texture: "rich moist woods, wooded slopes, ravines, along riverbanks and thickets." This helps us in one of two ways. If we landscape strictly appropriate to habitat, we know whether a plant is likely to fit in or not. If we are creating a habitat for a specific kind of plant in our landscape design, we know what sort of conditions it likes.

Additional help comes from the U.S. Fish and Wildlife Service, which developed "wetland indicators" in the 1980s to help support wetlands protection and preservation. Thousands of plant species were nationally and regionally categorized within these indicator sets, based on probability of occurrence in a wetland – floodplains, swamps, bogs, fens, seeps. (Pennsylvania is in Region 1).

Is a particular species more likely to be found in a wetland or an upland? Or some where in between? The result are helpful codes that appear all the time in discussions about native plants:

OBL – Obligate Wetland: occurs almost always (estimated probability 99%) under natural conditions in wetlands.

FACW – Facultative Wetland: usually occurs in wetlands (estimated probability 67%-99%), but occasionally found in non-wetlands.

FAC – Facultative: equally likely to occur in wetlands or non-wetlands (estimated probability 34%-66%).

FACU – Facultative Upland: usually occurs in non-wetlands (estimated probability 67%-99%), but occasionally found on wetlands (estimated probability 1%-33%).

UPL – Obligate Upland: occurs in wetlands in another region, but occurs almost always (estimated probability 99%) under natural conditions in non-wetlands in the regions specified. *If a species does not occur in wetlands in any region, it is not on the National List. If there's no code after the name, it is not found in wetlands.*

NI – No indicator: insufficient information was available to determine an indicator status; in the absence of an indicator, our discussion says nothing, but USDA relies on this for the same purpose in their materials.

To refine it even further, plus (+) and minus (-) signs in the FACW, FAC, and FACU categories indicate a tendency toward (+) wetland or away (-) from wetland.

If a species is designated UPL, it's probably going to prefer much dryer habitat than if it is designated OBL. For example, water lilies are always found in wet circumstances and cacti are usually found in dry ground. If it's FAC, it can handle being periodically flooded, but will also do fine on drier, often moist soil. FACU can infer a tendency toward upland, while FACW can infer a tendency toward wetland. While it's not by any means an absolute rule (many FACU plants are listed as being found in "wet meadows" or "moist woods"), it can help the landscaper group plants of similar nature for the sake of appropriate care with water supply.

And there's evidence to suggest that plants in the FACU, FAC and FACW categories, do a bit of fudging on their own. Many natives evolve in special ways, resulting in *ecotypes* or gene pools adapted to very specific circumstances. Not all Pennsylvania red maples (*Acer rubrum*) are the same. Some will do quite well in southern swampy areas, while others are genetically adapted to northern upland slopes.

These subtle variances create special challenges for conservation ecologists doing restoration work. The task is to find and install a correct ecotype for a specific, narrow region. The lesson for gardeners is to shop as locally as possible – and some vendors even identify ecotypes of the material they sell.

IS IT ENDANGERED?

Pennsylvania's Department of Conservation and Natural Resources publishes materials related to species that are protected because of some degree of peril: rare, threatened, endangered and extirpated. Our discussion of each species mentions those that are endangered or extirpated and a complete list of Pennsylvania's 540 rare, threatened, endangered and extirpated species appears in an appendix.

Endangered species offer us intriguing opportunities and challenges. Some find it enchanting to create a haven for them, and others get excited about anything rare. But it goes without saying that it is *not* appropriate to dig them up and transplant them from the wild. Even when skilled conservationists become involved in legitimate plant rescue operations, the task is extraordinary difficult and likelihood of failure is high. Stick to reputable nurseries that propagate plants legitimately.

SUN, SHADE AND POINTS IN BETWEEN

Veterans of native plant landscaping provide tips and suggestions and observations for success in gardening conditions, typically concerning light, soils and moisture.

Light conditions include:

Full sun – unobstructed sunlight throughout the entire day.

Sun – at least six to eight hours of direct sun daily.

Part sun – sunlight for a little over half the day, especially midday to afternoon, but also light shade coming from a high, thin canopy.

Part shade – sunlight for a little less than half the day, especially in the morning but also including moving pools of sunlight (dappled shade).

Shade – sunlight only in briefly moving pools of dappled light, or brief periods of sun early or very late in the day.

Full, or deep, shade – continuous shaded conditions, all day long.

Sun/shade terms are imprecise; one person's "part sun" can be another's "part shade," so it's generally best to err on the sunnier side. This is especially true of plants listed as "sun to part shade."

Additionally, many spring ephemerals are technically "part sun" to "sun" plants, but grow in deciduous shade, having bloomed in the sunshine available before tree canopies leaf out and sometimes going dormant before summer heat and dry periods arrive.

AN INTRODUCTION TO SOILS

An entire field of study is devoted to soil science – what it's made of, how it evolves, how it moves, where it came from and how it works. Every inch of Pennsylvania has been mapped, and a couple of free services allow us to identify a *soil series* within a half acre or so. The Pennystone Project's website lists all the soil patterns for all the counties, and has step-by-step instructions on how to identify yours within a few minutes.

Soils are often described as variants of *loams* – which means a soil composed of a reasonable combination of sands, silts and clays. *Rich* soils include substantial amounts of organic matter that often help retain moisture while being well-drained. *Humusy* soils are mineral topsoils that have a relatively thick layer of decomposed matter on or in the immediate surface.

Soil moisture is described as:

wet – frequently saturated and almost always moist, such as bogs, swamps and fens.

mesic – regularly moistened, but neither wet or dry for extended periods, common in many meadows and lower woodland slopes.

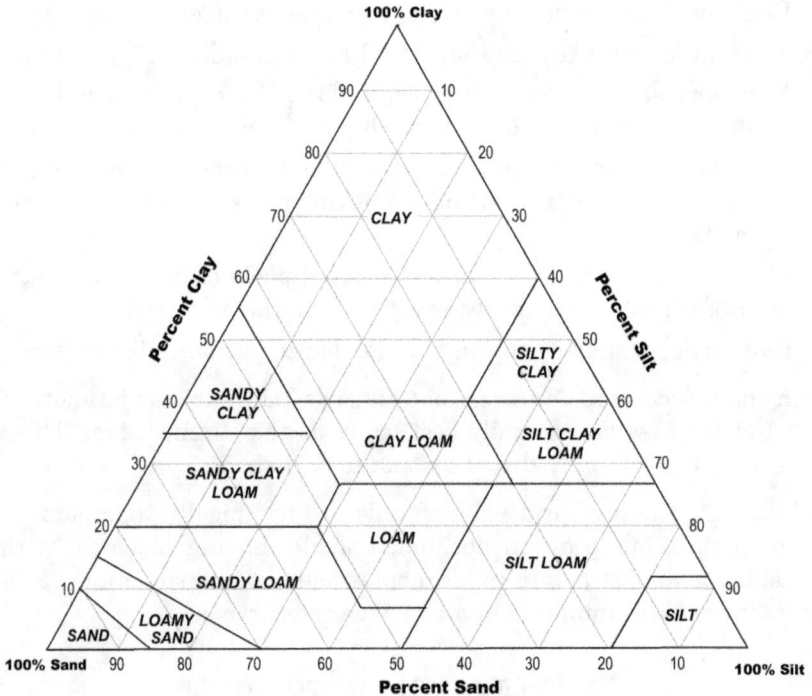

USDA chart defines common expressions relating to the mineral loams. Follow lines for any two of the three values (sand, silt and clay) to intersect points, which then defines the type of loam.

dry – generally dry, usually because it is well drained (sandy) – including higher slopes, but also some floodplains and prairies.

xeric – almost constantly dry, either as a consequence of infrequent water or being excessively well drained (thin soil ridgetops and high slopes facing south and west can often be dry to xeric).

mucky – very high in clays and silts, or in bogs almost entirely organic matter, constantly wet.

SOIL CHEMISTRY

In nature, the exact mineral composition of soil matters, sometimes a great deal. Sand, silt and clay are simply rock ground down to various sizes – which affects how easily water passes through it and how much air roots get. Plants draw minerals from the rock when water reacts with it to form solutions that roots can take up, so the chemical reactions often define how suitable a soil is for a specific species of plant.

How soil reacts (*soil reactivity*) is typically measured as a pH value to describe relative acidity or alkalinity.

On a scale of 0 to 14, pH 7.0 is neutral. The lower the value, the more acidic, and higher values are more alkaline. Because the scale is logarithmic, not linear, pH 6.0 is ten times more acidic than pH 7.0, and pH 5.0 is 100 times more acidic than pH 7.0. Very acidic habitats, such as bogs, can be less than pH 4.0, and mosses thrive in pH ranges of 5 to 6. Lawns and many garden vegetables prefer the pH 6.8 neighborhood.

Most native plants prefer an acidic to slightly acidic soil, but some are more comfortable with slightly alkaline soils. Those that do best right around 7.0 are said to prefer *circumneutral* soils.

Alkaline soils are common in Pennsylvania, mostly resulting from sedimentary deposits of limestone and dolomite. The expression *calcareous* is often used to describe slightly alkaline soils. On the other hand, bedrock composed of sandstones, siltstones and shales is most often acidic to varying degrees, and the leaf litter of many trees forms acidic humus layers.

Where data is available, the general and preferred pH ranges for species are listed. A complete county-by-county soil list is available at The Pennystone Project website (www.pennystone.com), along with instructions on how to locate the soil series in any location statewide.

PLANT AVAILABILITY

The commercial marketplace for native plants continues to grow. A number of nurseries have even developed cultivars of some species. Retail centers, as well as periodic plant sales by conservation-oriented organizations remain somewhat scattered, so shopping for natives often involves some travel or taking advantage of mail-order companies. To help connect buyers with reputable sellers (retail and wholesale), the University of Minnesota Libraries offers a free online service at http://plantinfo.umn.edu/. A criteria for being listed is a willingness to sell by mail-order – seeds, live plants or bare-root dormant plants.

In our discussion, each species listed was searched at Minnesota and, based on numbers of vendors listed, a plant was assigned a value of many, several, few or no sources. Those that were not found are listed here as "unavailable." Generally speaking, the closer the source of the plant to an individual garden, the more preferred; native plants may all be the same species, but many have genetically adapted to regional climates and consequently are more likely to thrive.

TREES AND SHRUBS

Abies balsamea (Balsam fir) – boreal and northern forests on mountain slopes, glaciated uplands and alluvial flats, peatlands, and swamps in pure, mixed coniferous, and mixed coniferous–deciduous stands, FAC. Mostly northeast (Northern Glaciated Allegheny Plateau); scattered northern tier. Grows to 65 feet; all soil textures from heavy clay to rocky; tolerates a wide range of soil acidity. Prefers cool, acidic wet–mesic sites, pH 5.1 to 6.0; many sources.

Acer negundo (Box–elder) – moist sites along lakes and streams, on floodplains and in low–lying wet places, FAC+. Mostly southeast (Central Appalachians, Piedmont, Atlantic Coastal Plain) and southwest (Southern Allegheny Plateau); scattered elsewhere. Grows 30 to 50 feet; wide variety of soils from gravel to clay but prefers well–drained deep, sandy loam, loam, or clay loam soils with a medium to rocky texture and a pH of 6.5 to 7.5; many sources.

Acer pensylvanicum (Moosewood) – moist, acid soils in deep valleys and on cool, moist, shaded, north–facing slopes, FACU. Statewide, except scattered southeast (Piedmont). Grows to 45 feet; small forest openings and under thinned overstories in part shade; prefers cool, moist well–drained loam; several sources.

Acer rubrum (Red maple) (*var. rubrum*) and Trident red maple (*var. trilobum*) – wet to dry sites in dense woods and in openings in low, rich woods, along the margins of lakes, marshes, and swamps, in hammocks, wet thickets, and on floodplains and stream terraces; also occurs in drier upland woodlands, low–elevation cove forests, dry sandy plains, and on stable dunes. FAC (*var. rubrum*) and FACW+ (*var. trilobum*); statewide. Grows 40 to 70 feet; wide variety of soils; develops best on moist, fertile, loamy soils but also dry, rocky, upland soils; many sources.

Acer saccharinum (Silver maple) – streamside communities and lake fringes, and occasionally in swamps, gullies, and small depressions of slow drainage, FACW. Statewide, especially southeast (Piedmont). Grows 50 to 80 feet; average, medium to wet soils in full sun to part shade. Prefers moist soils, but tolerant of poor dry soils; pH range 4.5 to 7.0; many sources.

Acer saccharum (Sugar maple) – rich, mesic woods and drier upland woods, on level areas or in coves, ravines and other sheltered locations on adjacent lower especially north–facing slopes. Often associated with stream terraces, stream banks, valleys, canyons, ravines, and wooded natural levees; occasionally found on dry rocky hillsides, FACU, statewide. Grows to 80 feet; wide variety of soils derived from shale, limestone and sandstone, but prefers deep, moist, fertile, well–drained sandy to silty loam; also associated with alluvial or calcareous soils. Intolerant of flooded soils and grows poorly on dry, shallow soils; pH 3.7 to 7.3 but prefers pH ranges 5.5 to 7.3; many sources.

Acer spicatum (Mountain maple) – cool woods where the climate is humid and precipitation is year–round, including flats, bogs, and along streams, but also occurs on drier and well–drained acidic soils such as talus slopes and cliff faces, FACU–; statewide. Grows to 35 feet; sun to part shade in moist cool acidic soil; a few sources.

Aesculus glabra (Ohio buckeye) – Bottomlands and moist stream banks, 60 to 80 feet, FACU+; mostly southwest (Southern Allegheny Plateau) and southeast (Piedmont). Average, well–drained soils in full sun to part shade; prefers fertile and moist soil; many sources.

Alnus incana ssp. rugosa (Speckled alder) – moist lowlands, frequently along streams and lakes; common in swamps and the older zones of bogs; statewide, except southeast (Piedmont). Shrub to 20 feet; sun to shade in moist rich loam; a few sources.

Alnus serrulata (Smooth alder or Hazel alder) – stream banks, ditches, edges of sloughs, swampy fields and bogs, and lakeshores, OBL. Statewide, especially southeast (Piedmont, Atlantic Coastal Plain), except north (northern Allegheny plateaus). Shrub to 20 feet; sun to shade in moist to wet circumneutral fine sandy loams, peats and mucks. Very flood tolerant. Alders fix nitrogen and thus serve as nutrient–giving pioneers in reclamation projects; a few sources.

Alnus viridis ssp. crispa (Mountain alder) – very rare as isolated individuals or in thickets adjacent to lakeshores, streams, bogs; on sandy to gravelly slopes and flats or cool, rocky wooded slopes; FAC; widely scattered and endangered. Typically 6 to 12 feet on rocky, dry, acidic but cool sites in full sun to shade; a few sources.

Amelanchier arborea (Shadbush) – swampy lowlands, dry open woodlands and sandy bluffs, rocky ridges, forest edges and fields, FAC–; statewide. Shrub or small tree to 48 feet; well–drained silty clay loam and poorly drained silt loams. White flowers in early spring; a few sources.

Amelanchier canadensis (Shadbush) – moist upland woods and edges, bogs, and swamps, FAC. Mostly southeast (Piedmont, Atlantic Coastal Plain), scattered elsewhere. Shrub or small tree to 20 feet; average, medium, well–drained soil in full sun to part shade. Tolerant of a somewhat wide range of soils. Often confused in the nursery trade with *A. arborea*. White flowers in spring; many sources.

Amelanchier humilis (Low juneberry) – dry open ground, rocky bluffs and lakeshores, FACU. Widely scattered, especially Allegheny Mountains. Shrub to 20 feet; sun to part shade in dry acidic sandy loam. White flowers in spring; a few sources.

Amelanchier laevis (Allegheny serviceberry, or smooth serviceberry) – thickets, open woods, sheltered slopes, roadside banks and wood margins; statewide. Shrub to 45 feet; full sun to part shade in average, mesic sandy loams. Tolerant of a wide range of soils, but prefers moist, well–drained loams. White flowers in spring; many sources.

Amelanchier sanguinea (Roundleaf serviceberry) – very rare on hillsides, woods; rocky slopes, barrens, UPL; widely scattered and endangered. Shrub or small tree to 20 feet; sun to part shade in dry to moist, rocky, well–drained soil. White flowers in spring; a few sources.

Amelanchier stolonifera (Low juneberry) – woods, old fields, fence rows and barrens, FACU; statewide, especially northern end of Central Appalachians. Colonizing shrub to 6 feet; full sun to part shade in mesic to moist, well–drained soil in full sun to part shade. Tolerant of a wide range of soils. White flowers in spring; several sources.

Amorpha fruticosa (False–indigo) – open woods, pond and stream edges, gravel bars in floodplains, roadsides, thickets, FACW; mostly southeast (Piedmont); scattered southwest. Grows 6 to 12 feet with violet to purple flowers in late spring. Grow in sun to part shade in moist sandy to clayey loams; many sources.

Andromeda polifolia var glaucophylla (Bog rosemary) – rare on moist to wet acidic peaty ground, OBL; mostly northeast (Northern Glaciated Allegheny Plateau); scattered northwest. To 18 inches.; part sun to part shade in acidic moist organic peats, sands and mucks. Pinkish–white flowers in spring; a few sources.

Aralia spinosa (Devil's walking stick) – upland and low woods, thickets, stream edges, palustrine wetlands and savannahs; prefers sites with deep, acidic, sandy peat soils, FAC. Statewide, especially west (Southern Allegheny Plateau). Shrub or tree to 32 feet; part shade in well–drained fertile to poor soils. Aggressive spreader via suckers; several sources.

Arctostaphylos uva–ursi ssp. coactilis (Bearberry or kinnikinnick) – very rare in dry nutrient–poor soils, often in open pine forests during intermediate succession; scattered northeast (Northern Glaciated Allegheny Plateau) and northwest (Western Glaciated Allegheny Plateau, Ontario and Erie Lake Plain); believed to be extirpated. Prostrate stems; sun to shade in dry to mesic uncompacted or loose rocky or sandy acidic soil. Intolerant of fertilizer. Pinkish white flowers in early spring; many sources.

Asimina triloba (Pawpaw) – Ravine slopes, stream banks and floodplains with deep, rich, moist soils ranging from sandy to clayey, 10 to 40 feet, FACU+; statewide except northern Allegheny plateaus. Average medium to wet soils but prefers acidic, fertile, moist soil. Sun to part shade, but becomes leggy in shade; many sources.

Baccharis halimifolia (Groundsel–tree) – rare in marshes (including salt), beaches and other sandy places and disturbed sites such as wet fields and roadsides, FACW; mostly southeast (Atlantic Coastal Plain) Grows up to 10 feet in circumneutral, wet to droughty, gravels to fine sands; wet sandy loams in part shade are preferred; a few sources.

Betula alleghaniensis (Yellow birch) – stream banks, swampy woods, and rich, moist, forested slopes, FAC, statewide. Grows to 100 feet; well–drained fertile loams and moderately well–drained sandy loams; several sources.

Betula lenta (Sweet birch) – rich, moist, cool forests, especially on protected slopes, to rockier, more exposed sites, FACU, statewide. Grows to 80 feet; part shade to shade in dry to moist slightly acidic rich, moist, well drained soil; several sources.

Betula nigra (River birch) – alluvial, often clay, soils on lowlands, floodplains, stream banks, and lake margins. Typically on sandbars and new land near streams, inside natural levees or fronts. Sometimes found on scattered upland sites, FACW. Mostly southeast (Central Appalachians, Piedmont). Grows to 100 feet; alluvial, clay soils in full sun to part sun with high soil moisture. Soil can be well or poorly drained as long as it is at or near field capacity year round. Can grow in highly acidic (pH less than 4) soils; many sources.

Betula papyrifera (Paper birch) – moist open upland forests, especially on rocky slopes, and sometimes in swampy woods, FACU. Mostly northeast (Northern Glaciated and Unglaciated Allegheny Plateaus), scattered elsewhere. Grows to 100 feet; sun to part sun in moist mineral–organic soil, pH above 5.0; prefers cooler north to northeast facing slopes with slow drainage and little competition; many sources.

Betula populifolia (Gray birch) – rocky or sandy open woods, moist to somewhat dry slopes, old fields, and waste places, FAC, statewide (mostly east), except southwest (Southern Allegheny Plateau). Grows to 32 feet; sun to shade in dry to moist, poor soils, wide range of pH; a few sources.

Calycanthus floridus var. laevigatus (Carolina allspice) – rare in deciduous and mixed woodlands, along streams and rivers, and woodland margins, FACU+; widely scattered statewide. Grows 6 to 10 feet, reddish–purple flowers in early summer; full sun to part shade in well–drained, medium moisture, average soil; prefers rich loams, and will grow taller in shade than in sun. Tends to sucker and will form colonies in the wild; many sources. A variety, *var. floridus* is introduced and has escaped cultivation, southwest.

Carpinus caroliniana (Hornbeam) – rich, deciduous forests along stream banks, on flood plains, and on moist hillsides, FAC; statewide. Tree to 30 feet; average, medium moisture soil in part shade to full shade. Prefers moist, organically rich soils; many sources.

Carya cordiformis (Bitternut hickory) – river flood plains, well–drained hillsides and limestone glades, FACU+; statewide. Grows to 100 feet; dry to moist rich, loamy or gravelly soil; a few sources.

Carya glabra (Pignut hickory) – deep flood plains, well–drained sandy soils, rolling hills and slopes, dry rocky soils, or thin soils on edge of granite outcrops, FACU–; statewide except north (Northern Glaciated and Unglaciated Allegheny Plateaus). Grows to 100 feet; light, well–drained, loamy soils derived from a variety of sedimentary or meta-morphic parent material, n full sun to part shade; a few sources.

Carya laciniosa (Shellbark hickory) – moist, rich bottomlands and slopes, especially along creeks and in cedar glades. FAC; mostly southeast (Piedmont). Grows to 100 feet in full sun on moist sandy to clayey soils of a wide pH range; a few sources.

Carya ovata (Shagbark hickory) – wet bottomlands, rocky hillsides, and limestone outcrops, FACU; statewide. Grows to 100 feet; humusy, rich, moist, well–drained loams in full sun to part shade; many sources.

Carya tomentosa (Mockernut hickory) – moist rocky open woods and slopes; less common on alluvial bottomlands; statewide except north (northern Allegheny plateaus). Grows to 100 feet; wide variety of moist soils; prefers finely textured, organic sandy loams; a few sources.

Castanea dentata (American chestnut) – rich deciduous and mixed forests, particularly with oak; statewide. Tree to 20 feet; moist, well–drained loams in full sun. Formerly very common and a forest dominant before dieback due to chestnut blight. Rarely lives longer than 15 to 20 years; several sources.

Castanea pumila (Chinquapin) – dry to moist slopes in open woodlands and forest understory as well as dry to wet sandy barrens. Mostly southeast (Piedmont and Coastal Plain). Grows 10 to 30 feet in well drained soils in full sun to part shade; a few sources.

Ceanothus americanus (New Jersey tea) – dry open plains and prairie–like areas, on sandy or rocky soils in woodland clearings, edges and slopes, on riverbanks or lakeshores; statewide. Shrub to 3 feet; sun to part shade in dry to mesic sandy rocky loam. White flowers in late spring; many sources.

Celtis occidentalis (Dogberry) – rich moist soil along streams, on flood plains and rocky wooded hillsides and woodlands, FACU; mostly southeast (Piedmont), scattered elsewhere. Grows to 110 feet; prefers moist, organically rich, well–drained soils in full sun. Tolerates part shade, wind, many urban pollutants and a wide range of soil conditions, including both wet, dry and poor soils; many sources.

Celtis tenuifolia (Dwarf hackberry) – shale banks and slopes along streams in open woods, dry wooded hillsides and limestone bluffs; mostly southeast (Central Appalachians, Piedmont). Shrub or small tree grows to 15 feet; sun to part shade in mesic to moist humusy, sandy loam; a few sources.

Cephalanthus occidentalis (Buttonbush) – swamps, bogs, lake margins and low wet ground, OBL; statewide except north (Northern Unglaciated Allegheny Plateau). Shrub to 10 feet; sun to part shade in moist, humusy soils in full sun to part shade. Grows well in wet soils, including flood conditions and shallow standing water. Adapts to a wide range of soils except dry; many sources.

Cercis canadensis (Redbud) – woodlands and stream banks that are neither excessively wet or dry or strongly acidic, 20 to 30 feet. Has a natural preference for, and can be used as an indicator of, alkaline soils. FACU–; mostly south, especially Southern Allegheny Plateau and Piedmont. Well–drained, moist deep soil in full sun to light shade. Popular for its dramatic display of pink flowers in spring; many sources.

Chamaecyparis thyoides (Atlantic white–cedar) – bogs and swamps, especially sphagnum, along the Atlantic and Gulf coasts, primarily coastal plain; scattered inland, OBL; scattered in southeast (Piedmont) and southwest (Southern Allegheny Plateau). Grows 35 to 70 feet in wet, acidic, sandy soils in part sun; a few sources.

Chamaedaphne calyculata var. angustifolia (Leatherleaf) – bogs and acidic wetlands, especially at higher elevations. OBL; mostly northeast (Northern Glaciated Allegheny Plateau) and northwest (Western Glaciated Allegheny Plateau, Erie and Ontario Lake Plain). Shrub to 5 feet; sun to part shade in acidic, peaty, moist to wet soils. White flowers in spring; a few sources.

Chimaphila maculata (Striped prince's pine) – moist woodlands in undisturbed organic litter of leaves and especially conifer needles; mostly southeast (Piedmont, Central Appalachians), scattered west. Subshrub, 4 to 12 inches; part shade to shade in dry, acidic sandy loam with leaf or needle litter, pH 4 to 5. White flowers in late summer; a few sources.

Chimaphila umbellata ssp. cisatlantica (Pipsisswea, or prince's pine) – upland woods and barrens; statewide except north (Northern Unglaciated Allegheny Plateau). Subshrub 4 to 12 inches; part shade to shade in dry, acidic sandy loam. White or pink flowers in late summer; a few sources.

Chionanthus virginicus (Fringe–tree) – bluffs, thickets, damp woods, 10 to 35 feet, FAC+. Mostly southeast (Piedmont, Atlantic Coastal Plain); widely scattered elsewhere. Grow in well–drained, average moisture soil in full sun to part shade; prefers moist fertile soils and rarely requires pruning. Tolerant of urban pollution, but not prolonged dry conditions; many sources.

Clethra acuminata (Mountain pepperbush) – very rare in deciduous, rocky forests Appalachian slopes, bluffs and ravines, typically on moist sites often near high–elevation streams; scattered southwest (Southern Allegheny Plateau) and endangered. Grows 12 to 20 feet in part shade on acidic, rocky soils, usually moist but can adapt to dryer circumstances. White flowers in mid–summer; a few sources.

Clethra alnifolia (Sweet pepperbush) – low wet woods, bogs and acidic swamps in moderately to poorly drained sites, FAC+; mostly east, especially Atlantic Coastal Plain. Shrub, 6 to 12 feet; average, medium to wet, well–drained soil in full sun to part shade. Adaptive to a wide range of soil, moisture and light conditions. Prefers part shade and consistently moist to wet, acidic soils. Tolerates full shade. pH 4.6 to 6.5. White flowers in summer; many sources.

Comptonia peregrina (Sweet–fern) – dry, sterile, sandy to rocky soils in pinelands or pine barrens, clearings, or woodlot edges; statewide, but scattered west. Shrub to 5 feet; sun to part shade in average, medium, well–drained soil in full sun to part shade. Prefers sandy, acidic loams, but tolerates poor soils. Spreads to form colonies. Tolerates wet conditions and wind, drought and a wide range of soils. Difficult to transplant after established; many sources.

Cornus alternifolia (Alternate–leaved dogwood) – moist woodlands, forest margins, stream and swamp borders, and near deep canyon bottoms; statewide. Shrub or small tree to 20 feet; sun to part shade in sandy, well–drained deep soils. White flowers in late spring; many sources.

Cornus amomum ssp. amomum (Red willow or Kinnikinik) – swamps, stream banks, moist woods, fields and thickets, FACW; statewide. Shrub to 10 feet. Two local subspecies: *amomum* and *obliqua*; part shade to shade in moist to wet acidic sandy loam. White flowers in late spring; many sources.

Cornus florida (Flowering dogwood) – mesic deciduous woods, on floodplains, slopes, bluffs, and in ravines, FACU; statewide, but scattered north (northern Allegheny plateaus). Tree to 30 feet; varied soils from moist, deep soils to light–textured, well–drained upland soils; prefers coarse to medium–textured acidic soils. White flowers in spring; many sources, including many garden centers.

Cornus racemosa (Silky dogwood) – swampy meadows, moist old fields, thickets, FAC–; statewide. Shrub 3 to 16 feet; sun to part shade in dry to mesic sandy loam. Tolerates wide range of soil conditions, including both moist and somewhat dry soils, and of city air pollution. White flowers in spring; many sources.

Cornus rugosa (Round–leaved dogwood) – well–drained rocky woods and cliffs; statewide, especially east. Shrub or small tree, 3 to 12 feet; part shade to shade in dry to mesic sandy acidic loam. White flowers in spring; a few sources.

Cornus sericea (Red–osier dogwood) – stream banks, swamps, moist fields, thickets, FACW+; mostly northwest (Western Glaciated Allegheny Plateau, Erie and Ontario Lake Plain); scattered elsewhere. Shrub to 10 feet; part shade in moist, circumneutral well–drained soil. Adaptable to a wide range of soil and climatic conditions. White flowers in spring. AKA *Cornus stolonifera*; many sources.

Corylus americana (American filbert) – moist to dry open woods, thickets, hillsides, roadsides, fencerows, and waste places, FACU–; statewide. Grows to 15 feet; average, medium, well–drained soil in full sun to part shade; forms thickets if suckers are not removed. White flowers in early spring; many sources.

Corylus cornuta (Beaked hazelnut) – moist to dry roadsides, woodland edges, thickets, fencerows, sometimes as an understory in open wood-lands, FACU–; statewide, mostly east, scattered west. Shrub to 20 feet; full sun to part shade in organically rich, medium moisture, well–drained circumneutral soils. Tolerates average garden soils, but not unamended heavy clays; several sources.

Crataegus chrysocarpa (Fireberry hawthorn) – rocky pastures, open woodlands and edges. Large shrub or small tree to 25 feet; sun to part sun in mesic to moist sandy loam; drought tolerant. White flowers in early summer; a few sources. AKA *Crataegus rotundifolia.*

Crataegus chrysocarpa var. chrysocarpa (Red–fruited hawthorn) – open woods, fields, roadsides and stream banks; statewide, especially southeast (Piedmont), except northeast (Northern Glaciated Allegheny Plateau). Shrub or small tree to 32 feet; sun to part sun in mesic to moist well drained sandy loam. Tolerates a wide range of soils as long as drainage is good, light shade and some drought, and many urban pollutants. White flowers in late spring. Also known as *Crataegus coccinea*; a few sources.

Crataegus crus–galli (Cockspur hawthorn) – woods, meadows, road-sides, thickets, especially in dry or rocky places, and slopes of low hills in rich soils, FACU; mostly southeast (Piedmont, Atlantic Coastal Plain); scattered elsewhere except north (northern Allegheny plateaus). Large shrub or small tree grows to 32 feet; sun to part sun in mesic to moist well drained sandy loam. Tolerates a wide range of well drained soils, light shade, some drought and many urban pollutants. White to pink flowers in late spring; many sources.

Crataegus dilatata (Broadleaf hawthorn) – thickets and calcareous hills, including pastures; scattered sites in the northern Allegheny Mountains. Grows to 20 feet in moist to wet soils in full sun to part shade; a few sources.

Crataegus mollis (Downy hawthorn) – fields, roadsides, alluvial thickets, woodland edges, FACU; scattered southeast (Atlantic Coastal Plain) and northwest (Erie and Ontario Lake Plain). Grows 35 to 75 feet in dry to moist soils in full sun to part shade. Avoid planting near red cedar (rust blight); susceptible to gypsy moth; a few sources.

Crataegus punctata (Dotted hawthorn) – open hardwood and co-nifer–hardwood forests; statewide. Large shrub or small tree to 40 feet; sun to shade in dry to moist circumneutral ordinary loams. White, pink, yellow flowers in late spring; a few sources.

Crataegus succulenta (Long–spined hawthorn) – woodland edges and thickets, pastures, rocky bluffs; scattered statewide, especially southeast (Piedmont) and central (Central Appalachians, Allegheny Mountains); grows to about 20 feet. Prefers dry sandy or rocky soils in part sun to dappled shade; a few sources.

Dasiphora fruticosa (Shrubby cinquefoil) – very rare in calcareous swamps and endangered in Pennsylvania; FACW. Typically grows in moisture retentive soils in swamps and moist rocky areas. Scattered sites in the Lehigh Valley. Grows 3 to 4 feet in full sun with yellow flowers in summer; prefers dry, circumneutral soil. AKA *Potentilla fruticosa*; a few sources.

Diervilla lonicera (Bush–honeysuckle) – typically on exposed rocky sites with dry to mesic well–drained soil; statewide. Shrub to 4 feet; part shade to shade in dry, rocky slightly acidic loam. Red, orange, yellow and purple flowers in summer; many sources.

Diospyros virginiana (Persimmon) – open woods, floodplains and old fields, seasonally flooded bottomlands, dry ridgetops and aban-doned agricultural land, FAC; mostly southeast (Piedmont, Central Appalachians, Atlantic Coastal Plain); scattered southwest (Southern Allegheny Plateau). Grows to 50 feet; dry to medium, well–drained soils in full sun to part shade. Wide range of soil tolerance, but prefers moist, sandy soils. Drought tolerant. Blooms late spring, edible fruit in the fall; many sources.

Dirca palustris (Leatherwood) – rich deciduous woods and thickets, FAC; scattered southwest. Shrub to 5 feet; full sun in moist, deep soils; prefers wet sites; pale yellow flowers in early spring; a few sources.

Epigaea repens (Trailing–arbutus) – moist to xeric pine or deciduous forests, clearings and edges, in sandy, rocky, or peaty soil; borders and banks; statewide. Creeping subshrub, about 6 inches, with white–pink flowers in early spring; part sun to part shade in dry sandy rocky acid loam. Can be difficult to transplant; a few sources.

Euonymus obovatus (Running strawberry–bush) – rich, dry to damp woodlands, thickets and slopes; mostly northwest (Western Glaciated Allegheny Plateau, Erie and Ontario Lake Plain). Grows 1 to 3 feet in rich, moist soils in part shade to shade; greenish–purple flowers in early summer; a few sources.

Fagus grandifolia (American beech) – rich deciduous and mixed–conifer forest, FACU; statewide. Grows to 80 feet; deep, rich, moist but well–drained soils in full sun to part shade. Intolerant of wet, poorly drained soils. Often forms thickets or colonies by suckering from the shallow roots; many sources.

Fraxinus americana (White ash) – middle, moderately–moist slopes and dry, cold ridges and mountaintops, FACU; statewide. Two varieties: *americana* (most common) and *biltmoreana* (southeast, Piedmont, Central Appalachians). Grows to 80 feet; deep, well–drained, moist soils with other hardwoods; many sources.

Fraxinus nigra (Black ash) – deciduous, coniferous, and mixed lowland forests, poorly drained swamps, bogs, gullies, depressions, valley flats, and stream and lake shores, FACW; statewide, especially southeast (Piedmont). Grows to 80 feet; moist to wet, deep, fertile, mineral or organic soils; several sources.

Fraxinus pennsylvanica (Green ash) – riparian areas such as floodplains and swamps, but is also in sites that periodically experience drought, FACW; mostly southeast (Piedmont, Atlantic Coastal Plain, Central Appalachians), scattered elsewhere. Grows to 80 feet; fertile, clay, silt, and/or loam soils that range from poorly to well drained; prefers constantly moist, humusy, well–drained soils in full sun; many sources.

Gaultheria hispidula (Creeping snowberry) – rare in wet woods and swamps and bogs on hummocks and tree stumps, FACW; mostly northeast (Northern Glaciated Allegheny Plateau), scattered north central and northwest. Creeping shrub to 6 inches.; part shade to shade in moist to wet cold humusy to peaty acidic soils, pH 4.0 to 5.0. White flowers in spring; a few sources.

Gaultheria procumbens (Teaberry) – oak woods or under evergreens; moist sites but tolerates moisture conditions ranging from dry to poorly drained, FACU; statewide. Creeping subshrub spreads from rhizomes; 4 to 8 inches with white flowers in spring; part shade to shade in mesic to moist sandy, well–drained organic loam. Prefers pH 4.5 to 6.0; many sources.

Gaylussacia baccata (Black huckleberry) – dry to wet acidic woods and thickets, often among oaks, FACU; statewide except north–central (Northern Unglaciated Allegheny Plateau). Shrub to 3 feet with white to pink flowers in early summer and fruit in late summer; part shade to shade in mesic to moist sandy organic loam. pH 4.0 to 6.0; a few sources.

Gaylussacia frondosa (Dangleberry) – dry to wet acidic oak woods and thickets, FAC; mostly southeast (Central Appalachians, Piedmont), scattered elsewhere. Grows to 6 feet, with white to pink flowers in early summer and fruit in late summer; part shade to shade in mesic to moist sandy organic loam, pH 4.0 to 6.5; a few sources.

Gleditsia triacanthos (Honey–locust) – well–drained upland woodlands and borders, rocky hillsides, old fields, fencerows and rich moist stream banks, bottomlands and floodplains, FAC–; statewide, especially southeast (Piedmont, Atlantic Coastal Plain). Grows to 65 feet; organically rich, moist, well–drained soils in full sun. Tolerant of a wide range of soils, wind, high summer heat, drought and saline conditions; several sources.

Gymnocladus dioicus (Kentucky coffee–tree) – moist woods, especially lower slopes, and floodplains, 60 to 80 feet. Suckers to form colonies in native habitats; mostly southeast (Piedmont, Atlantic Coastal Plain); scattered southwest. Grow in organically rich, moist soils in full sun; avoid heavy clay. Tolerates drought, poorer soils and urban environments; many sources AKA *Gymnocladus dioica*.

Hamamelis virginiana (Witch–hazel) – dry to moist woodlands, slopes, bluffs, and high hammocks, FAC–; statewide. Grows to 15 feet with yellow flowers in late fall to early winter; part shade to shade in mesic to moist sandy organic loam; prefers rich, deep soils. The familiar astringent is distilled from the bark of young shoots. Among the most widespread shrubs in the region; many sources.

Hydrangea arborescens (Wild hydrangea or sevenbark) – rich woods; rocky wooded slopes; stream banks and ravines, FACU; statewide, especially southwest (Southern Allegheny Plateau). Shrub to 6 feet with white flowers in summer; average, medium moisture, well–drained soil in part shade. Intolerant of drought; several sources.

Hypericum densiflorum (Bushy St..John's–wort) – rare in sphagnum bogs, swampy meadows, rocky river banks, seepage slopes, pond and lake margins, moist pinelands; FAC+; southwest (Southern Allegheny Plateau). Grows 18 inches to six feet with yellow flowers in summer. Prefers moist to wet organic clay loams in full sun, pH 5.5 to 5.7; a few sources.

Hypericum prolificum (Shrubby St John's–wort) – rocky ground, dry wooded slopes, uncultivated fields, gravel bars along streams and in low, moist valleys, FACU; mostly southwest (Southern Allegheny Plateau); scattered elsewhere except northeast (Northern Glaciated and Unglaciated Allegheny Plateaus). Shrub to 6 feet with yellow flowers in early summer; average, medium moisture, well–drained soil in full sun to part shade. Tolerates wide range of soils, including dry rocky or sandy soils. Also tolerates some drought; several sources.

Ilex montana (Mountain holly) – cool moist rocky woods; mostly northeast (Northern Glaciated Allegheny Plateau), scattered north (Western Glaciated and Northern Unglaciated Allegheny Plateaus and at higher elevations along the Allegheny front. Shrub or small tree, grows to 30 feet with white flowers in spring and fruit in early fall; sun to partial shade; well drained soil; a few sources.

Ilex mucronata (Catberry or mountain holly) – swamps, bogs, moist woods, fens, OBL; mostly north (Western and Northern Glaciated and Northern Unglaciated Allegheny Plateaus); scattered elsewhere. Shrub to 10 feet with white–yellow flowers in spring and fruit in late summer; sun to part shade in moist to wet silty organic loam; a few sources.

Ilex verticillata (Winterberry) – wet woods, swamps, bogs and moist shores, FACW+; statewide. Shrub to 15 feet; sun to part shade in moist acidic organic loam. Tolerates poorly drained soils, including swamps and bogs. Dioecious; only fertilized female flowers will produce the attractive red berries that are the signature of the species; many sources.

Itea virginica (Tassel–white) – very rare in swamps, wet woods, stream banks and moist coastal plain sites; OBL; mostly southeast (Atlantic Coastal Plain). Grows 3 to 5 feet with white flowers in summer. Prefers sun, but adapts to part shade. Grow in average medium to wet soil, especially humusy soils; a good rain garden shrub and popular for erosion control; a few sources.

Juglans cinerea (Butternut) – rich woods of river terraces and valleys, especially in coves, on stream benches and terraces and on slopes, in the talus of rock ledges, and on other sites with good drainage, FACU+; statewide. Grows to 100 feet; moist, organically rich, well–drained soils in full sun. Intolerant of shade; many sources.

Juglans nigra (Black walnut) – rich woods on wet bottomlands, dry ridges and slopes. Common on limestone soils, FACU; statewide except for north (northern Allegheny plateaus). Grows to 130 feet; deep, well–drained neutral soils that are moist and fertile; many sources.

Juniperus communis (Common juniper) – dry open woods, slopes, pastures; mostly southeast (Piedmont), scattered elsewhere Low growing, spreading shrub, with yellow flowers in early spring; part sun to part shade in dry to mesic sandy loam. Declining due to deer browsing. Fruits used to flavor gin; several sources.

Juniperus virginiana (Eastern red–cedar) – upland to low (especially early successional) woodlands, old fields and fence rows, glades and river swamps, FACU; mostly southeast (Piedmont, Central Appalachians). Grows to 65 feet; average, dry to moist, well–drained soils in full sun. Tolerates a wide range of soils and growing conditions. Prefers moist soils, but has the best drought resistance of any conifer native to the eastern U.S.; many sources.

Kalmia angustifolia (Sheep laurel) – sandy or infertile soil, bogs, old fields, dry woods, barrens. FAC; mostly northeast (Northern Glaciated Allegheny Plateau, Central Appalachians) and southeast (Piedmont). Grows to 3 feet with rose–pink to crimson flowers in early summer; part sun to part shade in mesic to moist sandy organic loam. pH 4.5 to 6; a few sources.

Kalmia latifolia (Mountain laurel) – dry upland sandy, acidic, rocky woods. FACU, statewide. Grows to 15 feet with white to pink flowers in early summer; part sun to part shade in dry to mesic, humusy, sandy loam, pH 4.5 to 6. Very slow growing. The state flower of Pennsylvania; many sources.

Kalmia polifolia (Bog laurel) – rare in peaty wetlands and bogs, OBL; northeast (Northern Glaciated Allegheny Plateau). Grows 6 to 36 inches with lavender flowers in summer; part sun to part shade in wet organic soils and peat; flood tolerant; a few sources.

Larix laricina (American larch or tamarack) – cold, wet to moist, poorly drained swamps, bogs, and muskegs; also along streams, lakes, swamp borders, and occasionally on upland sites, FACW; scattered north, especially northeast (Northern Glaciated Allegheny Plateau). Grows to 65 feet; sun to part sun in moist to wet acid soils; intolerant of shade, heat, polluted areas and of dry, shallow chalky soils, but adapts to sites slightly drier than natural habitat; many sources.

Ledum groenlandicum (Labrador–tea) – wetter sites with low subsurface water flow and low nutrients; poorly drained habitats such as boreal forests, open conifer bogs, treeless bogs, wooded swamps, wet barrens, and peatlands, OBL; northeast (Northern Glaciated Allegheny Plateau). Shrub to 3 feet with white flowers in early summer; sun to part shade in moist to wet acidic organic soils, peat and muck. Flood tolerant. Also known as *Rhododendron groenlandicum*; several sources.

Leiophyllum buxifolium (Sand–myrtle) – very rare on dry sandy barrens and thin moist mountain woods, FACU. Shrub to 3 feet with whitish–pink flowers in late spring to early summer; part shade in moist, acid sandy peaty soil. Does not tolerate drought. Possibly extirpated; a few sources. AKA *Kalmia buxifolia.*

Leucothoe racemosa (Fetter–bush) – rare in swamps and moist thickets, shrub–free bogs, along marshy stream banks and forest edges; southeast, especially Atlantic Coastal Plain. An important shrub species in palustrine wetlands with deep, acidic, sandy, peat soils, FACW. Grows to 10 feet with white to pink flowers in late spring to early summer; part shade on moist, sandy acidic loam. Also known as *Eubotrys racemosa;* a few sources.

Lindera benzoin (Northern spicebush) – moist sites in wooded bottomlands, ravines, valleys and along streams; found in many regional ecosystems, FACW–; statewide. Grows to 10 feet with yellow flowers in early spring; average, medium, well–drained soils in full sun to part shade, pH 4.5 to 6.5. Fall color is best in sunny areas. Tolerates full shade. Leaves used to make a mildly spicy herbal tea, hence the name; many sources.

Linnaea borealis var. americana (Twinflower) – rare in cool, dry to moist forests and woodlands, especially coniferous, in sandy acidic loam, and humus–rich swamps and barrens, FAC; widely scattered, mostly north. Trailing subshrub with pinkish–white flowers in spring; part shade to shade in moist to wet cool acidic humus. Low drought tolerance. pH 4 to 6; a few sources.

Liquidambar styraciflua (Sweetgum) – rich, moist, alluvial clay and loamy soils of river bottoms, especially on the Piedmont Plateau, 75 to 130 feet; FAC+; mostly southeast (Atlantic Coastal Plain, Piedmont); scattered elsewhere. Grow in deep, moist, alluvial loams, but very tolerant of different soils and sites; can be aggressive in sandy, moist soils. Rapid growth; many sources.

Liriodendron tulipifera (Tuliptree) – rich woodlands on hills, bluffs and low mountains, FACU; statewide, except north–central (Northern Unglaciated Allegheny Plateau). Grows to 150 feet with creamy–white flowers in spring; moist, organically rich, well–drained loams in full sun. Tolerates part shade; many sources.

Lonicera canadensis (Fly honeysuckle) – cool, dry to moist woods upland woods, thickets, swamps, fens and sometimes along streams, FACU; statewide, except scattered southeast (Piedmont) Grows to 5 feet with pale yellow flowers in late spring to early summer. Part sun to part shade in moist sandy organic loam; a few sources.

Lonicera oblongifolia (Swamp fly honeysuckle) – bogs, marshes, swamps, fens; OBL; mostly northwest (Western Glaciated Allegheny

Plateau), endangered. Grows less than 3 feet with white/yellow flowers in summer; prefers moist to wet alkaline soils (pH >7.2) in part shade to shade; a few sources.

Lonicera villosa (Waterberry) – very rare bogs, swamps, wet thickets, swamps, treed fens and stream banks; widely scattered and endangered. Shrub to 3 feet with pale yellow flowers in late spring to early summer; sun to part sun in moist to wet organic loam; a few sources.

Lyonia ligustrina (Maleberry) – low, alluvial woods and thickets, wet meadows, bogs, and lakeshores, FACW; statewide except Northern Unglaciated Allegheny Plateau, Western Glaciated Allegheny Plateau. Shrub to 10 feet with white flowers in late spring; part sun to part shade in mesic to moist sandy clay organic loam; a few sources.

Magnolia acuminata (Cucumber–tree) – scattered in cool moist oak–hickory forests, with a preference for bottomlands and north to east–facing, typically gentle slopes that are well–drained and deep; on steeper slopes it prefers coarser loams. Height ranges from 40 to 70 feet; statewide, especially west. The hardiest of the tree–sized magnolias, but intolerant of urban pollutants. Greenish–yellow flowers after 12 years. Grow in full sun to part shade in organically rich, well–drained moist loams; many sources.

Magnolia tripetala (Umbrella–tree) – rich woods and ravines, mainly in uplands, rarely on the coastal plain, FACU; mostly southeast (Piedmont, Atlantic Coastal Plain); scattered southwest. Grows to 30 feet with large white flowers in late spring; part shade in most, rich acidic, well drained sandy loam; a few sources.

Magnolia virginiana (Sweet–bay magnolia) – wet woods, swamps, swamp margins, savannas, hammocks, bogs, and floodplains, especially in acidic soils with poor to very poor drainage that are frequently flooded during winter or wet seasons, rarely in major river bottoms FACW+; mostly southeast (Piedmont, Atlantic Coastal Plain); scattered southwest. Grows 10 to 35 feet; fragrant white flowers in spring. Grow in acidic, medium to wet, rich organic soil in full sun to part shade; can tolerate wet, boggy soils; Many sources.

Malus coronaria var. coronaria (Sweet crabapple) – open woods, woodland edges and stream banks; statewide except north central (Northern Unglaciated Allegheny Plateau). Grows to 35 feet with pinkish–white flowers in spring; part shade in moist, well drained humusy soil. Fruit very tart and acidic; a few sources.

Morus rubra (Red mulberry) – low elevation moist thickets and forests, stream banks and depressions; FACU; mostly south, especially southeast (Piedmont, Central Appalachians) and southwest (Southern Allegheny Plateau). Grows to 15 to 35 feet; prefers well–drained, moist soils along streams or in sheltered coves; a few sources.

Myrica gale (Sweet–gale) – rare in bogs, shallow water of lake and stream edges, OBL.; northeast (Northern Glaciated Allegheny Plateau). Shrub to 5 feet with yellowish–green flowers in late spring; sun to part sun in wet to moist sandy loam; a few sources.

Myrica pensylvanica (Bayberry) – old fields, sand dunes, open woods, FAC. Mostly southeast (Piedmont, Atlantic Coastal Plain) and northwest (Erie and Ontario Lake Plain); widely scattered elsewhere. Grows to 6 feet with yellowish–green flowers in late spring; sun to part sun in dry to moist sandy clay loam. Prefers moist, peaty or sandy, acidic soils, but tolerates a wide range of soils and growing conditions. Groups of plants need at least one male plant to pollinate female plants for fruit. Fruits have waxy coating used to make traditional bayberry candles. AKA *Morella pensylvanica*; many sources.

Nyssa sylvatica (Sourgum or Black gum) – dry to middle and upper slopes and ridgetops, FAC; statewide except north–central (Northern Unglaciated Allegheny Plateau). Grows to 100 feet; average, medium to wet soils in full sun to part shade. Prefers moist, acidic soils. Tolerates poorly–drained soils and can grow in standing water; tolerates some drought and adapts to some dryish soils. Can spread by sucker growth; many sources.

Ostrya virginiana (Hop–hornbeam) – moist, open to forested hillsides to dry upland slopes and ridges, occasionally on moist, well–drained flood plains, FACU; statewide. Grows to 65 feet; average, medium, well–drained soil in full sun to part shade; many sources.

Oxydendrum arboreum (Sourwood) – subxeric open slopes and ridges occupied by oaks and Virginia pine; less common in mesic sites like coves and sheltered slopes. Also along well–drained lowland areas along Piedmont streams not subject to flooding, in gently rolling areas, FACU; mostly southwest (Southern Allegheny Plateau); scattered southeast. Grows 20 to 50 feet in full sun to part shade in well–drained, organically rich, moist soils. Part shade is tolerated, but flowering is diminished. Intolerant of urban pollution; many sources.

Paxistima canbyi (Canby's mountain–lover) – very rare on calcareous slopes and cliffs where soils are associated with dolomite. Mostly south central counties (Allegheny Mountains). Endangered in Pennsylvania. Grows 1 to 3 feet in part shade on fertile, well–drained soils. Greenish flowers in spring; a few sources.

Photinia floribunda (Purple chokeberry) – low woodlands, lake shores, stream banks, or at interface of marshes or bogs with adjacent uplands on sandy soils; southeast (Atlantic Coastal Plain). A natural hybrid between *Photinia melanocarpa* and *Photinia pyrifolia*; shrub, 8 to 12 feet; average, medium, well–drained soils in full sun to part shade. Wide range of soil tolerance including boggy soils. Best fruit production usually occurs in full sun. White flowers in late spring; a few sources. AKA *Aronia prunifolia*.

Photinia melanocarpa (Black chokeberry) – swamps, bogs, wet and dry woods, barrens. FAC, statewide. Shrub to 10 feet; sun to part shade in average, medium, well–drained soil. Tolerant of wide range of soils, including both dry and boggy soils. Best fruit production occurs in full sun. White flowers in late spring; many sources. AKA *Aronia melanocarpa*.

Photinia pyrifolia (Red chokeberry) – pine bottomlands; swamps and moist woods; open bogs, FACW, statewide. Shrub from 18 inches to 10 feet, depending on habitat.; sun to part sun in moist sandy loam. White flowers in late spring; many sources. AKA *Aronia arbutifolia*.

Physocarpus opulifolius (Ninebark) – wet woods, moist cliffs, sandy or rocky stream banks, gravel bars and moist thickets, FACW– ; statewide. Shrub to 10 feet with white to pink flowers in late spring; sun to part shade in mesic to moist, well–drained soil. Tolerates wide range of soil conditions, pH 5.1 to 6.5; many sources.

Picea mariana (Black spruce) – bottomlands, peat bogs and dry peat-lands, swamps, muskegs and transitional sites between peatlands and uplands, FACU–; mostly northeast (Northern Glaciated Allegheny Plateau); scattered elsewhere. To 65 feet; sun to shade in mesic to wet acidic humusy soils. Shallow root system makes this tree susceptible to wind throw; many sources.

Picea rubens (Red spruce) – cool upland to sub alpine forests in cli-mates with cool, moist summers and cold winters; on steep, rocky slopes with thin soils, and wet bottomlands; often on sites unfavorable for other species such as organic soils overlying rocks in mountainous locales, FACU; mostly northeast (Northern Glaciated Allegheny Plateau); widely scattered elsewhere. Grows to 100 feet on soils de-veloped from unsorted glacial drift and till deposited on the midslopes of hills and mountains with thick mor humus; a few sources.

Pinus echinata (Short–leaf pine) – dry upland slopes, ridges, plains, bluffs and ravines between 700 and 2,000 feet in elevation; UPL; mostly south–central (Central Appalachians). Grows 75 to 100 feet in dry, sandy to rocky acidic soils; prefers deep, well–drained soils having fine sandy loam or silty loam textures, often with clay components, in sun to part shade; a few sources.

Pinus pungens (Table–mountain pine) – dry, shaly to sandy, often rocky uplands between 1,500 and 4,000 feet elevation; UPL; mostly Central Appalachians. Rarely grows over 65 feet. Prefers shallow, strongly acidic stony, infertile and excessively drained soils in sun to part sun; a few sources.

Pinus resinosa (Red pine or Norway pine) – dry slopes and mountaintops and sandy soils in boreal forests, FACU; widely scattered, statewide. Grows to 120 feet; well–drained, dry to moist acidic to neutral soils in full to part sun. Tolerates poor soils; many sources.

Pinus rigida (Pitch pine) – upland or lowland, sterile, dry to boggy acidic forests and barrens, FACU; statewide. Grows to 100 feet; dry, thin, infertile, and sandy or gravelly soils, ranging from rapidly draining to swampy limestone and sandstone; a few sources.

Pinus strobus (Eastern white pine) – mesic to dry sites ranging from wet bogs and moist stream bottoms to xeric sand plains and rocky ridges, especially on northerly aspects and in coves, FACU; statewide. Grows to 130 feet; average, medium moisture, well–drained soil in full sun. Prefers full sun, fairly infertile sandy soils, such as well–drained outwash soils, in cool, humid climates with little hardwood competition. Tolerant of a wide range of soil conditions. Intolerant of many air pollutants such as sulfur dioxide and ozone; many sources.

Pinus virginiana (Virginia pine) – dry uplands, sterile sandy or shaly barrens, old fields, and lower mountains; barrens slopes and ridgetops. Mostly south, especially Central Appalachians, Southern Allegheny Plateau, Piedmont. Grows to 48 feet; full sun in sandy loam; will grow in poor, dry soils including clay; several sources.

Platanus occidentalis (Sycamore) – alluvial soils near streams and lakes and in moist ravines, sometimes on uplands and on limestone soils; cultivated in parks and gardens and as a street tree, FACW–; statewide. Grows to 160 feet; average, medium to wet, well–drained soils in full sun. Tolerates light shade. Prefers rich, humusy, consistently moist soils. Generally tolerant of most urban pollutants; many sources.

Populus balsamifera (Balsam poplar) – rare on river floodplains, stream and lake shores, moist depressions, and swamps, but will also grow on drier sites, FACW. Widely scattered statewide, endangered.

Grows to 100 feet; alluvial gravel, deep sand, clay loam, silt, and silty loam with abundant soil moisture is needed; several sources.

Populus deltoides (Eastern cottonwood) – low elevation floodplains, wet areas and river banks on rich, alluvial soils, especially bare mud left after flooding; FACU–; mostly east, especially southeast (Piedmont). Grows 65 to 130 feet in full sun, preferably in fertile, deep, and moist but well drained soil (avoid waterlogged soils); a few sources.

Populus grandidentata (Bigtooth aspen) – floodplains, gently rolling terrain, and lower slopes of uplands, FACU; statewide. Grows to 80 feet; light sandy loams, sands, and loamy sands above pH 4.0; a few sources.

Populus tremuloides (Quaking aspen) – moist upland woods, dry mountainsides, high plateaus, talus slopes, gentle slopes near valley bottoms, alluvial terraces, and along watercourses; statewide. Grows to 65 feet; soils ranging from shallow and rocky to deep loamy sands and heavy clays. Prefers sites that are well drained, loamy, and high in organic matter and nutrients; many sources.

Potentilla fruticosa (Shrubby cinquefoil) – very rare on damp rocky ground, usually on limestone, FACW; reported only in Monroe and Northampton counties, endangered. Grows to 3 feet with bright yellow flowers, early summer through frost; well–drained, reasonably rich soil, but will tolerate clay, rocky, or slightly alkaline soils; several sources.

Prunus americana (Wild plum) – riparian areas, but also moist to dry open to wooded prairie ravines, pastures, roadsides, fencerows, ditch banks, and natural drainage areas, FACU; statewide. Shrub or small tree to 20 feet with white flowers in spring; average, dry to medium, well–drained soils in full sun to part shade. Control spreading with sucker removal. Fruit used to make jams and jellies; many sources.

Prunus angustifolia (Chickasaw plum) – very rare in roadside thickets, pastures, fields, fencerows, stream banks and other disturbed areas, usually uplands and bottomlands in open and wooded–open edge sites; scattered in southeast (Piedmont). Grows up to 20 feet in full sun to part shade on a wide range of soils, except alkaline; does well in heavier clay–loam soils. a few sources.

Prunus maritima (Beach plum) – rare on sand dunes or sandy soils near the Atlantic coast; southeast (Atlantic Coastal Plain), endangered. Grows 6 to 12 feet with white flowers in spring, followed by fruit that attracts birds and other wildlife. Fruits are considered poisonous and should not be eaten. Grow in sandy to gravelly soils in full sun; many sources.

Prunus pensylvanica (Pin cherry) – areas characterized as water–shedding (rocky ridges, cliffs, dry woods, clearings) or water–receiving (sandy and gravelly banks, shores of rivers and lakes), FACU–; statewide. Shrub or tree to 40 feet with white flowers in spring; somewhat dry sites and shallow organic layers relatively low in nutrients. Soils very low in moisture may result in a shrub form of pin cherry; several sources.

Prunus pumila var. susquehanae (Sand cherry) – open habitats with little shade from trees or other shrubs, typically along edges of openings or in stands where canopy closure has not occurred; scattered southeast. Sites are typically dry and excessively drained. Shrub to 5 feet with white flowers in spring; sandy, gravelly, and rocky soils, dunes, beaches, and outwash plains; a few sources.

Prunus serotina (Wild black cherry) – mesic woods and second–growth hardwood forests and old fields, especially on the Allegheny Plateau, on nearly all soil types. Prefers middle and lower slopes of eastern and northern exposures than the dry soils associated with south– or west–facing slopes, FACU; statewide. Grows to 100 feet with white flowers in spring; average, medium–moisture, well–drained soils in full sun to part shade. Best in moist, fertile loams in full sun. Fruits used to make wines, jelly; many sources.

Prunus virginiana (Choke cherry) – very acid to moderately alkaline, well–drained limestone residuum soil with pH ranging from 3.5 to 7.6, often in oak–pine forests, FACU; statewide. Grows 3 to 20 feet with white flowers in spring; sun to shade in dry to moist, circumneutral limestone–based sandy loam; intolerant of poor drainage and prolonged flooding; many sources.

Ptelea trifoliata (Hoptree, Wafer ash) – gravelly areas, alluvial thickets and rocky slopes, FAC. Mostly northwest (Erie and Ontario Lake Plain) and southeast (Delaware River Valley); scattered elsewhere and endangered. Grows 10 to 35 feet in part shade to shade (will tolerate full sun) in well–drained, average, medium–moisture soils; many sources.

Quercus alba (White oak) – moist to fairly dry deciduous forests, usually on deeper, well–drained loams but sometimes on thin soils of dry upland slopes and sometimes on barrens, FACU. Grows to 100 feet; rich, moist, acidic, well–drained loams in full sun. Adapts to a wide variety of soil conditions with good drought tolerance. Natural hybrid with *Q. montana* is Saul oak; many sources.

Quercus bicolor (Swamp white oak) – low swamp forests, moist slopes, poorly drained uplands, FACW+; statewide. Grows to 100 feet; average, medium to wet, acidic soil in full sun; many sources.

Quercus coccinea (Scarlet oak) – poor soils of well–drained uplands, dry slopes and ridges, but sometimes on poorly drained sites; statewide except north central (Northern Unglaciated Allegheny Plateau). Grows to 100 feet; average, dry to medium, well–drained soil in full sun. Prefers dry, acidic, sandy soils; many sources.

Quercus falcata (Southern red oak, Spanish oak) – moist, but more often dry, sandy upland woodlands, typically south– and west–facing, sometimes on dry ridgetops, on or near the Atlantic Coastal Plain; FACU–; southeast (Atlantic Coastal Plain). Grows to 80 feet; sandy, loamy, or clay soils, most commonly on red clay and glacial soils; does well on calcareous soils; a few sources.

Quercus ilicifolia (Scrub oak) – dry thickets and barrens in sandy, rocky, well–drained, nutrient–poor soils; statewide, but scattered north. Shrub to 15 feet; sun to part sun in dry to mesic, acidic sandy or gravelly soils; a few sources.

Quercus imbricaria (Shingle oak) – mesic to somewhat dry uplands and slopes, sometimes in bottoms and ravines, FAC; mostly southwest (Southern Allegheny Plateau); scattered east. Grows 40 to 60 feet in full sun in well–drained, humusy, rich, medium moist soils; tolerant of dry soils. Formerly a source of shingles, hence the common name; many sources.

Quercus macrocarpa (Bur oak) – prairies, poorly drained areas, riparian slopes and bottomlands, typically on limestone and sometimes calcareous clays. Prominent in oak–basswood, upland oak–hickory and mix–oak communities, more often in coarsely–textured soil and less often on clays FAC–; mostly south, especially southwest (Southern Allegheny Plateau). Grows 60 to 80 feet in medium to dry, average, well–drained soils in full sun; prefers well–drained moist loams, but adapts; many sources.

Quercus marilandica (Blackjack oak) – dry, sterile soils on ridges, rocky outcrops, disturbed fields, glades and especially serpentine barrens; southwest (Piedmont, Atlantic Coastal Plain). Grows 30 to 50 feet in part shade on a variety of dry, acidic soils; a few sources.

Quercus montana (Chestnut oak) – rocky, xeric, upland forest, dry ridges, mixed deciduous forests on shallow soils usually on south and west–facing upper slopes, FACW; statewide. Grows to 80 feet; dry, rocky, infertile soil with a low moisture–holding capacity, although can grow best in rich, well–drained soils along streams; ridge dominance is suggested by its ability to withstand drought; several sources. AKA *Quercus prinus.*

Quercus palustris (Pin oak) – poorly drained clay soils in bottom-lands intermittently flooded during dormancy but not during the growing season, such as clay flats, depressions where water accumulates in winter, and clay ridges of first bottoms. Prefers level or near level moist uplands such as glacial till plains, FACW; statewide, except northern tier. Grows to 80 feet on average, medium to wet, acidic soils in full sun. Prefers moist loams. Tolerates poorly drained soils and some flooding; many sources.

Quercus phellos (Willow oak) – rare in bottomland flood plains, but also on stream banks, terraces and sometimes poorly drained uplands. Does best on clay loam ridges of new alluvium and diminishes from bottomland to higher terraces; FAC+; mostly southeast (Atlantic Coastal Plain, Piedmont). Grows 40 to 75 feet in full sun in well–drained, wet to medium average soils; tolerates light shade and urban pollution; many sources.

Quercus prinoides (Dwarf chestnut oak) – dry rocky soils, such as sandstone or shale outcrops associated with oak pine types; statewide except north (northern Allegheny plateaus). Shrub to 12 feet; part shade to shade in dry sandy loam; a few sources.

Quercus rubra (Northern red oak) – rich mesic slopes and well–drained uplands, occasionally on dry slopes or poorly drained uplands, sandy plains, rock outcrops, and the edges of floodplains, usually on north– and east–facing slopes. Often found in lower and middle slopes, in coves, ravines and on valley floors, FACU–; statewide. Grows to 100 feet; average, dry to medium moisture, acidic soil in full sun. Prefers deep fertile, sandy, finely–textured soils with good drainage and a relatively high water table. Soils are derived from a variety of parent materials including glacial outwash, sandstone, shale, limestone, gneiss, schist, or granite; many sources.

Quercus shumardii (Shumard oak) – very rare on mesic slopes and bottoms, stream banks and poorly drained uplands. Prefers rich sites with moist, well–drained loamy soils found on terraces, colluvial sites and bluffs adjacent to large and small streams; FAC+; south–central along the Allegheny front. Grows 40 to 60 feet in full sun in well–drained, acidic (will tolerate higher pH) dry to medium average soils. Tolerates wide soil range, including wet; many sources.

Quercus stellata (Post oak) – dry to xeric uplands with southerly or westerly exposure, terraces of smaller streams in well–drained soil, dry gravelly and sandy ridges, dry clays, prairies and limestone hills, woodlands and deciduous forests, UPL; southeast (Piedmont); scattered in Central Appalachians. Grows to 100 feet; rich, moist, acidic, well–drained coarse–textured loams in full sun. Adapts to a wide variety of soil conditions from poor dry sandy soils to moist heavy loams, especially where a heavy clay subsurface layer is within a foot of the surface or bedrock is within two or three feet. Also grows in deep sands and dry clay hills; a few sources.

Quercus velutina (Black oak) – xeric slopes and upland areas, especially with southerly or westerly facing slopes, occasionally on sandy lowlands and poorly drained uplands and terraces; statewide. Grows to 100 feet; moist, rich, well–drained sites, but sensitive to competition on these sites and is more often found on dry, nutrient–poor, coarse–textured soils, especially sandy or gravelly sites or heavy glacial clay hillsides; several sources.

Rhamnus alnifolia (Alder–leaved buckthorn) – rare in fens, calcareous marshes and wet thickets, OBL; mostly northwest (Western Glaciated Allegheny Plateau); widely scattered elsewhere. Shrub to 3 feet with greenish flowers in late spring; moist to wet rich organic loam, full to part sun; a few sources.

Rhododendron arborescens (Smooth azalea) – mountain bogs, forested swamps and stream banks, FAC; mostly southwest (Southern Allegheny Plateau), scattered elsewhere. Grows 10 to 35 feet in part shade in moist, acidic, well–drained soils. White flowers in late spring, among the last to bloom. Intolerant of drought; several sources.

Rhododendron atlanticum (Dwarf azalea) – very rare in flat, moist, pine woodlands and savannahs; reported only in southern York County and endangered. Grows 1 to 3 feet to form low colonies, sending up 1 to 3 foot, brief duration flowering stems with white to pinkish flowers. Grow in sandy, well–drained acidic soil; prefers a dry habitat; several sources.

Rhododendron calendulaceum (Flame azalea) – very rare on south– and west–facing slopes in submesic to subxeric rocky open mountain woodlands; reported only in Somerset County and believed to be extirpated. Grows 6 to 12 feet with red, orange or yellow flowers in late spring to early summer. Grow in well–drained, moist acidic soil in part shade; prefers pH range of 4.5 to 5.5; several sources.

Rhododendron canadense (Rhodora) – bogs, wet places with in-fertile, acidic soil, FACW; northeast (Northern Glaciated Allegheny Plateau). To 3 feet, with rose to purple flowers in spring; sun to part shade in mesic to wet cold acidic peaty soil; a few sources.

Rhododendron maximum (Rosebay) – dry to moist woods, swamps, stream banks. FAC; statewide. Grows to 16 feet with creamy white flowers in early summer; part sun to part shade in mesic to moist acid sandy loam, pH 4.5 to 6. Forms vast woodland and woods edge colonies; manage as with any hybrid rhododendron; several sources.

Rhododendron periclymenoides (Pinxter–flower) – mixed deciduous forests along stream bottoms, bogs, shaded mountainsides and ravines, FAC; statewide. Grows to 10 feet with white to pink flowers in spring; part sun to part shade in mesic to moist, well–drained acid soils in cool, moist locations. Best in acidic, humusy, organically rich, medium moisture, moisture–retentive but well–drained soils in part shade; pH 4.5 to 5.5; a few sources.

Rhododendron periclymenoides x prinophyllum (Azalea) – very rare in woods, thickets, swamp margins. Grows to 10 feet with white or pink flowers in spring; part sun to part shade in mesic to moist acid sandy loam, pH 4.5 to 5.5.White or pink flowers in spring. A natural hybrid; a few sources.

Rhododendron prinophyllum (Mountain azalea) – dry to moist woods thickets, rocky slopes, FAC; statewide. Grows to 10 feet with white to pink flowers in spring; part shade in rich humusy, acidic, medium moisture, well–drained soil in part shade; several sources.

Rhododendron viscosum (Swamp azalea) – swamps, bogs, stream margins and thickets, FACW+; mostly east (Northern Glaciated Allegheny Plateau, Piedmont, Atlantic Coastal Plain). Grows to 10 feet; part shade in moist to wet acidic silty loam. Flood tolerant. White flowers in spring; many sources.

Rhus copallinum (Shining sumac) – hillsides, open woods, glades, fields and along the margins of roadsides; statewide. Grows to 20 feet; full sun to part shade in dry to medium, well–drained soils. Intolerant of poorly drained soils; several sources. AKA *Rhus copallina*.

Rhus glabra (Smooth sumac) – open woodlands, prairies, dry rocky hillsides, canyons, and protected ravines; statewide. Grows to 15 feet; full sun to part shade in dry to medium, well–drained soils. Intolerant of poorly drained soils; many sources.

Rhus typhina (Staghorn sumac) – old fields, roadsides, woods edges, statewide. Shrub or small tree to 30 feet; full sun to part shade in dry to medium, well–drained soils. Intolerant of poorly drained soils; many sources.

Ribes americanum (Wild black currant) – moist woods, marshes and thickets, FACW; statewide. Grows to 6 feet with yellow flowers in spring; sun to shade in moist circumneutral soil; carries a disease that kills white pine; a few sources.

Ribes cynosbati (Prickly gooseberry) – moist, thin, usually rocky woods; statewide except southeast (Central Appalachians, Piedmont). Grows to 6 feet; part sun to part shade in moist rich loam. Yellow flowers; fruit: dull red to purple; a few sources.

Ribes hirtellum (Northern wild gooseberry) – moist, rocky woods; cliffs; bogs and fens, Calcareous marshes, swamps, FAC; scattered statewide. Shrub grows 2 to 4 feet with yellow flowers and dull red fruit; sun to shade in mesic to moist rocky circumneutral soils. Carries a disease that kills white pine; a few sources.

Ribes lacustre (Bristly black currant) – rare in mountain stream-sides, wet meadows, forests and cool wet woodlands, swamps, FACW; widely scattered north (northern Allegheny plateaus). Grows 3 to 4 feet with green flowers and black fruit; sun to shade in mesic to moist rocky circumneutral soils. Carries a disease that kills white pine; a few sources.

Ribes missouriense (Missouri gooseberry) – thickets, pastures, prairie ravines and rich upland woodlands on sites less than 2,000 feet elevation; endangered in Pennsylvania. Scattered in south–central counties (Central Appalachians). Grows 6 to 12 feet in part sun to part shade with white–greenish flowers in spring. Grow in loamy to rocky soil with organic matter to retain moisture, mesic to slightly dry conditions. Lack of flowers and fruit suggest too much shade; a few sources.

Robinia pseudoacacia (Black locust) – open woods on moist slopes and floodplains with a high probability of flooding in any given year, with pH minimum of 4.0, FACU–; statewide. Grows to 80 feet; rich, moist, limestone–derived soils; intolerant of heavy or poorly drained soils, although tolerant of periodic flooding. pH 4.0 to 8.2; many sources.

Rosa blanda (Meadow rose) – dry, open woods, hillsides, prairies, roadsides, widely scattered statewide. Shrub to 6 feet with pink flowers in early summer; full sun in dry rocky soils; several sources.

Rosa carolina (Pasture rose) – dry, rocky or sandy fields and meadows, UPL; statewide. Shrub to 3 feet with pink flowers in early summer; sun to part sun in moist to wet well–drained sandy soil; best flowering and disease resistance in full sun with good air circulation and mulch. Use as a native alternative to the invasive multiflora rose; many sources.

Rosa palustris (Swamp rose) – swamps; wet thickets; marshy shores of streams, ponds and lakes, OBL; statewide. Shrub, to 6 feet with pink flowers in summer; sun to part shade in moist to wet rich soil; many sources.

Rosa virginiana (Wild rose) – thickets, meadows, pastures, open woods, usually in a moist soil, FAC; widely scattered statewide except north–central (Northern Unglaciated Allegheny Plateau). Shrub to 6 feet with pink flowers in summer; sun to part sun in dry to mesic rich loam. Use as a native alternative to the invasive multiflora rose; many sources.

Rubus allegheniensis (Allegheny blackberry) – old fields, open woods, clearings, FACU; statewide. Stems to 6 feet with white flowers followed by black fruit; sun to part shade in mesic sandy loam, pH 4.5 to 7.5; a few sources.

Rubus canadensis (Smooth blackberry) – cool moist woods, rocky slopes, thickets; scattered north (northern Allegheny plateaus) and Allegheny Mountains. Stems 3 to 10 feet with white flowers followed by black fruit; part sun to part shade in moist sandy loam; a few sources.

Rubus flagellaris (Prickly dewberry) – rocky to shaly slopes and cliffs and in fields, FACU; statewide. Stems prostrate and rooting at tips, with white flowers becoming black fruits; part sun to part shade in dry to moist sandy loam; a few sources.

Rubus hispidus (Swamp dewberry) – bogs, swamps, moist woods, thickets and barrens, FACW; statewide. Trailing stems that root at tips with white flowers becoming black fruits; part sun to part shade in dry to moist sandy loam; a few sources.

Rubus idaeus var. strigosus (Red raspberry) – rocky woods, clearings and thickets, FAC–; statewide except Central Appalachians. Stems to 6 feet with white flowers becoming red fruit; part sun to part shade in dry to moist sandy loam; a few sources.

Rubus occidentalis (Black–cap raspberry) – open woods; bluffs; thickets; stream banks; wet meadows, roadsides and pastures; statewide. Stems 3 to 6 feet with white flowers becoming black fruits; part sun to part shade in dry to moist sandy loam; a few sources.

Rubus odoratus (Purple–flowering raspberry) – moist, shaded cliffs, ledges and rocky wooded slopes; statewide. Stems 3 to 6 feet with purple to maroon flowers becoming black fruit; full sun to part shade in mesic sandy loam; several sources.

Salix amygdaloides (Peach–leaved willow) – moist to mesic, sandy, silty or gravelly lake shores, marshes, swamps, floodplains and the valley or trough between sand dunes; FACW; mostly northwest (Erie and Ontario Lake Plain). Grows 35 to 65 feet on wet to damp limestone–based loams in sun to part shade; a few sources.

Salix bebbiana (Long–beaked willow) – upland deciduous woods, moist to dry thickets and edges; ideally in recent deposits of alluvial silts and gravels along waterways or in silted–in, abandoned beaver ponds, FACW–; statewide. Shrub or tree to 32 feet; sun to shade in mesic to moist silty loam. Short–lived and fast–growing. Susceptible to insect, disease, and wind damage; several sources.

Salix caroliniana (Carolina willow) – wet soils along stream banks and in swamps. To 20 feet; OBL, southwest (Southern Allegheny Plateau). Grow in continually moist to wet, organically rich silty–clay loams in full sun; a few sources.

Salix discolor (Pussy willow) – swamps and moist or wet woods, FACW. Shrub to 15 feet; sun to part sun in moist silty circumneutral loams; statewide. Short–lived and fast–growing; cut back heavily every few years to encourage vigorous new growth; many sources.

Salix eriocephala (Diamond willow) – banks of large streams, flood plains, wet meadows, shores and bottomlands, FACW+; statewide. Shrub to 20 feet; sun to part sun in moist to wet sandy loam. Short–lived and fast–growing; a few sources.

Salix exigua (Sandbar willow) – open to dense riparian communities along streams, gravel bars, lakeshores, and ditches, OBL; mostly west (Western Glaciated and Southern Allegheny Plateaus) and east (Delaware River Valley). Shrub or small tree to 30 feet; sun to part shade in moist to wet, sandy to gravelly loam. Favorable for stream stabilization because of profuse suckering; many sources.

Salix humilis (Upland willow) – moist barrens and dry thickets, FACU; statewide. Shrub to 10 feet; two local varieties: *humilis* and *tristis*; sun to part sun in mesic to moist loamy or sandy soil. Insert stems in the ground where they take root to form new stands. More drought tolerant than other willows; a few sources.

Salix lucida ssp. lucida (Shining willow) – wet soils, especially in and near swamps, marshes, peat bogs and on sand banks along creeks, FACW; statewide. Shrub or small tree to 20 feet; sun to part sun in moist to wet circumneutral clayey or silty loam. Prefers poor drainage; a few sources.

Salix myricoides – two varieties: *S. myricoides var. albovestita* (Shoreline willow) and *S. myricoides var. myricoides* (Broad–leaved willow). Scattered statewide, except northern tier counties. Sandy lakeshores, swamps and calcareous slopes; FAC. Grows 3.5 to 13 feet in full to part sun in moist sandy loam; a few sources.

Salix nigra (Black willow) – less sandy and wetter river margins, swamps, sloughs, swales, gullies, and drainage ditches, FACW+; statewide. Grows to 65 feet; fine moist to wet silt or clay, especially in saturated or poorly drained soil from which other hardwoods are excluded, with pH above 4.5. Not drought tolerant; many sources.

Salix petiolaris (Slender willow) – moist sedge meadows and swales, stream banks and openings in rich, moist, low deciduous woodlands; FACW+; scattered statewide. Forms clumps from 5 to 35 feet tall; prefers sunny sites in moist to wet rich loams; a few sources.

Salix sericea (Silky willow) – swamps, bogs, stream banks and low woods, OBL; statewide. Shrub to 15 feet; sun to part shade in moist to wet acidic sandy or clayey loam; a few sources.

Salix serissima (Autumn willow) – fens, treed bogs, wet thickets, gravelly stream banks and lake shores, typically on calcareous soils; OBL. Mostly northwestern counties, especially the Erie and Ontario Lake Plain and Western Glaciated Allegheny Plateau. Grows 5 to 15 feet in wet to wet–mesic circumneutral to alkaline silt and sand loams; a few sources.

Sambucus canadensis (American elder) – woods, fields, stream banks, moist fields and swamps, FACW; statewide. Shrub to 10 feet with white flowers in early summer and purple fruit in late summer; average, medium to wet well–drained soil in full sun to part shade. Prefers moist, humusy soils. Spreads by root suckers to form colonies; many sources.

Sambucus racemosa var. pubens (Red–berried elder) – stream banks, ravines, swamps, moist forest clearings and higher ground near wetlands, FACU; statewide. Shrub to 10 feet with white flowers in late spring becoming red fruit; sun to part sun in moist, well drained humusy soils; many sources.

Sassafras albidum (Sassafras) – open woods on moist, well–drained, sandy loam soils, dry ridges and upper slopes, fencerows and old fields, FACU–; statewide. Grows to 65 feet; average, medium, well–drained soil in full sun to part shade. Prefers moist, acidic, sandy–loamy soils, pH 6.0 to 7.0. Tolerates dry, sandy soils. Can be aggressive, especially following disturbance such as fire; many sources.

Shepherdia canadensis (Buffalo–berry) – rare on shaly, wet banks and lightly shaded depressions along Lake Erie; UPL; Mostly Erie County (Erie and Ontario Lake Plain). Grows 6 to 8 feet with inconspicuous yellow flowers in spring; grow in circumneutral to slightly alkaline moist, rocky soils in sun to part shade; a few sources.

Sorbus americana (American mountain–ash) – swamp margins, rocky hillsides, woodland edges, and roadsides, FACU; scattered statewide except southeast (Piedmont, Central Appalachians). Grows to 32 feet in newly–formed mineral–rich soils to shallow and infertile soils in cool, windy, and humid conditions; many sources.

Sorbus decora (Showy mountain–ash) – rare wet to mesic woods, cool moist rocky slopes, lake shores, FAC; northeast (Northern Glaciated Allegheny Plateau) and northwest (Erie and Ontario Lake Plain, Western Glaciated Allegheny Plateau); endangered. Grows to 35 feet; part shade to shade in moist, circumneutral, poor to well–drained mesic to wet soil; many sources.

Spiraea alba (Meadow–sweet) – wet prairies, especially open ground along streams, lakes and bogs, and moist meadows, FACW+; statewide. Grows to 6 feet with white to pink flowers in late summer; sun to part shade in mesic to wet, well–drained soil. Prefers full sun; soil should not be allowed to dry out; many sources.

Spiraea betulifolia var. corymbosa (Dwarf spiraea) – very rare on dry wooded slopes and steep shale hillsides, scattered in south–central counties (Allegheny Mountains). Grows 2 to 3 feet tall in average, well–drained soils in full sun; tolerates a wide variety of soils. White flowers in late spring on new wood; a few sources.

Spiraea tomentosa (Hardhack or Steeplebush) – meadows, old fields, pastures, bogs and swamps, FACU–; statewide. Grows to 3 feet with white to pink flowers in summer; sun to part sun in mesic to moist moderately acid soil; many sources.

Staphylea trifolia (Bladdernut) – bottomlands, woodland thickets and moist soils along streams, FAC; statewide except north–central (Northern Unglaciated Allegheny Plateau). Grows to 15 feet with white flowers in late spring; part shade to shade in dry to mesic sandy loam, but prefers a moist soil. pH 6.1 to 8; several sources.

Symphoricarpos albus var. albus (Snowberry) – warm, dry woodland hillsides and rocky, open forest slopes, warm moist slopes, riparian benches and terraces. FACU–; scattered west, especially Allegheny Mountains. Grows 3 to 6 feet with white flowers in early summer; sun to part shade in dry to moist circumneutral soil composed of infertile sands and gravels. Will grow in part shade, but prefers more open sites tending toward limestone substrate; many sources.

Symphoricarpos orbiculatus (Coralberry) – open woodlands, shaded woods, thickets, stream banks and river banks; characteristic of *Quercus stellata* (post oak) woodlands, UPL. Mostly southeast (Piedmont); scattered west. Grows 2 to 5 feet with pink flowers in spring; sun to part shade on well–drained, medium moist average soils. Forms extensive colonies by rooting at nodes that touch the ground; control spread by removing suckers and runners. Many sources.

Taxus canadensis (Canadian yew) – cool moist rocky slopes or ravines under mixed coniferous (rarely deciduous) forest canopy; statewide. Declining because of deer browsing, FAC. Shrub to 5 feet; sun to part shade in mesic to moist sandy circumneutral loam. Needs protection from winter sun and wind; a few sources.

Tilia americana var. americana (Basswood) – rich uplands on mid–slopes in mixed deciduous forests and occasionally swamps, FACU; statewide. Grows to 130 feet in sandy loams to silt loams; prefers moist to mesic, finer textured, well–drained loams. Generally intolerant of air pollution and urban conditions; many sources.

Toxicodendron vernix (Poison sumac) – wet soil of swamps, bogs, seepage slopes, and frequently flooded areas; in shady hardwood forests, OBL; statewide except north–central (Northern Unglaciated Allegheny Plateau). Grows to16 feet. Not a suitable landscape plant. All parts, in all seasons, will cause severe skin irritation if plant sap contacted; a few sources.

Tsuga canadensis (Canada hemlock, Eastern hemlock) – moist rocky ridges and hillsides, cool moist valleys, flats and ravines, especially on northern and eastern facing slopes, and swamp borders if peat and muck soils are shallow, usually above 1,200 feet, FACU; statewide. Grows to 100 feet; average, medium, well–drained soil in part shade to full shade. Prefers acidic cool, moist, humid conditions with good drainage; textures include sandy loams, loamy sands, and silty loams with gravel of glacial origin in the upper profile. Intolerant of drought and should be watered regularly in prolonged dry spells, particularly when young. Best sited in a location protected from strong winds. Currently under attack by *Adelges tsugae* (wooly adelgid), a pest from Japan; once infected, a tree is usually dead within a few years; many sources.

Ulmus americana (American elm) – alluvial woods, swamp forests, deciduous woodlands, fencerows, pastures, old fields, waste areas, FACW–; statewide. Grows to 130 feet; average, medium moisture, well–drained soils in full sun. Tolerant of light shade. Prefers rich, moist loams. Adapts to both wet and dry sites. Generally tolerant of urban conditions and often planted as a street tree. Once a very common species, it fell victim to a fungus imported from Europe; many sources.

Ulmus rubra (Red elm or slippery elm) – moist rich soils on lower slopes, alluvial flood plains, stream banks, riverbanks and river terraces, and wooded bottom lands, sometimes on drier, limestone–origin sites, FAC–; statewide. Grows to 65 feet; average, medium moisture, well–drained soils in full sun. Tolerant of light shade. Prefers rich, moist loams. Adapts to wet and dry sites. Generally tolerant of urban conditions; a few sources.

Vaccinium angustifolium (Low sweet blueberry) – dry woods and barrens, acidic soils, FACU; statewide. Grows to 30 inches with white flowers in spring and dark blue fruit in late summer; part sun to part shade in dry to mesic sandy loam; several sources.

Vaccinium corymbosum (Highbush blueberry) – dry to wet woods, thickets, stream banks, bogs in acidic soil, FACW–; statewide, especially east. Grows to 10 feet with white flowers in spring and dark blue fruit in late summer; sun to part shade in dry to mesic sandy organic loam. Parent plant of almost all hybrid blueberries; several sources.

Vaccinium macrocarpon (American cranberry) – peaty woodlands, seepy areas and sphagnum bogs, OBL; statewide, especially northeast (Northern Glaciated Allegheny Plateau). Trailing shrub with white flowers in spring and the familiar red cranberry in late summer; sun to part shade in damp, acidic (pH 4.0 to 5.2), organically rich, well–drained soil in full sun; several sources.

Vaccinium myrtilloides (Sour–top blueberry) – wet thickets and barrens, FAC; mostly northwest (Western Glaciated Allegheny Plateau) and northeast (Northern Glaciated Allegheny Plateau); scattered elsewhere. Shrub to 30 inches with greenish–white flowers in spring and dark blue fruit in late summer; sun to part shade in moist acidic sandy loam; a few sources.

Vaccinium oxycoccos (Small cranberry) – bogs, especially in cool areas, OBL; mostly northeast (Northern Glaciated Allegheny Plateau). Trailing shrub with white flowers in spring followed by red fruit; sun to part shade in moist to wet acidic sandy loam; a few sources.

Vaccinium pallidum (Lowbush blueberry) – dry, rocky hillsides, upland ridges, rocky outcrops and ledges, sandy knolls, shale barrens and upland swamps; statewide. Shrub to 3 feet with white flowers in spring and dark blue–purple fruit in late summer; part sun to part shade in dry to mesic sandy loam; a few sources.

Vaccinium stamineum (Deerberry) – dry woods, openings, barrens and clearings. FACU; statewide. Shrub to 6 feet with white flowers and spring and green fruit when ripe in late summer; part sun to part shade in mesic sandy clay loam; a few sources.

Viburnum acerifolium (Maple–leaved viburnum) – upland forests, woodlands, ravine slopes and hillsides in well–drained, moist soils; particularly tolerant of acid soils, UPL; statewide. Shrub to 6 feet with white flowers in spring; part sun to part shade in mesic to moist rich sandy loam; pH 5.1 to 6; several sources.

Viburnum cassinoides (Witherod) – swamps, moist upland woods and clearings and exposed rock crevices, FACW; statewide. Shrub to 15 feet with white flowers in spring; full sun to part shade in well–drained moist loams, but tolerates a wide range of soils including boggy ones; many sources.

Viburnum dentatum (Southern arrow–wood) – moist woods and along stream banks. FAC; mostly southeast (Piedmont). Grows 6 to 10 feet with white flowers in spring; sun to shade in wet to dry acidic soils and sandy loams; among the most adaptable of all the viburnums. Suckers freely from the base and is easily transplanted; many sources.

Viburnum lantanoides (Hobblebush) – rich, moist acidic woods, stream banks, ravines and swamps, FAC; mostly north (Western and Northern Glaciated, Northern Unglaciated Allegheny Plateaus) and Allegheny Mountains. Shrub to 6 feet with white to pink flowers in late spring; part sun to part shade in moist sandy loam. Trailing stems take root where they touch the ground, creating hazards for walkers, hence the name; a few sources.

Viburnum lentago (Nannyberry) – woods, swamps and thickets with rich, moist soil, FAC; statewide, especially southeast (Piedmont).

Shrub to 15 feet with white flowers in spring; part sun to part shade in average, medium, well–drained soil; prefers mostly gravelly sandy loam; many sources.

Viburnum nudum (Possum–haw) – rare in low woods, swamps, bogs, OBL; southeast (Atlantic Coastal Plain) and endangered. Grows 5 to 12 feet with white flowers in spring; prefers moist loams in full sun to part shade, but tolerates wide range of soils; a few sources.

Viburnum opulus var. americanum (Highbush cranberry) – swampy woods, bogs, lake margins, pastures, thickets, slopes and moist low places, FACW; widely scattered south, especially southeast (Piedmont). Shrub to 15 feet with white flowers in spring; full sun to part shade in moist to wet circumneutral (but not limestone) well–drained soil. Prefers loams with consistent moisture, but tolerates a wide range of soils. AKA *Viburnum trilobum*; many sources.

Viburnum prunifolium (Black–haw) – successional woods, thickets, old fields, roadsides, FACU; statewide except north (Western and Northern Glaciated and Northern Unglaciated Allegheny Plateaus). Shrub or small tree to 25 feet with white flowers in spring; sun to part shade in dry to mesic sandy loam. Tolerates drought; many sources.

Viburnum rafinesquianum (Downy arrow–wood) – rocky woods, old fields, dry slopes and banks; widely scattered statewide. Shrub to 5 feet with white flowers in spring; part sun to part shade in dry to mesic rocky sandy loam. White flowers in spring; a few sources.

Viburnum recognitum (Northern arrow–wood) – swamps, boggy woods, wet pastures, stream banks, FACW–; statewide. Shrub to 15 feet with white flowers in spring; part shade to shade in moist, humusy well–drained acidic loam; a few sources.

Viburnum trilobum (Highbush cranberry) – swamps, thickets, fens and wet woods; mostly northwest (Western Glaciated Allegheny Plateau). Shrub to 15 feet with white flowers in spring; full sun to part shade in moist to wet circumneutral (but not limestone) well–drained soil. Prefers loams with consistent moisture, but tolerates a wide range of soils. Also known as *Viburnum opulus var. americanum*; many sources.

Zanthoxylum americanum (Prickly–ash) – calcareous soils or diabase along streams, on river bluffs, rocky hillsides and ravines and along roadsides; FACU; Mostly southeast (Central Appalachians, Piedmont). Grows 12 to 35 feet with inconspicuous flowers in rocky, calcareous soils (circumneutral to pH 7.2) in sun; a few sources.

APPARENTLY NOT AVAILABLE

The following 19 woody perennials do not appear to be commercially available:

Amelanchier bartramiana (Mountain juneberry)
Amelanchier intermedia (Shadbush)
Amelanchier obovalis (Coastal juneberry)
Crataegus flabellata (Fanleaf hawthorn)
Crataegus intricata (Biltmore hawthorn)
Crataegus pruinosa (Frosted hawthorn)
Ilex beadlei (Mountain holly)
Ilex laevigata (Smooth winterberry)
Quercus prinoides (Dwarf chestnut oak)
Rhamnus alnifolia (Alder–leaved buckthorn)
Ribes glandulosum (Skunk currant)
Ribes rotundifolium (Wild gooseberry)
Rubus enslenii (Southern dewberry)
Rubus pensilvanicus (Blackberry)
Rubus pubescens (Dwarf blackberry)
Rubus recurvicaulis (Dewberry)
Rubus setosus (Bristly blackberry)
Salix candida (Hoary willow)
Spiraea alba x latifolia (Meadow–sweet)

PERENNIAL FORBS

Aconitum uncinatum (Blue monkshood) – rare in rich, wet areas near streams and springs and low woods; occasionally in less mesic woods and clearings. Southwestern counties (Southern Allegheny Plateau). Grows to 4 feet, violet–purple flowers in spring, in part shade in moist, calcareous fertile soil. Does well in open woodlands; may be ignored by rabbits and deer. All parts are poisonous; a few sources.

Acorus americanus (Sweet flag) – Very rare emergent semi–aquatic in silty soil in shallows, ponds, marshes and quiet water less than 20 inches deep. Northwest (Erie and Ontario Lake Plain); endangered. Grows to 6 feet, yellow to brown flowers in late spring on fine–textured moist to wet soils (pH range of 5.6 to 7.2) in full sun to part shade. A vigorous spreader in wet soils and works well for retaining soil at the edge of a stream or pond; a few sources.

Actaea pachypoda (Dolls–eyes) – rich, open upland woods and thickets, statewide. Grows 12 to 30 inches, white flowers in late spring; part shade to shade in moist sandy humusy loam, pH 5 to 6; many sources.

Actaea podocarpa (American bugbane) – Rare in rich coves and rich northern hardwood forests. Southwestern counties (Southern Allegheny Plateau). Grows to about 30 inches in a clump with flower stems 5 to 6 feet bearing bottlebrush–like, branched racemes to 20 inches long of fluffy, creamy white flowers in summer. Prefers humusy, moisture–retentive soils in part shade to shade, sheltered from strong winds. Foliage scorches if too dry. AKA *Cimicifuga americana*; a few sources.

Actaea racemosa (Black cohosh, black snakeroot) – rich moist woods, wooded slopes, ravines, along riverbanks and thickets, statewide. Grows 3 to 8 feet, white flowers on tall racemes in early summer, similar to *A. podocarpa,* which blooms earlier. Part shade to shade in moist rich humus, pH 5 to 7; many sources.

Actaea rubra (Red baneberry) – usually upland hardwood and mixed–wood forest habitats on fresh or moist, fine–textured mineral soils. Mostly northeast and northwest (Northern and Western Glaciated Allegheny Plateaus). Grows 12 to 30 inches, white flowers in late spring; part sun to open shade in moist humus rich loam, pH 5 to 6; many sources.

Agastache nepetoides (Yellow giant hyssop) – generally upland moist, rich, open woodland areas, thickets and woodland borders, FACU. Mostly southern, especially southeast (Piedmont). Grows 3 to 5 feet, greenish–yellow flowers in late summer; full sun in moist rich loam; many sources.

Agastache scrophulariifolia Purple giant hyssop) – moist woods and thickets; statewide, except northern tier, especially southeast (Piedmont). Grows 3 to 5 feet, purple flowers in late summer; sun to part shade in moist rich humus, pH 6 to 7. Shade tolerant, but prefers sun; many sources.

Ageratina aromatica (Small–leaved white–snakeroot) – Rare in pine–oak and oak–hickory upland woodlands, sand ridges and burned pinelands, mostly southeast (Piedmont). Grows to 4 feet in sun to part shade with white flowers in late summer; prefers sandy, well drained soil. AKA *Eupatorium aromaticum;* a few sources.

Agrimonia parviflora (Southern agrimony) – moist to wet woods and thickets, FAC; statewide except scattered north. Grows up to 45 inches, yellow flowers in late summer; part shade to shade in moist sandy loam; a few sources.

Agrimonia striata (Roadside agrimony) – moist upland woods and thickets, FACU–; statewide except southern tier. Grows up to 36 inches, yellow flowers in late summer; part shade to shade in moist sandy loam, pH 5 to 6; a few sources.

Aletris farinosa (Colic–root, True unicorn root) – Rare in moist bogs, dry to mesic prairies, and dry, upland woods and thickets; FAC. Scattered statewide, most concentrated in southeastern counties (Piedmont, Atlantic Coastal Plain); endangered. Grows 2 to 3.5 feet in full sun to part shade in humusy moist soil with white flowers in late spring to mid–summer; a few sources.

Alisma subcordatum (Broad–leaved water–plantain) – aquatic; shallow ponds, stream margins, marshes, and ditches, OBL; statewide. Grows 12 to 36 inches, pink to white flowers in summer; sun to part sun in silty loam in ponds and pond edges; several sources.

Alisma triviale (Broad–leaved water–plantain) – Rare in shallow, muddy marshes, ditches, ponds and stream margins; OBL. Mostly western counties (Erie lake plain, western and southern Allegheny plateaus); endangered. Grows 2 to 3 feet in full to part sun in boggy soils, wet pond margins or in shallow water. Whorls of white flowers in summer; a few sources.

Allium canadense (Wild onion) – upland glades, bluffs, open woods, prairies and disturbed sites, FACU; statewide except for the highest elevations on the Allegheny Plateau. Grows 8 to 12 inches, pink to white flowers in early summer; full sun to part shade in moist rich loam, pH 6.5 to 7; several sources.

Allium cernuum (Nodding onion) – moist soils in cool mountainous regions. Mostly southwest (Southern Allegheny Plateau, Allegheny Mountains), scattered elsewhere. White flowers in spring. Grow in well–drained soil, especially sandy loams in full sun to light shade; does best in full sun with light afternoon shade and will naturalize by self–seeding and bulb offsets; many sources.

Allium tricoccum (Ramp) – moist ground in rich upland woods, depressions, streamside bluffs, and colluvial slopes, FACU+; statewide except for the Central Appalachians. Grows up to 20 inches, white flowers in spring; deciduous shade (needs sun in early spring) in rich moist mesic loam. pH 6.8 to 7.2; many sources.

Anaphalis margaritacea (Pearly everlasting) – dry, sandy or gravelly soil of fields, woods, edges and roadsides; statewide, mostly north and east. Grows 1 to 3 feet, white flowers in late summer; average, medium, well–drained soil in full sun to part shade. Prefers full sun and somewhat dry, sandy conditions; many sources.

Anemone canadensis (Canada anemone) – moist thickets and open woodlands, meadows and wet prairies, clearings and the shores of lakes and streams; occasionally in swampy areas. FACW. Mostly northwest (Western Glaciated Allegheny Plateau and Erie and Ontario Lake Plain). Grows 12 to18 inches, white flowers in early summer. Best in moist, humusy but well–drained soils in part shade; tolerates full sun. A very aggressive spreader (rhizomes and seed), ideal for naturalizing large areas, but a favorite browse of deer; many sources.

Anemone cylindrica (Thimbleweed) – rare in dry open woods, prairies, pastures, roadsides. Observed in Erie and Centre counties; endangered. Grow in sun to part shade in dry, rocky soils; many sources.

Anemone quinquefolia (Wood anemone) – moist upland open woods and thickets, banks and shady roadsides, FACU; statewide. Grows 4 to 8 inches, white flowers in spring; part shade to shade in damp to moist rich loam, pH 5 to 6; a few sources.

Anemone virginiana (Virginia anemone) – upland rocky and dry open woods, slopes, thickets and prairies; statewide. Grows up to 12 inches, greenish–white flowers in early summer, followed by attractive seed pods that persist into fall; sun to part shade in dry to moist sandy loam; many sources.

Angelica atropurpurea (Purple–stemmed angelica) – swamps, moist meadows, stream banks and wet woods, OBL; statewide except for higher elevations on the Allegheny Plateau and the central Appalachian ridges and valleys. Grows 3 to 10 feet, white flowers in summer; full sun to dappled shade in medium to wet soils; many sources.

Angelica venenosa (Hairy angelica) – dry open woods, roadsides, banks, serpentine barrens and old fields; statewide, mostly south. Grows up to 6 feet, white flowers in mid–summer; full sun to part shade in dry, sandy to gravelly soil; a few sources.

Antennaria neglecta (Overlooked pussytoe) – mesic to dry prairies, slopes of upland open woodlands, dry meadows in woodland areas, savannahs, shale glades, eroded clay banks, pastures, abandoned fields, and roadsides; mostly southeast (Piedmont). Grows up to 6 inches, brown/gray flowers in spring; sun to part sun in dry to moist clay loam, pH 5.5 to 7.5; a few sources.

Antennaria parlinii (Parlin's pussytoe) – open woods and fields; statewide, especially southeast (Piedmont). Grows up to 8 inches, white flowers in spring; sun to part sun in dry, sandy, well drained loam; a few sources.

Antennaria plantaginifolia (Plantain–leaved pussytoe) – dry open woods, pastures, fields, rocky barrens; statewide, especially Central Appalachians and Piedmont. Grows up to about 10 inches, white flowers in spring; sun to part sun in dry, sandy, well drained loam, pH 4 to 7; several sources.

Antennaria virginica (Shale–barren pussytoe) – Dry, shaly barrens in the Allegheny Mountains (south–central counties) where it roots into rock crevices to form thick mats. Spreads slowly by runners to form silvery mats in dry, partly shady, poor soil, an ideal ground cover for such sites, including rock gardens. Prefers sun to part sun with southern to western exposure; blooms in spring on 15 inch stalks; a few sources.

Aplectrum hyemale (Puttyroot) – rich moist woods and bottomlands, FAC. Mostly southeast (Piedmont), scattered elsewhere. Grows 12 to 24 inches, purple flowers in early summer; part shade to shade in moist rich humus; several sources.

Apocynum androsaemifolium (Pink dogbane) – well–drained upland forest sites, open hillsides and ridges, especially on dry, fresh, sandy and coarse loamy soils; statewide. Also found in clearings and fields, along forest margins, on roadsides and disturbed ground. Grows 8 to 32 inches, pink flowers in early summer; sun to part shade in dry, sandy loam, pH 5 to 6; a few sources.

Apocynum cannabinum (Indian hemp) – upland open woods, pastures, waste ground, disturbed sites, wooded slopes, on roadsides and along railroads, FACU; statewide. Grows up to 5 feet, pink flowers in early summer; sun to part sun in dry to moist sandy loam; several sources.

Aquilegia canadensis (American columbine) – open, steep, rocky wooded bluffs of streams and stream banks, wooded slopes of deep ravines, limestone bluffs and ledges, borders and clearings in deciduous or mixed woods or thickets, FAC; statewide. Grows up to 32 inches, yellow and red flowers in late spring; sun to part shade in average well–drained soil, pH 5 to 7. Prefers rich, moist soils in light to moderate shade, with pH of 6 to 7; many sources.

Arabis glabra (Towercress) – fields, open woods, ledges, usually in dry soil. Pennsylvania distribution includes most eastern, northern and southwestern counties. Grows 16 to 40 inches, greenish–white flowers in late spring; part sun to shade in dry to moist rocky clay loam; a few sources.

Aralia nudicaulis (Wild sarsaparilla) – dry, upland open woods and thickets with thin soil, FACU; statewide. Grows 12 to 36 inches, greenish flowers in spring; part sun to shade in dry to moist rich humus, pH 5 to 7; several sources.

Aralia racemosa (Spikenard) – rich wooded slopes, ravines, moist ledges and bluffs; statewide. Grows up to 6 feet, greenish flowers in early summer; part sun to part shade in moist rich humus; many sources.

Arisaema dracontium (Green–dragon) – Wet to mesic deciduous woodlands, thickets, and bottoms; FACW. Scattered statewide, especially southeast (Piedmont). Grows 1 to 3 feet, green–brown flowers in late spring similar to Jack–in–the–Pulpit in spring. Prefers constantly moist soil rich in organic matter; does poorly in clay soils. Grows well in moist conditions along streams or ponds; part sun to part shade. Goes dormant in summer. Roots contain calcium oxalate and are poisonous in an uncooked state; handle roots and seed pods with great care; a few sources.

Arisaema triphyllum (Jack–in–the–pulpit) – moist low woods, swamps, bogs and floodplains, FACW–; statewide. Grows up to 36 inches, with the familiar greenish flowers in spring; part shade to full shade in constantly moist soil rich in organic matter, pH 5 to 6; many sources.

Aristolochia serpentaria (Virginia snakeroot) – rich, rocky upland woods, thickets, ravines and slopes, UPL; mostly south. Grows up to 20 inches, greenish–white flowers in spring; part shade to shade in dry to moist sandy loam; a few sources.

Arnoglossum atriplicifolium (Pale Indian plantain) – open woods, fields and on moist banks; statewide except northern tier (Western and Northern Glaciated and Northern Unglaciated Allegheny Plateaus). Grows up to 9 feet, yellow flowers in late summer and early fall; sun to part shade in dry to moist sandy loam, pH 4 to 5.5; several sources. AKA *Cacalia atriplicifolia.*

Arnoglossum reniforme (Great Indian–plantain) – wet to mesic prairies and savannahs. Scattered southwest (Southern Allegheny Plateau) and southeast (Piedmont). White flowers in summer; grows to 8 feet. Grow in full sun in moist, rich well–drained loam. AKA *Cacalia muhlenbergii*; a few sources.

Aruncus dioicus (Goat's–beard, bride's feathers) – moist, rich woods in mountainous areas, FACU; mostly southwest (Southern Allegheny Plateau). White flowers in late spring; grows to 4 to 6 feet, open habit. Grow in part shade in rich, medium to wet well–drained soils; tolerates flooding. Often found in better garden centers; many sources.

Asarum canadense (Wild ginger) – the understory of upland deciduous forests (rarely coniferous); statewide. Grows 6 to 12 inches, brownish–purple flowers in early spring; part shade to full shade in moist humus, pH 4 to 7. Slowly spreads by rhizomes to form large colonies. Not related to the culinary spice, but has been used as a substitute, hence the name; many sources.

Asclepias amplexicaulis (Blunt–leaved milkweed) – dry fields and upland open woods, usually in sandy soil. Mostly east and in the Central Appalachians. Grows 12 to 36 inches, greenish–pink flowers in summer; sun to part sun in dry, sandy loam; a few sources.

Asclepias exaltata (Poke milkweed) – rich upland woods and woods edges, FACU; statewide. Grows 12 to 32 inches, greenish–purple flowers in early summer; part shade to shade in dry to moist sandy loam, pH 5.5 to 7; a few sources.

Asclepias incarnata (Swamp milkweed) – floodplains and wet meadows, OBL; statewide. Grows up to 5 feet, pink–rose flowers in early summer; full to part sun in constantly moist rich loam; many sources.

Asclepias syriaca (Common milkweed) – dry, upland woods edges fields and prairies; statewide. Host species for monarch butterflies. Grows 3 to 6 feet, very fragrant purple–whitish flowers in early summer; sun to part sun in dry sandy loam, pH 4 to 7; many sources.

Asclepias tuberosa (Butterfly weed) – dry fields, roadsides and shale barrens; statewide especially southwest (Southern Allegheny Plateau), central (Central Appalachians) and east (Piedmont). Grows 12 to 30 inches, orange–yellow flowers in early summer; sun to part shade in dry to medium wet, well drained sandy loam, pH 4.5 to 6.8; many sources.

Asclepias variegata (White milkweed) – upland dry or rocky woods, sandy open ground, ravine bottoms, low woods, slopes, ridges and along roadsides, FACU, endangered. Mostly southeast (Piedmont). Grows up to 36 inches, white to pinkish flowers in early summer; sun to part shade in dry sandy loam; a few sources.

Asclepias verticillata (Whorled milkweed) – open woods, dry slopes, serpentine barrens on dry rocky sandy soil, mostly southeast (Piedmont). Grows 8 to 20 inches, white–greenish flowers in summer; sun to part sun in sandy loam, pH 4.8 to 6.8; many sources.

Asclepias viridiflora (Green milkweed) – dry rocky slopes, serpentine barrens, rocky prairies, glades; mostly south, especially southeast (Piedmont). Grows 12 to 32 inches, greenish flowers in summer; sun to part sun in dry sandy loam; a few sources.

Astragalus canadensis (Milk–vetch) – rocky roadsides, shale barrens, limestone ledges and banks, FAC; southwest (Southern Allegheny Plateau), scattered elsewhere. Grows up to 5 feet, white flowers in early summer; sun to part shade in mesic to moist sandy loam; many sources.

Aureolaria virginica (Downy false–foxglove) – dry open deciduous woods; statewide, especially southeast. Grows 20 to 60 inches, yellow flowers in late summer; part shade to shade in dry sandy loam, pH 4 to 6; a few sources.

Baptisia australis (Blue false–indigo) – edges of woods, prairies and limestone glades in circumneutral soils. Mostly west (Southern and Western Glaciated Allegheny Plateaus). Purple flowers in late spring.

Grow in well drained, dry to medium circumneutral soils in full sun (best) to part shade. Drought and poor–soil tolerant; many sources.

Baptisia tinctoria (Wild indigo) – dry, open woods and clearings in sandy soil; statewide except Northern Glaciated and Northern Unglaciated Allegheny Plateaus. Grows up to 36 inches, yellow flowers in summer; sun to part shade in dry to moist sandy loam. pH 5 to 7, but prefers acidic soils; several sources.

Blephilia ciliata (Wood–mint) – Swamps, thin woods, meadows, limestone bluffs, woodland slopes and calcareous hillsides. Mostly west (Western Glaciated and Southern Allegheny Plateaus). Grows 9 to 18 inches, lavender flowers in summer; prefers average, dry to mesic, circumneutral, well–drained soils in full sun to part shade; a few sources.

Boltonia asteroides (Aster–like boltonia) – very rare and endangered in moist to wet, gravelly to sandy rocky shores and river beds in full sun; FACW. Observed in Dauphin, York and Lancaster counties. Grow in well–drained, medium soils, toward dryer and less fertile soils. Rich moist soils will result in plants that tend to flop and need support; poor dry soils will result in shorter plants with smaller flowers; several sources.

Brasenia schreberi (Purple wendock) – aquatic; ponds, lakes, and sluggish streams, with pink to yellow flowers in summer; ponds with intermediate to low nutrient values, OBL. Mostly northeast (Northern Glaciated Allegheny Plateau), scattered elsewhere. Grow in full sun to part shade in still to slow moving standing water; a few sources.

Calopogon tuberosus (Grass–pink) – bogs, fens and wet meadows, pine and oak savannahs, grasslands and swales, FACW+; mostly east, scattered elsewhere. Grows 12 to 30 inches, pink–purple and yellow flowers in summer; sun to part sun in wet, rich sandy acidic loam; a few sources.

Caltha palustris (Marsh marigold) – wet woods, stream banks, muddy meadows, OBL; statewide. Grows up to about 15 inches, yellow to white flowers in spring and early summer; sun to part shade in wet, muddy humus rich loam; many sources.

Camassia scilloides (Wild hyacinth, Atlantic camas) – very rare in mesic to moist prairies and meadows as well as open weeds; FAC. Mostly southwestern counties (Southern Allegheny Plateau); endangered. Grows 1 to 2 feet, white flowers in spring; prefers moist but well–drained limestone–based sandy loam. Green in spring only, then dormant for the year; a few sources.

Campanula americana (Tall bellflower) – moist upland woods, on rocky wooded slopes and stream banks, FAC; statewide except Western and Northern Glaciated and Northern Unglaciated Allegheny Plateaus. Grows up to 6 feet, blue to white flowers in summer; part shade to shade in moist silty loam; several sources.

Campanula rotundifolia (Harebell) – dry, rocky upland slopes, bluffs and cliffs, FACU. Mostly east and scattered throughout the Central Appalachians. Grows up to 6 feet, blue flowers in summer; sun to shade in dry rocky sandy loam, pH 5 to 7; several sources.

Cardamine diphylla (Crinkleroot toothwort) – rich woods and floodplains, FACU; mostly north and west (Allegheny plateaus). Grows up to 12 inches, white flowers in spring; sun to part shade in moist to wet humus–rich loam; a few sources.

Cardamine maxima (Large toothwort) – Very rare in rich woods, shady ravines, ledges steep forested slopes and moist alluvial bottoms and banks. Scattered, mostly central to west. Grows 1 to 3 feet, purple flowers in spring; prefers part shade to shade in rich, humusy soil; a few sources.

Cardamine pratensis (Cuckoo–flower) – swamps, wet meadows and alluvial woods, OBL. Scattered north and east. Grows 8 to 20 inches, white to pink flowers in spring; full sun to part shade in cool, moist soils; a few sources.

Caulophyllum thalictroides (Blue cohosh) – moist rich deciduous and mixed forests; statewide except limestone substrates in the Central Appalachians. Grows 12 to 30 inches, greenish yellow/purple flowers in early spring; shady woodland areas in rich, moist, soils that do not dry out; pH 4 to 7; many sources.

Ceratophyllum demersum (Coontail) – aquatic; quiet waters of lakes and ponds, rivers, streams, swamps, generally submerged, sometimes free floating, OBL; mostly northwest and southeast, scattered elsewhere. Flowers early summer, fruit in late summer; silty garden ponds ranging from fresh to slightly brackish; several sources.

Chamaelirium luteum (Devil's bit or Fairywand) – dry–wet open woods, clearings, barrens in humus–rich soil; FAC; mostly southeast (Piedmont) and scattered elsewhere. Grows to 40 inches, white to yellow flowers in late spring; sun to part shade in dry, rich sandy loam, pH 5 to 7; several sources.

Chamerion angustifolium ssp. circumvagum (Fireweed) – mesic woods edges and recent clearings in open sandy ground; usually a pioneer species after forest fires, FAC; statewide. Grows 3 to 12 feet, purple–pink flowers in summer; disturbed sandy loam in full sun to part shade; forms dense clumps and spreads aggressively; many sources.

Chelone glabra (White turtlehead) – wet open woods, swamps and stream banks, OBL; statewide. Grows 20 to 30 inches, white to pinkish flowers in summer; sun to part shade in moist rich loam, but prefers full sun, pH 5.5 to 7; many sources.

Chrysogonum virginianum (Green–and–gold) – Very rare in moist to dry woodlands and forests, clearings and edges, especially over limestone. South–central (Blue Ridge Mountains); endangered. Grows 3 to 6 inches and spreads via rhizomes to form an attractive ground cover. Yellow flowers from March into July, but will continue to bloom with moisture into the fall. Grow in part sun to full shade in average soils, but prefers moist, rich organic soil; a few sources.

Chrysopsis mariana (Golden aster) – Rare in open areas of pine and oak woodlands, scrub, natural rock outcrops, fields and roadside embankments; UPL. Mostly southeast (Atlantic Coastal Plain and Piedmont); endangered. Grows up to 12 inches, yellow flowers in late summer on open to partly shaded, disturbed clay to sandy soils; a few sources.

Cicuta maculata var. maculata (Beaver–poison or water hemlock) – swamps, marshes, wet meadows, stream banks and ditches, OBL; statewide. Grows up to 8 inches, white flowers in summer; moist to wet silty organic loam in sun to part sun. All parts highly toxic and may be fatal if eaten; a few sources.

Cirsium muticum (Swamp thistle) – swamps, bogs, stream banks and wet meadows, OBL; statewide. Grows 3 to 6 feet, purple flowers in summer; sun to part sun in moist to wet rich loam; a few sources.

Claytonia caroliniana (Carolina spring beauty) – moist, rocky upland wooded slopes, open woods and thickets, FACU; north and west (Allegheny plateaus). Grows 6 to 12 inches, white to pinkish flowers in spring; part sun to part shade in moist to wet rich loams, pH 5 to 6; a few sources.

Claytonia virginica (Spring beauty) – moist woods and meadows, often on alluvial soils, FACU; statewide. Grows 6 to 12 inches, white to pinkish flowers in spring; sun to part shade in moist loam, pH 5 to 7; many sources.

Clinopodium arkansanum (Calamint) – moist dolomite alvars, open flats and bald knobs, fens, limestone glades and bluffs, and wet prairies and meadows, as well as stream gravel bars; FACU. Northwest (Erie and Ontario Lake Plain). Grows 2 to 8 inches in mats with white to purple flowers from June through late September. Prefers neutral to slightly alkaline, mesic and well–drained soils in full sun, but tolerates light shade. AKA *Calamintha arkansana;* a few sources.

Clintonia borealis (Blue bead lily) – shady, cool moist woods and thickets, mostly in the mountains, FAC; statewide except southeast (Piedmont). Grows up to 16 inches, yellow flowers in late spring, fruit a blue berry in summer; part shade to shade in moist humusy loam, pH 4 to 6; a few sources.

Clintonia umbellulata (Speckled wood–lily) – Rich hardwood forests, especially in coves, ravines, and banks. Mostly west (Western Glaciated and Southern Allegheny plateaus).Grows 1 to 3 feet, white flowers in late spring; prefers acidic, humus–rich (peaty) soils in damp, cool, part shade to shade, and serves as a good groundcover for shady sites. Short–creeping underground stems form dense patches; a few sources.

Collinsonia canadensis (Horse balm) – moist rich woods and on wooded floodplains and ravines, often on limestone substrates, FAC+; statewide. Grows to 48 inches, yellow flowers in summer; part shade to shade in dry to moist organic loam, pH 6 to 7; a few sources.

Comarum palustre (Marsh cinquefoil) – emergent aquatic; swamps, bogs and peaty lake margins, OBL. Northeast (Northern Glaciated Allegheny Plateau) and northwest (Western Glaciated Allegheny Plateau and Erie and Ontario Lake Plain). Grows 8 to 24 inches, red–purple flowers in summer; full sun in mucky, peaty soil along pond edges; a few sources. AKA *Potentilla palustris.*

Commelina erecta (Erect dayflower) – Very rare in hummocks, shale barrens, sand dunes and rocky woods including scrub oak and pine woodlands, as well as roadsides and railroad rights of way. Only one southeastern site reported and now believed to be extirpated. Grows in typically prostrate style on stems up to 3 feet long that lie on the ground, with blue and white flowers that last just one day from May to October in part shade on dry, sandy soils; a few sources.

Conoclinium coelestinum (Mistflower) – along streams, in low woods and woods margins, wet meadows, ditches. FAC. Mostly south, especially Piedmont and Southern Allegheny Plateau. Pale blue flowers in late summer. Grow in well–drained, medium moist soils in full sun to part shade; prefers full sun. Aggressive spreader through rhizomes and will form large colonies. Cut back in summer for denser habit. AKA *Eupatorium coelestinum;* many sources.

Conopholis americana (Squaw–root) – rich oak or beech woods, where it is parasitic on oaks; mostly south, scattered elsewhere. Grows up to 6 inches, pale brown to yellowish flowers in late spring; part shade to shade in dry to moist sandy loam, pH 4 to 6; a few sources.

Coptis trifolia ssp. groenlandica (Goldthread) – rich, damp, mossy woods bogs and swamps, often associated with hemlock and mosses, FACW; mostly north, scattered elsewhere. Grows 6 to 8 inches, white flowers in early spring; shade in moist, acidic, humusy loam, pH 4 to 5; a few sources.

Cornus canadensis (Bunchberry) – cool, damp woods, bogs and swamp edges, FAC–. Mostly north; scattered south. Grows 4 to 8 inches, white flowers late spring and fruit in late summer; part shade to shade in moist, rich humus, pH 4 to 5; many sources.

Corydalis sempervirens (Rock harlequin) – dry rocky woods, woodland outcrops and open areas on poor gravelly soil; statewide. Grows 12 to 30 inches, pinkish–white to purple flowers in late spring to early fall; sun to part shade in dry sandy loam, pH 5 to 6; several sources.

Cryptotaenia canadensis (Honewort) – moist woods, wooded stream banks, seeps; FAC; statewide. Grows 10 to 30 inches, white flowers late spring to early summer; part shade in moist, sandy loam; several sources.

Cunila origanoides (Common dittany) – dry open woods, shaly slopes, and serpentine barrens. Mostly southeast (Central Appalachians, Piedmont); scattered southwest (Southern Allegheny Plateau); part sun to part shade in dry, sandy rocky loam; a few sources.

Cypripedium acaule (Pink lady's slipper) – dry to wet acidic upland forests, bogs, and brushy barrens; FACU; statewide. Grows 6 to 16 inches, pink flowers late spring; part shade to shade in well mulched, dry to moist sandy acidic loam, pH 4 to 5. Very difficult to transplant because of long, thin root system and soil preferences; several sources.

Cypripedium candidum (Small white lady's–slipper) – Very rare in wet to mesic prairies and meadows, fens and very rarely in open wooded sites; OBL. Believed to be extirpated. Grows 6 to 16 inches in calcareous, wet to moist soils rich in organic matter in sun to part sun, with white flowers in late spring; a few sources.

Cypripedium parviflorum var. parviflorum (Lesser yellow lady's slipper) – dry deciduous and deciduous–hemlock forests, usually on slopes, FAC+. Scattered statewide, endangered. Grows 8 to 30 inches, yellow flowers in spring; part shade to shade in rich dry to moist acidic sandy loam; a few sources.

Cypripedium parviflorum var. pubescens (Large yellow lady's slipper) – moist, rich, rocky woods and slopes, bogs and swamps, FAC+; statewide, endangered. Grows 8 to 30 inches, yellow flowers, spring; sun to part shade in moist to wet silty loam, pH 5 to 7, but prefers 6.5 to 7; several sources.

Cypripedium reginae (Large white lady's slipper) – very rare in hardwood and coniferous fen forests and meadows, hillside seeps, fen and moist meadows, wet prairies and seeping cliffs. FACW; mostly northwest (Western Glaciated Allegheny Plateau) and widely scattered in Central Appalachians. Largest and most showy of the native orchids, with white and pink flowers in late spring to early summer. Grow in full sun to part shade in moist to wet rich, circumneutral soils; several sources.

Dasiphora fruticosa (Shrubby cinquefoil) – Very rare in swamps, bogs, meadows and moist rocky sites, especially calcareous sites; mostly east (Lehigh Valley) and endangered; FACW. Grows 3 to 6 feet, typically prostrate, in full sun on circumneutral loams, often for erosion control purposes. AKA *Potentilla fruticosa*; a few sources.

Delphinium exaltatum (Tall Larkspur) – Very rare on rocky slopes of barrens and open deciduous woods, usually on calcareous substrates as well as shale, mostly southwestern counties (Southern Allegheny Plateau, Allegheny Mountains); endangered. Grows 4 to 6 feet, blue flowers in summer in full sun to part sun. Prefers fertile, mesic well–drained circumneutral soils perhaps with some afternoon shade; a few sources.

Delphinium tricorne (Dwarf larkspur) – Rare on thin, deciduous forest slopes, moist ravines, thicket edges, partially shaded cliffs along streams and moist prairies, mostly southwest (Southern Allegheny Plateau); UPL. Grows 8 to 18 inches in rocky to loamy soils ranging from slightly dry to mesic; prefers light dappled shade or part sun. Dark purple flowers in early spring; a few sources.

Desmodium canadense (Showy tick–trefoil) – dry open woods and fields, FAC; mostly east and west, scattered center. Grows 20 to 40 inches, blue to violet flowers late summer; sun to part shade in dry to moist sandy loam; many sources.

Desmodium glutinosum (Sticky tick–clover) – dry to moist rich woods; statewide except for limestone substrates counties in the Central Appalachians. Grows 12 to 36 inches, with pink to purple flowers in summer; part shade to shade in moist, rich loam; a few sources.

Desmodium paniculatum (Tick–trefoil) – clearings and edges of moist or dry upland woods, UPL; statewide except north–central (Northern Unglaciated Allegheny Plateau). Grows 12 to 36 inches, violet to purple flowers, late summer; sun to part shade in dry to moist sandy loam. pH 6 to 7; a few sources.

Desmodium sessilifolium (Sessile–leaved tick–trefoil) – very rare in rocky open woodland, limestone glades, dry sandy savannas, prairies; believed to be extirpated. Grows 18 to 36 inches in full sun to part sun in dry, sandy soil; tolerates loamy or rocky soils. Purple flowers in summer; a few sources.

Dicentra canadensis (Squirrel corn) – deciduous woods, often among rock outcrops, in rich loam soils; scattered statewide except limestone–substrate Central Appalachians. Grows up to 10 inches, white flowers in early spring; part shade to shade in moist, rich sandy loam, pH 6 to 7; several sources.

Dicentra cucullaria (Dutchman's breeches) – deciduous woods and clearings, in rich loam soils; statewide. Grows to 10 inches, white flowers in early spring; part shade to shade in dry to moist, rich sandy loam, pH 6 to 7; many sources.

Dicentra eximia (Wild bleeding heart, fringed bleeding heart) – very rare in rich woods and on cliffs; prefers damp woods with oak mulch; widely scattered sites northeast and southwest; endangered. Grows 10 to 15 inches, pink to purple flowers in early spring; part shade to shade in dry to moist rich loam. pH 4 to 7 but prefers 4.5 to 5.5; many sources.

Disporum lanuginosum (Yellow mandarin) – Rich moist, deciduous woodlands and coves, mostly west (Western Glaciated Allegheny Plateau, Southern Allegheny Plateau, Allegheny Mountains). Grows 1 to 3 feet, greenish–white bell–shaped flowers in spring; prefers humus rich, moist, acidic soil in part shade to shade of deciduous trees. AKA *Prosartes lanuginosa;* a few sources.

Dodecatheon meadia (Shooting–star) – rare in wet to dry prairies and moist open rocky woods and rocky slopes. FACU; endangered. Widely scattered, mostly southeast. Grows 12 to 15 inches, with white, pink and rarely purple flowers in spring; medium, well–drained (especially sandy) soils in sun to full shade. Prefers moist, humusy soils in part shade. Intolerant of poor wet soils, especially in winter; many sources.

Doellingeria umbellata (Flat topped white aster) – moist woods, fields and floodplains, FACW; statewide. Grows 3 to 6 feet, white flowers in late summer to early fall; sun to part shade in moist to wet sandy loam, pH 5 to 6; many sources.

Drosera intermedia (Spatulate–leaved sundew) – open peat and along edges of bogs and glacial lakes, OBL; northeast (Northern Glaciated Allegheny Plateau), scattered southeast (Piedmont). Aquatic carnivore; grows 3 to 10 inches, with white flowers; full sun in pond margins in moist to wet rich peaty loam; a few sources.

Drosera rotundifolia (Round–leaved sundew) – sphagnum bogs and peaty edges of bogs, OBL; statewide, especially northeast (Northern Glaciated Allegheny Plateau). Grows 3 to 10 inches, white to pink flowers. Aquatic carnivore; grow in full sun in pond margins in moist to wet rich peaty loam; a few sources.

Echinacea laevigata (Appalachian coneflower, smooth coneflower) – Very rare in open woods, barrens, clearcuts, dry limestone bluffs and fields; believe to be extirpated. Grows up to 4 feet, purple flowers in summer in sunny, well–drained sites rich in calcium and magnesium with low competition (the reason it has historically been rare); a few sources.

Elephantopus carolinianus (Elephant's foot) – Rare in open pine and mixed forests, typically with sandy soils, as well as serpentine barrens, mostly extreme southeastern counties (Piedmont, Atlantic Coastal Plain); FACU. Grows 2 to 3 feet on dry sandy soils in sun to part shade with white to lavender flowers in late summer, often used as a ground cover in dry, difficult areas; a few sources.

Elodea canadensis (Ditch–moss) – Aquatic, free floating in shallow, mostly calcareous waters of ponds, lakes, creeks and rivers, OBL; statewide. Flowers in summer; grow in neutral soil at the base of shallow ponds; several sources.

Epilobium coloratum (Purple–leaved willow–herb) – moist fields, shores and floodplains, OBL; statewide. Grows up to 3 feet, pink to white flowers in late summer; sun to part sun in rich, moist sandy loam; a few sources.

Erigeron philadelphicus (Daisy fleabane) – openings and margins of upland woods, marsh and stream edges, fields, roadsides, lawns, and other open, disturbed sites, FACU; statewide. Grows 8 to 40 inches, with white–pale lavender flowers in early summer; part sun in mesic to dry sandy loam; a few sources.

Erigeron pulchellus (Robin's plantain) – bottomland, especially along creeks; ravines, swamp edges, dry to moist woods, slopes and woodland edges, prairies and meadows, FACU; statewide. Grows to 8 feet, blue to pink–white flowers from late spring through summer; part shade in moist, rich, sandy loams; a few sources.

Eryngium aquaticum (Marsh eryngo, rattlesnake master) – Very rare in river swamps, marshes, pine wetlands, pond banks and gravelly shores, mostly Atlantic Coastal Plain, believed to be extirpated; OBL. Biennial that grows 3 to 6 feet, with greenish flowers in summer, in part sun to part shade in wet, somewhat acidic soils; a few sources.

Erythronium albidum (White trout–lily) – Rare in mesic floodplains and bottomlands, upland forests and woodlands, typically silt to clay loams, mostly southern counties, especially Southern Allegheny Plateau; FACU. Grows 6 to 12 inches, white–yellow flowers in spring to form extensive colonies in part shade to shade in acidic, moist, humusy soils; easiest to grow from corms rather than seed; a few sources.

Erythronium americanum (Yellow trout lily) – open deciduous moist woods and rich slopes with deep humus–rich loam; statewide. Grows up to 8 inches, yellow flowers in spring; part shade in dry to moist sandy loam, pH 5 to 7; many sources.

Eupatorium altissimum (Tall eupatorium, tall boneset) – Dry rocky slopes, thickets, clearings, openings in upland forests, limestone glades, abandoned fields, favors disturbed areas to form large colonies, mostly south; FACU. Grows to 4 feet in full to part sun with mesic to dry conditions, circumneutral to alkaline in loam, clay or gravel soils; white flowers in late summer; a few sources.

Eupatorium fistulosum (Trumpet weed) – mesic to moist fields, meadows and thickets, FACW; statewide. Grows up to 10 feet, pink–purple flowers in late summer and fall; sun to part sun in moist, rich sandy loam, pH 5.5 to 7; many sources.

Eupatorium maculatum (Spotted Joe–pye–weed, spotted trumpetweed) – floodplains, thickets and swamps, FACW. Mostly north (Western and Northern Glaciated and Northern Unglaciated Allegheny plateaus), scattered elsewhere. Grows up to 6 feet, purple flowers late summer; sun to part sun in moist silty clay loam, pH 5.5 to 7; many sources.

Eupatorium perfoliatum (Boneset) – flood plains, bogs, swamps and wet meadows, FACW+; statewide. Grows up to 5 feet, white flowers in late summer and fall; sun to part sun in moist to wet rich loam; many sources.

Eupatorium purpureum (Joe–pye–weed) – mesic to moist open woods and fields, FAC; statewide. Grows up to 6 feet, pink to purple flowers in late summer and fall; sun to part shade in moist to wet rich sandy loam; many sources.

Eupatorium rugosum (White snakeroot) – rich rocky woods, at the base of cliffs and rock outcrops, and in thickets and fields, FACU–; statewide. Grows 12 to 60 inches, white flowers in summer and fall; average, medium to wet, well–drained soils in full sun to part shade. Prefers part shade in moist, humusy soils, pH 6 to 7. AKA *Ageratina altissima*; many sources.

Eupatorium sessilifolium (Upland eupatorium) – dry wooded slopes and roadsides; statewide except for glaciated plateaus. Grows 24 to 60 inches, white flowers in summer and fall; sun to part shade in dry, rocky sandy loam; a few sources.

Euphorbia corollata (Flowering spurge) – dry open woods and shale barrens, fields and sandy waste ground. Southern and western counties in Pennsylvania; scattered elsewhere. Grows up to 3 feet, white flowers in late summer; full sun in dry to mesic sandy loam; several sources.

Euphorbia purpurea (Glade spurge) – Very rare in rich, cool, stream valleys, seeps, swamps in the Appalachians and Piedmont, especially in circumneutral to calcareous soils; FAC, endangered. Grows to 3 feet, purplish flowers in spring in part shade to shade; a few sources.

Eurybia divaricata (White wood aster) – dry to mesic, deciduous and mixed deciduous woods, edges and clearings; statewide. Grows 10 to 35 inches, with white flowers in autumn; part shade to shade in dry to moist, sandy loam, pH 5 to 7; many sources.

Eurybia macrophylla (Bigleaf aster) – moist, often rocky upland woodlands; statewide. Grows 10 to 35 inches, white flowers in autumn; sun to part shade in dry to moist sandy loam, pH 6 to 7; many sources.

Euthamia graminifolia (Grass–leaved goldenrod) – moist fields, roadsides, ditches and shores, FACU+; statewide. Two varieties: *graminifolia* and *nuttalli*. Grows up to 5 feet, yellow flowers in late summer and fall; sun to part sun in dry to moist sandy loam; several sources.

Euthamia graminifolia (Grass–leaved goldenrod) – Moist prairies and meadows, roadsides, shorelines, old fields, statewide; FAC. Two local varieties: *graminifolia* and *nuttalli*. Grows up to 5 feet, yellow flowers in late summer and fall; sun to part sun in dry to moist sandy loam; a few sources.

Filipendula rubra (Queen–of–the–prairie) – moist meadows, thickets and roadsides, FACW. Scattered statewide. Grows 3 to 6 feet, pink flowers in early summer; average, medium to wet, well–drained soil in full sun to part shade. Prefers consistently moist, fertile, humusy soils; many sources.

Fragaria vesca spp. americana (Woodland strawberry) – deciduous wooded slopes; scattered statewide. Grows 6 to 8 inches, white flowers in spring and fruit in early summer; part shade to shade in moist sandy loam; many sources.

Fragaria virginiana spp. virginiana (Wild strawberry) – dry to moist open woodlands and clearings, typically in disturbed areas, FACU; statewide. Grows 6 to 8 inches, white flowers in spring and fruit in early summer; part sun to part shade in dry to moist sandy loam; many sources.

Frasera caroliniensis (American columbo) – rare on dry slopes, abandoned fields and open woods; mostly northwest (Western Glaciated Allegheny Plateau). Grows to 8 feet with green–brown–purple flowers in summer. Prefers part sun to part shade in well drained, moist, peaty acidic soils. AKA *Swertia caroliniensis;* a few sources.

Galearis spectabilis (Showy orchis) – moist, calcareous woodlands, thickets, and old fields; statewide, especially southeast (Piedmont). Grows 4 to 8 inches, pink to purple flowers in spring; part shade to shade in moist rich loam. pH 5 to 6; a few sources.

Galium boreale (Northern bedstraw) – upland rocky woods, slopes, wet fields, fens, roadside banks, FACU; statewide, especially in Central Appalachians and Piedmont regions. Grows 1 to 3 feet, white flowers in late summer; average, medium, well–drained soils in part shade. Prefers moist soils where it will often spread by creeping roots and self–seeding; several sources.

Gentiana alba (Yellowish gentian) – Rare on wooded hillsides, limestone glades, rocky bluffs; FACU, scattered statewide, but believed to be extirpated. Grows 1 to 2 feet tall with yellowish–green flowers in late summer; prefers full to part sun in mesic, rich soils containing sand, silt or clay; a few sources.

Gentiana andrewsii var. andrewsii (Bottle gentian) – wet fields and moist, open woods, FACW; mostly west (Southern Allegheny Plateau) and southeast (Piedmont, Central Appalachians). Grows up to 3 feet, blue flowers in late summer; sun to part shade in moist to wet sandy humusy loam; many sources.

Gentiana clausa (Meadow closed gentian) – moist meadows, stream banks, and open woods in moist acidic soil, FACW; statewide. Grows up to 3 feet, blue flowers in late summer; sun to part shade in moist to wet rich acidic loam, pH 4 to 5; a few sources.

Gentiana villosa (Striped gentian) – Pine barrens and open woodlands, as well as serpentine barrens, mostly southeast (Piedmont) and endangered. Grows to 2 feet; flowers are white with purple stripes in autumn. Prefers sun to part sun in mesic, organically rich but well–drained soils; a few sources.

Geranium maculatum (Wood geranium) – rich open upland woods, shaded roadsides and areas of fields, FACU; statewide. Grows 18 to 24 inches, with pink–purple flowers in spring; part sun to part shade in moist humusy loam, pH 5 to 7; many sources.

Geum canadense (White avens) – upland dry to mesic open woodlands, woodland edges and openings and thickets, FACU; statewide. Grows 16 to 40 inches, white flowers in early summer; sun to part shade in dry to moist sandy loam; a few sources.

Geum laciniatum (Herb–bennet) – mesic savannahs, thickets and woodland borders and moist meadows, FAC+; statewide. Grows 16 to 40 inches, with white flowers in summer; sun to part shade in moist, rich loam, pH 4 to 6; a few sources.

Geum rivale (Water avens) – bogs, peaty meadows and calcareous marshes, OBL; mostly northwest (Western Glaciated Allegheny Plateau), and scattered north. Grows 6 to 24 inches, flowers are yellowish with purple veins in early summer; full sun in wet, silty, rich circumneutral loam; a few sources.

Gillenia trifoliata (Bowman's–root) – dry to moist, upland woods and rocky banks; statewide, less common along northern tier. Grows 24 to 36 inches, white flowers in late spring and early summer; part shade to shade in moist, slightly acidic rich, rocky soil. AKA *Porteranthus trifoliatus*; many sources.

Goodyera pubescens (Downy rattlesnake plantain) – dry to moist warm, deciduous or coniferous forests, FACU–; mostly southeast (Piedmont), scattered elsewhere. Grows 8 to 16 inches, with white flowers in summer; part shade to shade in dry to moist silty–sandy loam, pH 5 to 6; many sources.

Hasteola suaveolens (Sweet–scented Indian–plantain) – Shaded stream banks, rich woods, wet meadows; OBL. Scattered, mostly west (Central Appalachians, Western Glaciated and Southern Allegheny Plateaus). Grows 2 to 5 feet, white to cream flowers in late summer to early fall; prefers wet to wet–mesic well–drained somewhat organic soils. AKA *Cacalia suaveolens;* a few sources.

Helenium autumnale (Common sneezeweed) – meadows, moist riverbanks, wet fields, alluvial thickets and swamps, FACW+; statewide. Grows 3 to 5 feet, yellow flowers in late summer to fall; sun to part sun in moist to wet rich loam, pH 5.5 to 7; many sources.

Helianthemum bicknellii (Bicknell's hoary rose) – sandy, dry rocky slopes, open woods and prairies. Mostly southeast (Piedmont); scattered elsewhere and endangered. Grows 8 to 24 inches, with yellow flowers in summer; sun to part shade in dry, sandy soil loam; a few sources.

Helianthemum canadense (Frostweed) – dry sandy or rocky ground, open woods and barrens. Mostly southeast (Piedmont); scattered elsewhere. Grows 6 to 12 inches, yellow flowers in early summer; sun to part shade in dry, gravelly loam; a few sources.

Helianthus angustifolius (Swamp sunflower) – Very rare in sandy, open ground, including swamps, lower Bucks County, but believed extirpated; FACW. Grows 1 to 3 feet, yellow flowers in late fall; prefers wet somewhat circumneutral soils in part shade and a good choice for bog or pond planting; a few sources.

Helianthus decapetalus (Thin leaved sunflower) – open woodlands, woodland edges, savannahs, meadows, thickets and lightly shaded areas along rivers, FACU; statewide. Grows 2 to 5 feet, yellow flowers in late summer; part sun to part, especially dappled, shade in moist sandy loam. Can be aggressive; a few sources.

Helianthus divaricatus (Woodland sunflower) – dry open woods and wooded slopes, thickets, shale barrens and roadsides; statewide. Grows up to 5 feet, yellow flowers in late summer; part sun to part shade in dry to mesic sandy loam, pH 5 to 7. Aggressive spreader; several sources.

Helianthus giganteus (Swamp sunflower) – wet fields, swamps and ditches, FACW; mostly southeast (Piedmont) and west (Southern Allegheny Plateau), scattered elsewhere. Grows 6 to 10 feet, yellow flowers in late summer and fall; sun to part sun in moist, rich silty loam; a few sources.

Helianthus hirsutus (Hairy sunflower) – Dry, open sites including roadsides and woodland, especially oak, edges; mostly southwest (Southern Allegheny Plateau). Grows 2 to 5 feet in full to part sun in loamy to sandy soils that are mesic to dry. Yellow flowers in late autumn; easy to grow, but can be an aggressive spreader; a few sources.

Helianthus microcephalus (Small wood sunflower) – Open, upland woods, rocky slopes and along roadsides, mostly west (Western Glaciated and Southern Allegheny Plateaus). Grows to 5 feet in full sun and prefers average to circumneutral, well drained soil. Yellow flowers from summer into fall; a few sources.

Helianthus occidentalis (Sunflower) – very rare in prairies, dry meadows, fields, glades and occasionally rocky open woods. UPL; reported only in Warren County. Yellow flowers in summer, 2 to 4 feet; dry to medium, well drained soils in full sun. Tolerates a wide range of dry to moist soils, but intolerant of heavy clays. Spreads by rhizomes to form large colonies; many sources.

Helianthus strumosus (Rough–leaved sunflower) – fields, dry, open, upland woods and woodland edges; statewide. Grows up to 7 feet, yellow flowers in summer. Possibly hybridizing with *Helianthus divaricatus*; sun to part shade in dry, sandy loam, pH 5.5 to 7; several sources.

Heliopsis helianthoides (Ox–eye) – open and sometimes rocky woods, thickets, prairies, stream banks; statewide. Grows up to 5 feet, with yellow flowers in late summer; full sun to part shade (where it may require support) in dry to moist sandy loam, pH 5.6 to 6.8; many sources.

Hepatica nobilis (Liverleaf) – rich woods and dry rocky upland slopes; statewide. Two varieties – *obtusa* and *acuta* (sharp and round lobed leaves, respectively). Grows 6 to 8 inches, lavender to purple flowers in early spring; part shade to shade in dry sandy loam. pH 4 to 7, but prefers pH 4.5 to 6. Also known as *Hepatica americana*; a few sources.

Heuchera americana (Alum–root) – rich woods, rocky slopes, shaly cliffs on rich, well–drained humus, FACU–; mostly southeast (Piedmont) and west (Southern Allegheny Plateau), scattered elsewhere. Grows 12 to 30 inches, greenish–white to pink flowers in spring; part sun to part shade in dry, sandy well–drained humusy loam. pH 5 to 7; many sources.

Hibiscus laevis (Halberd–leaved rose–mallow) – rare along muddy alluvial shorelines and in swamps and marshes, sometimes in standing water, mostly southeast (Piedmont). Grows 5 to 7 feet in full to part sun with white to pink flowers in summer (flowers require sunlight to open properly). Prefers continually moist to wet organically rich soil; a few sources.

Hibiscus moscheutos (Rose–mallow) – marshes, wet meadows, swampy open forests. OBL. Mostly southeast (Piedmont, Atlantic Coastal Plain), scattered elsewhere. Large white flowers with crimson center in summer, 3 to 8 feet. Very late to appear in spring, then grows rapidly. Best in moist soils rich in organic matter; soil should not dry out and regular watering with fertilization helps. Tolerates light shade, but does best in full sun with good air circulation; many sources. AKA *Abelmoschus moschatus.*

Hieracium kalmii (Canada hawkweed) – clearings, roadsides and in prairies. Mostly northeast (Northern Glaciated Allegheny Plateau); scattered elsewhere. Grows 6 to 48 inches, yellow–orange flowers in late summer; sun to part sun in dry to moist sandy loam; a few sources.

Hieracium scabrum (Rough hawkweed) – open fields, clearings, woods edges; statewide. Grows 8 to 48 inches, yellow–orange flowers, late summer and fall; sun to part sun in dry sandy loam; a few sources.

Hieracium venosum (Rattlesnake weed) – dry, upland woods including slopes and edges; statewide except north–central (Northern Unglaciated Allegheny Plateau). Grows up to 32 inches, orange–yellow flowers, summer; part shade to shade in dry to moist organic clay sandy loam; a few sources.

Houstonia caerulea (Bluets or Quaker ladies) – dry to mesic meadows, fields, upland open woods, and woods edges, FACU; statewide. Grows up to 16 inches, blue flowers with yellow centers in spring; sun to part shade in moist rich sandy loam, pH 5.5 to 7; a few sources.

Houstonia longifolia (Long–leaved bluets) – Dry wooded slopes, shale barrens and sandy fields, mostly south, especially Central Appalachians. Grows 1 to 3 feet, white, pink or purple flowers in early summer. Prefers dry to moist, acidic, sandy to gravelly loams in full sun to part shade. A good choice for rock gardens and relatively easy to cultivate; a few sources.

Houstonia purpurea var. purpurea (Purple bluets) – Very rare in open, moist rocky woodlands, stream banks and rocky slopes; scattered sites southwest (Southern Allegheny Plateau). Grows 6 to 8 inches, pale blue white flowers in early summer; prefers part shade to shade in acidic, well drained, moist, loamy soils; a few sources.

Houstonia serpyllifolia (Creeping bluets, Thymeleaf bluets) – Rare along streams and meadows; southwest (Southern Allegheny Plateau); believed to be extirpated. Grows 2 to 3 inches, light blue to lilac flowers in mid to late summer. Spreads by stolons to form a colony in moist sandy and slightly acidic soil in part sun to part shade (requires sunlight to bloom). Good for rock walls or flagstone paths; a few sources.

Hydrastis canadensis (Goldenseal) – mesic deciduous forests, often on clay soils. Mostly southeast (Piedmont) and southwest (Southern Allegheny Plateau). Tiny white flowers in spring, followed by dramatic red fruit. Grow in well drained, medium soil in part shade; prefers soils well composted with much leaf mold; many sources.

Hydrocotyle americana (Marsh pennywort) – swampy thickets, boggy fields, wet woods and lake margins, OBL; statewide. Low creeping habit with white flowers in summer; sun to part shade in moist to wet marshy soils; a few sources.

Hydrocotyle umbellata (Water pennywort) – Very rare in muddy shorelines and shallow water, principally southeast (Atlantic Coastal Plain); believed to be extirpated, OBL. Grows less than 12 inches in sun to shade in continually moist to wet muddy to sandy soil, including standing water up to 4 inches. Spreads to form a ground cover and bears white flowers in summer. Good for ponds and wetlands; a few sources.

Hydrophyllum canadense (Canadian waterleaf) – rocky upland wooded slopes, ravines and moist woods, FACU. Mostly southwest (Southern Allegheny Plateau), scattered elsewhere. Grows 12 to 20 inches, white–pink to purple flowers in summer; part shade to shade in moist humusy soil; a few sources.

Hydrophyllum virginianum (Virginia waterleaf) – mesic wooded slopes and stream banks and in thickets, FAC; statewide. Grows 12 to 30 inches, white flowers in spring; part shade to shade in moist humusy loam, pH 6 to 7; a few sources.

Hypericum punctatum (Spotted St. John's–wort) – floodplains, thickets, moist fields and along roadsides, FAC–; statewide. Grows 20 to 40 inches, yellow flowers in summer; sun to part sun in dry to moist sandy loam; a few sources.

Hypericum pyramidatum (Great St. John's–wort) – alluvial shores and in moist to mesic fields, rocky banks, and swamps, FAC. Scattered mostly east and northwest. Grows 30 to 60 inches, yellow flowers in summer; sun to part sun in dry to moist rich sandy loam, pH 5 to 6. AKA *Hypericum ascyron*; many sources.

Hypoxis hirsuta (Yellow star grass) – dry to mesic meadows, fields, clearings, barrens and dry woods, FAC; statewide, except north–central (Northern Unglaciated Allegheny Plateau). Grows up to 15 inches, yellow flowers in spring to summer; sun to part shade in dry to wet sandy loam, pH 4.5 to 7; several sources.

Ionactis linariifolius (Stiff–leaved aster) – dry rocky woods and edges; typically in acidic soils in pine–oak or pine–hickory woods, ridgetops, upland slopes and glades. Mostly east (especially Piedmont). Grows 12 to 24 inches, violet flowers in late summer to fall; average, dry to medium, well–drained soil in full sun to part shade. Prefers acidic, sandy soils; pH 4 to 7; a few sources.

Iris cristata (Dwarf crested iris) – very rare in rich woods, ravines and bluffs. Endangered; mostly southwest (Southern Allegheny Plateau); scattered elsewhere. Pale blue to purple flowers in spring, rarely white. Grow in well drained soil rich in organic matter and with medium moisture, sun to part shade; prefers part shade and will tolerate close to full shade; if grown in sun, keep soil constantly moist. Does well on well–drained slopes; many sources.

Iris versicolor (Northern blue flag iris) – marshes, bogs and wet meadows, OBL; statewide except north and south central high elevations. Grows 24 to 60 inches, blue–violet flowers in late spring or early summer; sun to part sun in moist to wet rich silty loam, especially in pond margins; many sources.

Iris virginica (Southern blue flag) – Rare in wetlands such as the margins of lakes, ponds and streams, mostly extreme northwest (Erie and Ontario Lake Plain) and endangered; OBL. Grows 1 to 3 feet, blue–violet flowers in early summer; prefers wet, acidic, boggy, sandy soils in full sun. Ideally roots should be under water for extended periods of time, otherwise they will grow slightly smaller in average garden soils that are uniformly moist. Spreads by rhizomes to form colonies; a few sources.

Jeffersonia diphylla (Twinleaf) – open rocky slopes and outcrops as well as rich moist woods, typically over limestone or other calcareous rock. Mostly southwest (Southern Allegheny Plateau); scattered south–central and southeast. Very brief bloom with a single white flower in early spring; generally grown for its unique foliage. Grow in well–drained, mulched, circumneutral, continually moist humusy soils in part shade; tolerates full shade; many sources.

Justicia americana (Water–willow) – Along the banks of or in the shallow waters of rivers, ponds, and lakes, statewide; OBL. Grows 1 to 3 feet, flowers that are white or light violet, with purple spots or other markings in the throat, throughout the summer. Aquatic; grow in moist soil or in a few feet of water in full sun to part shade. Forms colonies on or near shorelines, including rocky riffles and shoals. Rhizomes and roots provide important spawning sites for many fish species and habitat for invertebrates; a few sources.

Krigia biflora (Dwarf dandelion) – moist fields and meadows, FACU. Mostly west (Southern Allegheny Plateau) and East (Piedmont and north along the Delaware River Valley), scattered elsewhere. Grows 4 to 24 inches, yellow flowers from late spring into fall; sun to part sun in dry to moist sandy loam; a few sources.

Laportea canadensis (Wood–nettle) – rich moist deciduous forests, often along seepages and streams, FACW; statewide. Grows 20 to 40 inches, tiny white flowers in spring; part shade to shade in moist, humusy loam. Stinging hairs on all parts causes brief burning or itching; a few sources.

Lathyrus japonicus var. glaber (Beach pea) – Very rare on sand plains and dunes and sandy to gravelly shores, extreme northwest (Erie and Ontario Lake Plain); FACU–. Trailing perennial that grows up to 3 feet, pink–magenta flowers in summer; full to part sun in moist, sandy, well–drained soil; a few sources.

Lathyrus palustris (Marsh pea) – moist meadows, sand plains, swamps and thickets, FACW+. Scattered statewide, mostly southeast (Piedmont), and endangered. Grows up to 3 feet, red–purple flowers in early summer; moist to wet rich loam in full to part sun; a few sources.

Lathyrus venosus (Veiny pea) – Woodland slopes, sandy to rocky shorelines, railroad banks; scattered throughout mostly south, especially the Lehigh Valley. Grows 1 to 3 feet in a trailing habit in part shade with pink to purple flowers in summer. Prefers dry to mesic average soils; a few sources.

Lemna minor (Duckweed) – aquatic; still water of nutrient–average to nutrient–rich lakes and ponds, and in streams, swamps and ditches, OBL; statewide except for high Alleghenies. Grow in shallow ponds and water features with slow–moving to still water; several sources.

Lemna trisulca (Star duckweed) – cool–temperate aquatic; nu-trient–average, quiet waters rich in calcium, forms tangled colonies in lakes, ponds, bogs, marshes, streams, OBL. Scattered, mostly east and northwest. Grow in shallow ponds and water features with slow–moving to still water; a few sources.

Lespedeza capitata (Round–headed bush–clover) – upland woods, thickets, prairies, glades and along streams, FACU–. Mostly southeast (Piedmont), scattered elsewhere. Grows 20 to 60 inches, yellow–white flowers, late summer; sun to part sun in dry to moist sandy loam; many sources.

Lespedeza hirta (Bush–clover) – dry prairies, savannahs, fields, meadows; statewide, except north–central (Northern Unglaciated Allegheny Plateau). Grows 24 to 48 inches, yellow flowers in summer; sun to part shade in dry sandy loams; a few sources.

Lespedeza hirta (Bush–clover) – Dry prairies, savannahs, fields, meadows, statewide, except most northern tier counties. Grows 24 to 48 inches, yellow flowers in summer; sun to part shade in dry sandy loams. Natural hybrids: *x intermedia* (Nuttall's bush clover), *x virginica* (bush–clover); a few sources.

Lespedeza violacea (Slender bush–clover) – dry upland woods, thickets and openings. Mostly southeast (Piedmont), scattered elsewhere. Grows 12 to 30 inches, violet–purple flowers in late summer; part sun to part shade in dry sandy loam; a few sources.

Lespedeza virginica (Slender bush–clover) – dry fields, stony banks, rocky woods. Mostly southeast (Piedmont), scattered elsewhere and absent in north (Western and Northern Glaciated and Northern Unglaciated Allegheny Plateaus). Grows 12 to 40 inches, violet–purple flowers in summer; sun to part shade in dry sandy loam; a few sources.

Liatris scariosa (Northern blazing–star) – Three varieties found in Pennsylvania: *var. scariosa* on limestone and sandstone outcrops, rock ledges, shale banks, flood plains and dry woods; *var. nieuwlandii* in prairies, glades, bluffs, open woods, red clays and rocky limestone soils; and *var. novaeangliae* in sandy fields and woodlands. All three mostly in Ridge and Valley province of the Central Appalachians, and all UPL. Grows 2 to 4 feet in full sun with lavender flowers in late summer. Prefers dry sandy to rocky, well–drained soils and while it will grow taller in fertile loams it may also need staking to support it. Intolerant of winter wet soils; a few sources.

Liatris spicata var. spicata (Blazing–star) – moist fields, meadows and swamps, usually over limestone, FAC+; southeast (Piedmont) and west (Southern Allegheny Plateau). Grows up to 6 feet, blue–purple flowers in late summer; sun to part sun in moist rich sandy loam. pH 5.5 to 7; many sources.

Lilium canadense (Canada lily) – wet meadows, moist rich woods especially edges, stream sides and river alluvia, bogs, marshes and swamps, FAC+; statewide. Grows up to 6 feet, yellow or red flowers in early summer; sun to part sun in moist to wet organic loam. pH 4 to 7; several sources; several sources.

Lilium philadelphicum (Wood lily) – open dry woods, borders and clearings on well–drained soil, FACU+; mostly Central Appalachians and east; scattered elsewhere. Grows up to 3 feet, orange–red flowers in early summer; part sun to part shade in dry to moist sandy loam. pH 5 to 7; several sources.

Lilium superbum (Turk's–cap lily) – moist meadows and thickets, pine barrens, swamp edges and bottoms, gaps and openings in rich forests; FACW+, statewide, but sparse in northeast and northern Piedmont. Yellow–orange with maroon spotted flowers in spring; prefers well–drained, average soils, mesic to wet in full sun to part shade. Spreads to form colonies; many sources.

Linum striatum (Ridged yellow flax) – moist meadows, wet open ground and wet open woods, FACW. Mostly south, especially Piedmont, scattered north. Grows 12 to 36 inches, yellow flowers in summer; sun to part shade in moist rich loam; a few sources.

Lithospermum caroliniense (Golden puccoon) – Very rare in open woods, sandy barrens and grasslands; endangered. Grows 1 to 3 feet, yellow flowers in late spring; prefers full to part sun with dry to dry-mesic sandy soils. Difficult to germinate and transplant, hence it is rarely cultivated; a few sources.

Lobelia cardinalis (Cardinal flower) – wet meadows, swamps, river-banks and lake shores, FACW+; statewide. Grows 20 to 36 inches, with red flowers in late summer; sun to part sun in moist to wet, humus rich, sandy loam, pH 5.5 to 7; many sources.

Lobelia inflata (Indian–tobacco) – upland dry to mesic woods, old fields, meadows and along roadsides, FACU; statewide. Grows up to 36 inches, blue to white flowers in late summer; sun to part sun in dry to moist sandy loam; many sources.

Lobelia puberula (Downy lobelia) – Rare in serpentine barrens and moist, sandy open ground such as prairies or fields and gravel pits, mostly southeast (Piedmont) and endangered; FACW–. Grows up to

30 inches in full to part sun with blue–violet flowers in late summer. Prefers moist to wet sandy loams; a few sources.

Lobelia siphilitica (Great blue lobelia) – swamps, moist meadows, stream banks and ditches, FACW+; statewide. Grows up to 5 feet, blue flowers in summer; sun to part sun in moist to wet silty loam; many sources.

Lobelia spicata var. spicata (Spiked lobelia) – dry to mesic fields and open woodlands, FAC–; mostly south, sparse to absent in northern tier (glaciated and unglaciated plateaus). Grows up to 36 inches, with pale blue to white flowers in summer; sun to part shade in dry to moist sandy loam; several sources.

Ludwigia alternifolia (Seedbox) – swampy fields, wet woods, and the borders of streams and pond and lake shores, FACW+; statewide, except northern tier. Grows 16 to 48 inches, yellow flowers in early summer; sun to part shade in moist sandy loam. Common name comes from box–like seed pods; several sources.

Ludwigia palustris (Marsh–purslane) – swamps, wet meadows, muddy shores, stream banks, ditches, OBL; statewide. Prostrate, creeping, floating stems; full sun in moist to wet mucky soils, including shallow water; a few sources.

Ludwigia peploides ssp. glabrescens (Primrose–willow) – Rare in silty, muddy shorelines and shallow water, and regarded by many as troublesome aquatic noxious weed that invades water ecosystems and can clog waterways; OBL. Southeast (Atlantic Coastal Plain). Grows creeping stems up to 12 feet long with yellow flowers in summer; full sun in mud or shallow standing water. Trim anytime to restrain spread; a few sources.

Lupinus perennis (Blue lupine) – dry fields, woods edges and along roadsides in sandy acidic soil. Mostly Central Appalachians and Piedmont, scattered elsewhere. Grows 8 to 24 inches, blue flowers in spring and early summer; sun to part sun in dry to moist acidic sandy loam, pH 5.5 to 7; many sources.

Lycopus americanus (Water–horehound) – mesic to moist hillsides and fields, moist thickets, wet ditches and swamps, OBL; statewide. Grows 6 to 24 inches, small white flowers in summer; sun to part shade in moist to wet rich, mucky soils; several sources.

Lysimachia ciliata (Fringed loosestrife) – low moist ground and old fields, in floodplains and on stream banks, FACW; statewide. Grows 16 to 48 inches, yellow flowers in early summer; sun to part sun in moist sandy rich loam; a few sources.

Lysimachia hybrida (Lance–leaved loosestrife) – swamps, wet meadows, fens and pond margins, OBL. Mostly east (Piedmont, Delaware River Valley) and widely scattered elsewhere. Grows up to 5 feet, yellow flowers in early summer; full to part sun in mesic to moist organic, clay to sandy/rocky loam; a few sources.

Lysimachia quadrifolia (Whorled loosestrife) – dry to mesic hardwood forests, lowlands, fens, moist clearings, roadsides, and fields, rocky thickets and slopes, FACU–; statewide. Grows up to 3 feet, yellow flowers in early summer; full sun to part shade in a wide range of moist soils; a few sources.

Lysimachia terrestris (Swamp–candles) – swamps, flood plains, fens, bogs, stream banks, pond and lake margins and wet ditches, OBL; statewide. Grows 16 to 30 inches, yellow flowers in early summer; sun to part sun in moist rich loam; a few sources.

Lysimachia thyrsiflora (Tufted loosestrife) – bogs, swamps, marshes and wet woods, OBL. Northeast and north (glaciated plateaus). Grows 12 to 30 inches, yellow flowers in early summer; sun to part shade in moist to wet rich loam; a few sources.

Lythrum alatum (Winged loosestrife) – swamps, marshes, fens, borders of lakes, areas along rivers and drainage ditches; FACW+, scattered and endangered, but most in southeast (Piedmont). Grows 3 to 6 feet, pink to purple flowers in late spring through summer. Prefers full sun in moist to wet sites, and is aquatic. Soil should be poorly drained and high in organic matter. Not to be confused with *Lythrum salicaria* (Purple Loosestrife), an invasive species, but *L. alatum* can be aggressive and is listed as a noxious weed in some states and banned for sale in Michigan; a few sources.

Maianthemum canadense (Canada mayflower) – dry to moist woods, rich and often sandy clearings, FAC–; statewide. Grows 6 to 8 inches, white flowers in late spring; part shade to shade in dry to moist sandy acidic loam, pH 4 to 5; several sources.

Maianthemum racemosum (False Solomon's–seal, feathery false lily–of the–valley) – dry to moist deciduous woodlands, FACU–; statewide. Grows up to 3 feet, with white flowers in late spring; part shade to shade in dry to moist humusy loam, pH 4 to 6; many sources.

Maianthemum stellatum (Starry false lily–of–the–valley) – moist to wet woods, marginal woodlands, oak openings and on stream banks,

FACW. Mostly southeast (Piedmont) and northwest (Western Glaciated Allegheny Plateau); scattered elsewhere. Grows up to 24 inches, white flowers in spring; part shade to shade in moist to wet rich loam. pH 4 to 5; several sources.

Maianthemum trifolium (Threeleaf false lily–of–the–valley) – often dense clonal patches in sphagnum bogs, and wet forests, OBL. Northeast and northwest (Northern Glaciated and Western Glaciated Allegheny Plateaus); scattered elsewhere. Grows up to 8 inches, white flowers in spring; part shade to shade in moist to wet rich loam; a few sources.

Medeola virginiana (Indian cucumber root) – mesic woods and moist slopes; statewide. Grows 12 to 24 inches, greenish–yellow flowers in late spring; moist to wet soils in part shade to full shade, pH 4 to 6; several sources.

Meehania cordata (Heart–leafed meehania, Meehan's mint) – Woodland slopes and banks, mostly southwest (Southern Allegheny Plateau). Grows 3 to 6 inches in part shade to shade with lavender blue flowers in late spring. Tolerates dense shade and sun (as long as soil is moist). Good ground cover for shade and woodland gardens; a few sources.

Mentha arvensis (Field mint) – swamps, wet meadows and moist banks, FACW; statewide. Grows 12 to 24 inches, blue–lavender flowers in fall; part shade in mesic to moist rich loam; a few sources.

Menyanthes trifoliata (Bogbean or Buckbean) – aquatic; bogs, sphagnum swamps and shallow water of ponds and lakes, OBL. Mostly northeast (Northern Glaciated Allegheny Plateau), scattered elsewhere. White flowers in late spring; grow in water gardens in mud or containers submerged in shallow water (3 inches over rhizome) in full sun to part shade. Best in acidic, peaty soils; several sources.

Mertensia virginica (Virginia bluebells) – river bottoms and floodplains, moist woodlands and forest clearings. FACW; statewide except Allegheny Mountains and Northern Unglaciated Allegheny Plateau. Grows 12 inches, blue flowers in very early spring before leaves are out; foliage dies back to the ground when the plant goes dormant in early summer. Grow in well–drained, average moist soil in part shade to full shade; prefers rich, moist soils. Slowly spreads by rhizomes, but freely from seed; many sources.

Mimulus alatus (Winged monkey–flower) – seeps, swamps, stream edges, openings in floodplain forests, throughout except northeast and most concentrated in southeast (Piedmont, Ridge and Valley provinces);

OBL. Grows up to 3 feet tall with blue flowers in summer. Prefers part sun with consistently moist to wet rich soil with substantial organic matter; tolerates full sun and light shade; a few sources.

Mimulus moschatus (Muskflower) – wet shores, seeps and spring–fed swales, OBL. Mostly east (Delaware River Valley); scattered elsewhere. Creeping habit, with yellow flowers in summer; muddy moist to wet margins of garden water features in full sun to part shade; a few sources.

Mimulus ringens (Allegheny monkey flower) – sunny pond edges, swamps and wet meadows, OBL; statewide. Grows up to 6 inches, blue flowers in summer; sun to part sun in moist to wet rich loam; many sources.

Mitchella repens (Partridgeberry) – dry to moist upland woods and sandy bogs, FACU; statewide. Trailing stems to 12 inches. White flowers in late spring, with long–lasting red fruits following; part shade to shade in moist rich humus. pH 4 to 5; many sources. Technically a subshrub.

Mitella diphylla (Bishops cap) – rich, cool shaded sites in moist open woods and along stream banks, FACU; statewide. Grows 4 to 16 inches, white flowers in early spring; part shade to shade in moist rich sandy loam. pH 5 to 7, but prefers 6.0; many sources.

Mitella nuda (Naked mitrewort) – very rare cool, mossy, mixed woods and cedar swamps, FACW–. Northeast and northwest (glaciated plateaus); endangered. Grows 2 to 4 inches, greenish–yellow flowers in late spring; part shade to shade in moist rich organic loam; a few sources.

Moehringia lateriflora (Blunt–leaved sandwort) – moist to dry woodlands and moist to mesic meadows, gravelly shores, swales, and low woods, FAC. Mostly east and west of the Central Appalachians. Grows up to 24 inches, white flowers in late spring; mesic to moist sandy loams in full sun to part shade; a few sources.

Monarda clinopodia (White bergamot) – moist woods, fields and floodplains; statewide. Grows up to 36 inches, white–yellow flowers in summer; sun to part shade in dry, rocky, sandy loam; a few sources.

Monarda didyma (Bee balm) – rich moist fields, meadows; bottomlands, thickets, woods and especially stream banks, FAC+; mostly west and east of the Central Appalachians. Grows 2 to 4 feet, red flowers in late summer; sun to part sun in medium to wet, moisture–retentive soils. Prefers rich, humusy soils in full sun, pH 5.5 to 7; many sources.

Monarda fistulosa var. mollis (Horsemint) – moist to wet prairies and upland open woods; statewide. Grows 20 to 48 inches, lavender flowers in late summer; sun to part sun in dry to moist sandy loam, pH 5.5 to 7. UPL; many sources.

Monarda media (Bee balm) – rich moist acidic soil on stream banks, thickets, low woods and ditches. Mostly west (Southern Allegheny Plateau); scattered east. Grows up to 36 inches, purple flowers in summer; part shade in moist rich loam; a few sources.

Monarda punctata (Spotted bee–balm) – rare in savannahs, prairies, meadows and pastures; UPL; endangered. Widely scattered statewide. To 24 inches, greenish pink flowers in spring to summer. Grow in full sun in dry, sandy circumneutral soils. Drought tolerant; many sources.

Nelumbo lutea (American lotus) – rare in ponds, lakes, marsh pools and swamps, as well as backwaters of reservoirs and lingering ponds in floodplains of major rivers. OBL. Creamy–white flowers in late spring to early summer. Widely scattered, mostly southeast (Atlantic Coastal Plain). Grow in any still–water pond or submerged pot; saucer–shaped leaves are up to 12 inches in diameter and plant requires room to spread/reproduce; many sources.

Nuphar advena (Spatterdock, or yellow pond lily) – aquatic; lake margins, ponds, slow moving streams, swamps and tidal marshes, OBL; statewide, mostly Central Appalachians and Piedmont. Grows in 1 to 3 feet of water in full sun to part shade. Can be grown in containers for water gardens; for natural ponds, plant rhizomes directly in the muddy bottom of poor sandy soil; a few sources. AKA *Nuphar lutea*

Nymphaea odorata (Fragrant water–lily) – aquatic; quiet waters of acidic or alkaline ponds, lakes, sluggish streams and rivers, pools in marshes, ditches, canals, or sloughs, OBL. Mostly northeast (Northern Glaciated Allegheny Plateau), scattered elsewhere. White flowers from late spring to early fall; shallow ponds in silty to sandy soil; several sources.

Oenothera biennis (Evening primrose) – dry fields, waste ground, and along roadsides, FACU–; statewide. Grows 20 to 60 inches, yellow flowers in late summer to fall; sun to part sun in dry to moist sandy loam; many sources.

Oenothera fruticosa (Sundrops) – mesic meadows, fields and along roadsides, FAC; statewide. Grows 8 to 30 inches, yellow flowers, early summer. Two local subspecies, *fruticosa* and *glauca*; sun to part shade in dry to moist sandy loam, pH 5.5 to 7; several sources.

Oenothera perennis (Sundrops) – mesic pastures, shale slopes and along roadsides, FAC; statewide. Grows 4 to 24 inches, yellow flowers in early summer; sun to part sun in dry to moist sandy loam; a few sources.

Opuntia humifusa (Eastern prickly–pear cactus) – sandy habitats, especially openings on dry sometimes wooded hillsides; mostly southeast (Piedmont). Spreading, prostrate habit with yellow flowers in summer; sun to part sun in dry sandy loam, pH 5.5 to 7; many sources.

Orontium aquaticum (Goldenclub) – aquatic; shallow water of bogs, marshes, swamps, and streams, OBL; Central Appalachians and east, especially in northern Piedmont. Grow in water gardens in containers submerged in 6 to 18 inches of water in full sun. Leaves tend to emerge in water 6 to 9 inches deep, but mostly float in water 12 to 18 inches deep; several sources.

Osmorhiza claytonii (Sweet–cicely) – rich upland woods and wooded slopes, FACU; statewide except for Central Appalachians. Grows 15 to 30 inches, white flowers in early summer; part shade to shade in moist rich loam; several sources.

Osmorhiza longistylis (Anise–root) – upland dry to mesic wooded areas, shaded slopes and ravines, FACU; statewide. Grows 15 to 30 inches, white flowers in early summer; part sun to part shade in moist rich loam; a few sources.

Oxalis stricta (Common yellow wood–sorrel) – dry to mesic fields, lawns, gardens in shallow sandy loams to loamy tills, UPL; statewide. Prostrate to 20 inches, yellow flowers in summer; sun to part sun in dry to moist sandy loamy till, pH 4 to 6; a few sources.

Oxalis violacea (Violet wood–sorrel) – dryish, acidic soils in glades, rocky open woods, fields and prairies, stream banks. Mostly south, especially southeast (Piedmont). Grows 6 to 9 inches, violet flowers in spring; part sun to part shade in dry to moist sandy loam; pH 4 to 7 but prefers 6 to 6.5; a few sources.

Oxypolis rigidior (Cowbane) – swamps, bogs, meadows, and moist sandy shores, OBL. Mostly southeast (Piedmont) and southwest (Southern Allegheny Plateau). Grows 4 to 5 feet, white flowers in late summer; sun to part shade in wet, sandy or clay loam; a few sources.

Packera aurea (Golden ragwort) – floodplains and in moist fields and woods, FACW; statewide. Grows 12 to 32 inches, yellow flowers in early summer; sun to part shade in moist to wet rich loam. AKA *Senecio aureus*; many sources.

Packera obovata (Ragwort, squaw weed) – moist fields, meadows, upland woods and calcareous slopes. Western, south central and southeastern counties (including Carbon and Monroe) in Pennsylvania; scattered elsewhere Grows up to 30 inches, yellow flowers in early summer; sun to part shade in circumneutral humusy loam. AKA *Senecio obovatus*; a few sources.

Packera paupercula (Balsam ragwort) – moist meadows, peaty thickets, stream banks, prairies, meadows; in rocky, loamy soil; FAC. Mostly southwest (Southern Allegheny Plateau, Allegheny Mountains), scattered elsewhere. Grows up to 30 inches, with yellow flowers in early summer; sun to part sun in moist sandy rich loam. FAC. AKA *Senecio pauperculus*; a few sources.

Panax quinquefolius (Ginseng) – rare in cool, moist, rich mesic woods, often on north–facing slopes; statewide. Grows up to 24 inches, greenish flowers in spring, red fruit in fall; moist, fertile, organically rich, medium moisture soils in part shade to full shade; pH 4 to 7 but prefers 4.5 to 6; many sources.

Parnassia glauca (Grass–of–parnassus) – boggy meadows or seeps on calcareous soils, OBL. Mostly east (Hudson Valley Province) and west (Southern Glaciated Allegheny Plateau and Erie and Ontario Lake Plain); endangered. Grows 10 to 20 inches, white flowers in late summer; moist to wet organic loams in full sun to part shade; a few sources.

Parthenium integrifolium (American fever–few, wild quinine) – rare in dry to mesic woodlands and prairies. Widely scattered and considered extirpated. White flowers in early summer. Grow in well–drained, dry to medium average soils in full sun; many sources.

Pedicularis canadensis (Forest lousewort) – open dry upland woods, old fields, woods edges and mesic grasslands, FACU; statewide. Grows 6 to 16 inches, yellow to purple flowers in spring; sun to part shade in dry sandy loam; a few sources.

Pedicularis lanceolata (Swamp lousewort) – Swamps, fens, boggy sedge meadows and swales; parasitic on the roots of other plants. Throughout, but most concentrated in southeast (Piedmont); FACW. Grows 1 to 2 feet, yellow flowers in late summer; prefers full to part sun with wet to moist circumneutral loamy soils; a few sources.

Peltandra virginica (Green arrow–arum) – emergent aquatic; bogs, swamps and ditches, and edges of ponds, lakes, and rivers, OBL; mostly east (Piedmont, Atlantic Coastal Plain, Northern Glaciated Allegheny Plateau) and west (Western Glaciated Allegheny Plateau), scattered elsewhere. Grows 2 to 3 feet, green flowers in spring; water garden, bog, or pond areas in part shade, muddy soil in shallow water; a few sources.

Penstemon canescens (Grey beard–tongue) – Dry, rocky, shale outcrops and wooded slopes; in south, mostly Allegheny Mountains. Grows 12 to 18 inches in full sun with pale to dark violet flowers in late spring. Average, dry to mesic, well drained loams. Ideal for borders and rock gardens; a few sources.

Penstemon digitalis (Beards tongue, Talus slope penstemon) – old fields, meadows, prairies and mesic open woods and margins, FAC; statewide. Grows up to 60 inches, white flowers in summer; average, dry to medium moisture, well–drained soil in full sun to part sun; many sources.

Penstemon hirsutus (Northern beard–tongue) – dry to mesic, open rocky slopes, fields, and roadside banks. Scattered statewide, mostly east (Piedmont, Central Appalachians) and west (Southern Allegheny Plateau). Grows 15 to 32 inches, violet to purple flowers in early summer; sun to part sun in dry rocky sandy loam; pH 5.5 to 6.5; several sources.

Penstemon laevigatus (Eastern beard–tongue) – Moist meadows, rich wooded hillsides, roadsides; FACU. Mostly southwest (Southern Allegheny Plateau). Grows 1 to 3 feet, full sun to shade, with purple flowers in early summer. Prefers moist, organic soils; a few sources.

Persicaria amphibia (Water smartweed or Water knotweed) – aquatic, found in very wet prairies and along shorelines, in swamps, ponds, and quiet streams, in mud or floating on still fresh water, OBL; statewide, especially in the Delaware River Valley. Two varieties; *emersum* (leaves don't float) and *stipulaceum* (leaves float); full sun to part sun in wet mucky soil or in water gardens. AKA *Polygonum amphibium;* not to be confused with the invasive *Polygonum cuspidatum* (Japanese knotweed); a few sources.

Persicaria hydropiperoides (Mild water–pepper) – wet banks and clearings, shallow water, marshes, moist prairies, ditches, OBL. Mostly southeast (Piedmont, Central Appalachians), scattered elsewhere. Grow in full sun in mucky soil, standing water; a few sources. AKA *Polygonum hydropiperoides var. hydropiperoides.*

Persicaria punctata (Dotted smartweed) – Shallow water and lake, pond and stream edges, swamps, marshes, and floodplain forests, OBL; statewide. Grows 18 to 24 inches, white flowers in summer; prefers full to part sun in moist to wet mucky soil high in organic matter and tolerates standing water. AKA *Polygonum punctatum var. punctatum;* a few sources.

Persicaria virginiana (Jumpseed) – rich deciduous forests, floodplain forests, dry to moist woodlands and thickets, FAC; statewide. Grows 15 to 40 inches, white flowers in spring; sun to part shade in rich sandy loam. AKA *Polygonum virginianum;* several sources.

Phlox divaricata ssp. divaricata (Wild blue phlox, Sweet William) – rich, moist deciduous forests and bluffs, FACU. Mostly southwest (Southern Allegheny Plateau); scattered elsewhere; absent in Northern Glaciated and Unglaciated Allegheny Plateaus. Grows up to 12 inches, pale blue to white flowers in spring; humusy, medium moisture, well–drained soil in part shade to full shade. Prefers rich, moist, organic soils, pH 5 to 7; many sources. Another subspecies, *laphamii (*southeast, Piedmont) is introduced, not native, and escaped from cultivation.

Phlox maculata (Meadow phlox, Wild sweet–William) – Wet meadows, swamps, abandoned fields and thickets, low moist woods and riverbanks, FACW; statewide. Grows 12 to 32 inches, pink–rose to purple flowers in early summer; moderately fertile, medium moisture, well–drained soil in full sun to light shade. Prefers moist, organically rich soils in full sun; a few sources.

Phlox paniculata (Summer phlox, Fall phlox) – meadows, thickets and along stream banks, often on calcareous substrate, FACU; statewide. Grows up to 6 feet, pink flowers in early summer; sun to part sun in moist to wet sandy rich loam, pH 5 to 7; many sources.

Phlox pilosa (Downy phlox) – rare in dry open woodlands, prairies, roadsides and thickets. FACU. Southeast (Piedmont) and endangered. Lavender flowers in spring. Grow in sun to part shade in sandy to rocky slightly acidic, well–drained soils; many sources.

Phlox stolonifera (Creeping phlox) – rich open woods and stream banks. Mostly southwest (Southern Allegheny Plateau). Grows 4 to 6 inches, violet to rose purple flowers in spring; part shade to shade in dry to moist rich loam, pH 6 to 7; many sources.

Phlox subulata ssp. subulata (Moss pink) – dry rocky ledges, slopes, clearings and fields. Mostly southeast (Piedmont), scattered elsewhere. Grows to about 6 inches, pink, purple or white flowers in spring; sun to part sun in dry sandy loam, pH 5.7 to 7.5. Listed as endangered; several sources. Another subspecies, *brittonii,* is very rare on shale barrens in the southwest (Southern Allegheny Plateau).

Phryma leptostachya (Lopseed) – rich woods, rocky limestone slopes and swamps, UPL; statewide except north (Western and Northern Glaciated and Northern Unglaciated Allegheny Plateaus). Grows 1 to 3 feet, purple flowers in summer; part sun to part shade in moist, rich circumneutral loam; a few sources.

Phyla lanceolata (Fog–fruit) – Rare in wet to moist forests and along lakes, ponds and streams, OBL; scattered throughout, but most common southeast (Piedmont). Grows 6 to 20 inches in sun to part sun with pink to white flowers in spring; spreads to form a dense mat in average soil. Good groundcover for wet areas or pond edges; a few sources.

Physalis heterophylla (Ground cherry) – fields, sandy or cindery open ground and cultivated areas; mostly southeast (Piedmont) and west (Southern Allegheny Plateau), scattered elsewhere. Grows 8 to 36 inches, yellow flowers in late summer; sun to part sun in dry, sandy loam; a few sources.

Physostegia virginiana (False dragonhead) – stream banks and along moist shorelines. Scattered statewide except northern tier (northern Allegheny plateaus). Grows up to 36 inches, pinkish–purple flowers in late summer; part sun to part shade in moist rich loam, pH 5 to 6.5; many sources.

Phytolacca americana (Pokeweed) – moist to mesic thickets, clearings and forest openings, open ground and along roadsides. FACU+; statewide. Grows up to 10 feet, with greenish–white flowers in summer to fall; part sun to part shade in dry to moist sandy loam, pH 5 to 6; several sources.

Platanthera ciliaris (Yellow fringed orchid) – bogs, moist meadows, and moist to wet woods, FACW; mostly southeast (Central Appalachians and Piedmont). Grows 15 to 40 inches, orange–yellow flowers in summer; sun to part shade in moist, rich loam; a few sources.

Platanthera clavellata (Clubspur orchid) – bogs, shores, moist woods, thickets, sunny openings, in damp deep humus; FACW+; statewide, except for southwest (Southern Allegheny Plateau). Grows 5 to 15 inches, white flowers in late summer; sun to part sun in moist to wet sandy rich loam, pH 5 to 6; a few sources.

Podophyllum peltatum (Mayapple) – medium wet, well–drained soil in mesic woods, especially maple woods and clearings, FACU; statewide. Grows 12 to 18 inches, white flowers in spring followed by green fruits that yellow when ripe. Spreads by rhizomes to form huge colonies and appears to be ignored by deer; part shade to shade in dry to moist humusy loam, pH 4 to 7; many sources.

Pogonia ophioglossoides (Rose pogonia) – sphagnum bogs, fens, moist acidic sandy meadows and prairies, open wet woods, pine savannahs, sandy–peaty stream banks, and seepage slopes, OBL. Mostly eastern third of the state; scattered central and west. Grows 4 to 16 inches, pink flowers in summer; full to part sun in moist to wet acidic humusy loam; a few sources.

Polemonium reptans (Spreading Jacob's ladder, Greek valerian) – low moist woods, wooded floodplains, thickets at the base of cliffs and moist ground near streams, FACU; statewide. Grows 6 to 20 inches, light blue flowers in spring; part shade to shade in moist, rich sandy loam, pH 5 to 7. Cut back to avoid shaggy appearance after bloom, will green up again. Spreads by free–seeding, not rhizomes; many sources.

Polemonium vanbruntiae (Jacob's ladder) – very rare sphagnum glades, swamps, and marshes, FACW; reported only in Wayne, Sullivan, Berks and Somerset counties. Grows up to 36 inches, blue flowers in summer; moist rich humusy soils in sun to part shade. Listed as endangered. AKA *Polemonium caeruleum ssp. van–bruntiae*; a few sources.

Polygala paucifolia (Bird–on–the–wing) – rich dry to mesic rocky upland woods and wooded slopes, FACU; statewide except for far western edge. Grows 3 to 6 inches, rose–purple flowers in spring; part shade to shade in moist rich loam, pH 4 to 6; a few sources.

Polygonatum biflorum (Smooth Solomon's seal) – dry to moist woods in fertile, loamy soil; tall, robust plants are known as *var. commutatum*, FACU; statewide. Grows up to 6 feet, but more typically around 3 feet, with white–greenish flowers in spring and dark purple fruits following; part shade to shade in dry to moist rich loam. pH 4 to 6 but prefers 5 to 6.5; many sources.

Polygonatum pubescens (Hairy Solomon's seal) – fertile, humus–rich moisture retentive well–drained soil in cool, shaded, dry to moist woods, wooded slopes and coves; statewide. Grows up to 36 inches, white–greenish flowers in spring; part shade to shade in dry to moist humusy sandy loam; pH 4 to 6 but prefers 5 to 6.5; many sources.

Pontederia cordata (Pickerel–weed) – emergent aquatic; pond and lake margins and swampy edges of lakes and streams, OBL. Mostly east (Northern Glaciated Allegheny Plateau, Delaware River Valley) and west (Western Glaciated Allegheny Plateau). Grows 2 to 4 feet above water with light blue flowers in late summer to fall; full sun in mud at the margins of a pond or in containers of rich organic loams in a water garden under 3 to 5 inches of water; many sources.

Potamogeton amplifolius (Bigleaf pondweed) – aquatic; waters of lakes, ponds, streams, and rivers, OBL. Mostly east (Northern Glaciated Allegheny Plateau, Delaware River Valley) and northwest (Western Glaciated Allegheny Plateau). Green flowers in summer; full sun in shallow ponds in silty loam; a few sources.

Potamogeton natans (Floating pondweed) – aquatic; quiet or slow–flowing waters of ponds, lakes, and streams, OBL. Northeast and northwest; scattered elsewhere. Stems to 6 feet and green flowers in summer; full sun in ponds in silty loam; a few sources.

Potamogeton nodosus (Longleaf pondweed) – aquatic; clear to turbid waters of lakes, streams, rivers, and sloughs, OBL; statewide, especially southeast (Piedmont). Greenish–white flowers in summer. Serves as an oxygenator in water gardens; grow in aquatic containers of sandy loam or rooted in muddy pool bottoms at depth of 6 to 24 inches, full sun to part shade; a few sources.

Potamogeton pectinatus (Sago pondweed) – Shallow brackish to alkaline waters of lakes, streams, rivers, and estuaries, OBL; scattered throughout, especially along the Susquehanna and lower Delaware Rivers. Grows up to 6 feet on nearly all bottom substrates in fresh to saline and alkaline water less than 10 feet deep, but poorly in waters with high turbidity. Considered a problem in recreational and irrigation waters; a few sources.

Potamogeton perfoliatus (Perfoliate pondweed) – aquatic; lakes, streams, rivers, and bays; statewide. Green flowers in summer; full sun in water features and ponds in silty loam; a few sources.

Potamogeton praelongus (White–stem pondweed) – Very rare in waters ranging from neutral to alkaline of lakes, rivers, and streams; OBL. Mostly northwest (Erie and Ontario Lake Plain) and endangered. Grow in full sun in water 3 to 10 feet deep in a soft sediment soil; prefers alkaline water. Tiny flowers in summer; a few sources.

Potentilla anserina (Silverweed) – Very rare on gravelly to sandy moist shores, OBL; northwest (Erie and Ontario Lake Plain) and southeast (Atlantic Coastal Plain). Grows 6 to 9 inches in full sun in moist sandy loams to sand with yellow flowers in summer; most often used for erosion control and bank stabilization. AKA *Argentina anserina; a few sources.*

Potentilla arguta (Tall cinquefoil) – dry upland rocky ledges, fields and woods, UPL. Mostly along the Delaware River, widely scattered elsewhere. Grows 15 to 40 inches, white flowers in early summer; sun to part shade in dry sandy loam; many sources.

Potentilla simplex (Old–field cinquefoil) – dry upland woods, fields, meadows and along roadsides, FACU–; statewide. Prostrate stems to 20 inches, yellow flowers in late spring; sun to shade in dry, sandy loam. pH 5.5 to 7; a few sources.

Potentilla tridentata (Three–toothed cinquefoil, shrubby fivefingers) – rare on dry ridge tops and in open woods, northeast (Northern Glaciated Allegheny Plateau), and endangered. Grows 1 to 10 inches, white flowers in summer; sun to part shade in dry to moist sandy loam, pH 5.5 to 7. AKA *Sibbaldiopsis tridentata*; a few sources.

Prenanthes alba (White rattlesnake root) – moist open woods, along shady roadsides and in thickets, FACU. Statewide, especially southeast (Piedmont). Grows up to 8 inches, white and pinkish–lavender flowers in late summer into fall; part shade to shade in moist, well–drained soils. AKA *Nabalus albus*; a few sources.

Prenanthes racemosa (Glaucous rattlesnake–root) – Very rare in bogs, marshy flats, tall–grass prairies, wet meadows and sandy alluvial soils of stream banks; FACW– and believed to be extirpated. Grows 3 feet, pinkish flowers in summer in full sun in wet to mesic, well drained sandy loams; a few sources.

Prunella vulgaris ssp. lanceolata (Heal–all) – mesic fields, upland woods, floodplains, and along roadsides, FACU+; statewide. Grows up to 24 inches, violet–blue to pink or white flowers in summer and fall; sun to part sun in moist rich loam; several sources.

Pycnanthemum incanum (Mountain mint) – moist old fields, thickets, and barrens. Mostly southeast (Central Appalachians, Piedmont), scattered elsewhere. Grows up to 36 inches, with purple to white flowers in late summer; sun to part sun in dry moist sandy loam; a few sources.

Pycnanthemum muticum (Mountain mint) – moist woods, thickets, meadows and swales, FACW. Mostly southeast (Piedmont), scattered elsewhere. Grows 15 to 30 inches, purple to white flowers in late summer; sun to part shade in moist rich loam, pH 5.5 to 7.5; several sources.

Pycnanthemum tenuifolium (Mountain mint) – moist fields, stream banks and floodplains, FACW. Mostly southeast (Piedmont), scattered elsewhere. Grows 20 to 30 inches, purple to white flowers in late summer; sun to part sun in moist rich loam; a few sources.

Pycnanthemum virginianum (Mountain mint) – boggy fields, moist woods and floodplains, FAC; Mostly southeast (Piedmont), scattered elsewhere. Grows up to 36 inches, purple to white flowers in late summer; sun to part shade in moist, sandy loam, pH 5.5 to 7; many sources.

Pyrola elliptica (Shinleaf) – bogs, fens, swamps and moist to wet coniferous woods; statewide. Grows 6 to 12 inches, white flowers in early summer; part shade to shade in dry to moist acidic loam, pH 4 to 6; a few sources.

Ranunculus fascicularis (Early buttercup) – rare in dry upland woods, grasslands and thickets, FACU. Scattered southeast; endangered. Grows 4 to 10 inches, yellow flowers in spring; sun to shade in dry sandy loam; a few sources.

Ranunculus flammula var. ovalis (Creeping spearwort) – muddy, wet ground, including shores to shallow water; observed only in Pike, Northampton, Montour, Dauphin, Lancaster and Philadelphia counties; believed to be extirpated. Prostrate stems to 20 inches, yellow flowers in summer; sun to part sun in moist to wet rich loam; a few sources.

Ranunculus hispidus var. hispidus (Hairy buttercup) – rich dry to mesic woods, usually oak–hickory, and meadows, FAC; statewide. Grows 5 to 20 inches, yellow flowers in spring; sun to part shade in dry to moist rich loam, pH 5 to 6; a few sources.

Ranunculus hispidus var. nitidus (Hairy buttercup) – wet, low woodlands, swamps, marshes and thickets, statewide; FACW. Grows 5 to 10 inches, yellow flowers in late spring; sun to part shade in moist to wet rich loam; a few sources.

Ranunculus recurvatus (Hooked crowfoot) – rich, low moist woods, FAC+; statewide. Grows 6 to 20 inches, yellow flowers in early summer; part shade to shade in moist rich loam; a few sources.

Ratibida pinnata (Prairie coneflower) – rare in prairies and thickets, as well as woodland edges. Mostly west (Southern Allegheny Plateau); believed to be extirpated. Yellow flowers in summer; grow in well–drained medium moisture average soils in full sun. Prefers sandy and clay soils, but tolerates poor, dry soils. Grow in average, medium moisture, well–drained soil in full sun; many sources.

Rhexia mariana (Maryland meadow–beauty) – rare in savannas and meadows; marshes and bogs, especially the Atlantic Coastal Plain; OBL and endangered. Grows 1 to 3 feet in full to part sun in slightly acidic, mesic to wet, fertile sandy loams. White to pink flowers in summer; good for water gardens and pond areas; a few sources.

Rhexia virginica (Meadow beauty or Handsome Harry) – rich, acidic sandy soil in moist open areas, OBL. Mostly southeast (Piedmont), scattered elsewhere. Grows 10 to 40 inches, dark pink flowers in late summer; sun to part shade in wet rich sandy loam; a few sources.

Rudbeckia fulgida var. fulgida (Eastern coneflower, black–eyed Susan) – prairies, pastures, open woods; FAC; mostly southeast (Central Appalachians, Piedmont), scattered elsewhere. Grows 2 to 4 feet, yellow to orange flowers in summer. Tolerant of hot, humid summers and some light shade; grow in well–drained, dry to medium average soil in full sun; many sources.

Rudbeckia fulgida var. speciosa (Coneflower, Orange coneflower) – mesic open woodlands and fields, mostly southeast (Piedmont); FAC. Grows 2 to 4 feet in full to part sun with yellow flowers in summer; prefers loamy, well drained, moderately moist soils; a few sources.

Rudbeckia hirta (Black–eyed Susan) – mesic prairies, plains, meadows, pastures, savannahs, woodland edges and openings, FACU–; statewide. Grows up to 36 inches, orange–yellow flowers in late summer. Two local varieties – *hirta* and *pulcherrima*; full sun in average, dry to medium, well–drained soils. Prefers moist, organically rich soils; many sources.

Rudbeckia laciniata (Cutleaf coneflower) – moist, rich soils in fields, floodplains, open woods and thickets, FACW; statewide. Grows 2 to 9 feet, yellow flowers in late summer; sun to part shade in moist sandy loam, pH 5 to 7; many sources.

Rudbeckia triloba (Three–lobed coneflower) – mesic to wet woodlands, thickets, pastures, roadsides and meadows, frequently on limestone, FACU; statewide. Grows 18 to 60 inches, yellow to orange flowers in late summer; sun to part sun in dry to moist sandy loam; many sources.

Ruellia caroliniensis (Carolina petunia) – very rare in sandy, open upland woodlands and stream banks; believed to be extirpated. Grows 1 to 3 feet, purple flowers in summer in part shade on moist to dry sandy soil; prefers soils without humus that are nutrient poor; a few sources.

Ruellia humilis (Fringed–leaved petunia) – very rare in woodland openings and edges, thickets; UPL. Reported only in Franklin County;

endangered. Pale lavender flowers throughout summer, especially if kept moist. Grow in well–drained, dry to medium moisture average soils in full sun to part shade; many sources.

Ruellia strepens (Limestone petunia) – rare in open woodlands and rich wooded slopes and bluffs, typically over limestone; mostly south (Central Appalachians and Piedmont); FAC. Grows 1 to 3 feet, lilac to lavender flowers, summer, in part shade on well drained, organically rich, circumneutral soils; tolerates nearly full shade; a few sources.

Rumex altissimus (Tall dock) – river bottomlands and wet woods margins in rich alluvial soils, FACW–. Mostly southeast (Piedmont); scattered elsewhere. Grows up to 50 inches, reddish–green flowers in early summer; sun to part sun in moist, rich sandy loam; a few sources.

Rumex verticillatus (Swamp dock) – bogs, marshes, wet swampy meadows, swamps, wet alluvial woods and swales, including shallow water; OBL. Mostly northwest (Western Glaciated Allegheny Plateau). Grows 3 to 5 feet, white–green flowers in late spring to early summer. Prefers light shade to full sun in wet, mucky soil, including standing water; a few sources.

Sagittaria graminea var. graminea (Grass–leaved sagittaria) – aquatic; streams, lakes and mudflats, erect or immersed or submerged in shallow water. OBL. Mostly eastern third of the state, scattered west. Blooms in summer; full sun in shallow water in silty soil; a few sources.

Sagittaria latifolia var. latifolia (Wapato, or duck potato) – aquatic; wet ditches, pools, and margins of streams, lakes and ponds, OBL; statewide. Grows 12 to 48 inches, white flowers in summer; plant in mud at the margins of a pond or in containers in a water garden, either along the shore or in up to 6 to 12 inches of water; many sources.

Sagittaria rigida (Arrowhead) – aquatic; calcareous shallow water and shores of ponds, swamps, and rivers, occasionally in deep water, OBL. Scattered statewide, especially in eastern streams. Grows up to 3 feet, white flowers in late summer; plant in mud at pond edges or in containers in a water garden, either along the shore or in up to 6 to 12 inches of water; a few sources.

Sagittaria subulata (Subulate arrowhead) – rare along streams and brackish bays and mud flats in tidal shore areas, especially southeast (Atlantic Coastal Plain); OBL. Grows 8 to 16 inches in silty to sandy soils. Often sold as an aquarium plant; a few sources.

Salvia lyrata (Lyre–leaved sage) – rock, rich open woods, wet to dry meadows and alluvial areas, in well–drained sand or loam, UPL; mostly southeast (Piedmont), scattered elsewhere. Grows 1 to 2 feet with purple flowers in late spring; medium to wet, average soils in full sun; prefers moist sandy soils, and tolerates very light shade. Tolerates heat and humidity; many sources.

Sanguinaria canadensis (Bloodroot) – moist to dry upland woods and thickets, especially on flood plains and shores or near streams on slopes, FACU; statewide. Grows 2 to 6 inches, white flowers early spring; part shade to shade in dry to moist rich sandy loam, pH 5 to 7, and spreads to form small colonies; many sources.

Sanguisorba canadensis (American burnet) – swamps, bogs, meadows and floodplains, FACW+; mostly southeast (Piedmont); scattered elsewhere. Grows up to 50 inches, white flowers in summer; sun to part sun in moist to wet rich loam, pH 5.5 to 7; a few sources.

Sarracenia purpurea (Pitcher plant) – sphagnum bogs and peatlands, fens, swamps, wet conifer woodlands, lake and pond margins, OBL. Mostly northeast (Northern Glaciated Allegheny Plateau) and northwest (Western Glaciated Allegheny Plateau), scattered elsewhere. Grows 4 to 8 inches, maroon to red flowers in early summer; full sun in acidic, humusy muck that is constantly damp but not watery, pH 4.5 to 5.5; a carnivore requiring insects for nutrition, several sources.

Saururus cernuus (Lizard's–tail) – wet soils and mud in lowlands and stream and lake edges, including still standing fresh or slightly brackish water to a depth of 6 inches; OBL; scattered throughout except for Northern Glaciated and Unglaciated Allegheny Plateaus. White flowers in late summer. In water gardens, plant in containers in shallow water, about 6 inches deep. In natural ponds, plant in sandy to muddy pond margins under shallow water or in boggy, moist soil. Prefers full sun to part shade, but will flower in full shade. Rhizomes spread to create colonies; many sources.

Saxifraga micranthidifolia (Lettuce saxifrage) – rare in seepage areas and shaded streambeds, often among mossy rocks; OBL. Mostly southwest (Southern Allegheny Plateau) and the Lehigh Valley (Lower New England Section). Grows 1 to 3 feet, white flowers in late spring; prefers part shade to shade in continually moist, humusy soils; a few sources.

Saxifraga pensylvanica (Swamp saxifrage) – wet woods, bogs and swamps, OBL; statewide. Grows 8 to 30 inches, greenish–white flowers in late spring; part shade in moist to wet circumneutral soils; a few sources.

Saxifraga virginiensis (Early saxifrage) – rock crevices on dry to mesic rocky slopes, FAC–; statewide except north–central (Northern Unglaciated Allegheny Plateau). Grows 4 to 12 inches, white flowers in spring; sun to part sun in dry to moist sandy loam, pH 5.5 to 7; a few sources.

Scrophularia lanceolata (Lanceleaf figwort) – low woods, thickets, stream banks, and along moist roadsides, FACU+; statewide, especially southeast (Piedmont). Grows up to 6 feet, with yellowish–green flowers in summer; part shade to shade in moist, rich sandy loam; a few sources.

Scrophularia marilandica (Eastern figwort) – alluvial woods, river banks, moist shores and along roadsides, FACU–; statewide. Grows up to 10 feet, purple–brownish flowers in summer; part shade to shade in moist, rocky, rich loam; a few sources.

Scutellaria incana (Downy skullcap) – open rocky woods, clearings, on slopes and along streams, statewide except for northern–most counties and most common on the Southern Allegheny Plateau. Grows 2 to 3 feet in sun to part shade with blue flowers in early autumn; prefers average, well–drained soil, especially dryer sandy to clay soils; a few sources.

Scutellaria integrifolia (Hyssop skullcap) – swamps, bogs and moist fields, FACW. Southeast, especially Central Appalachians and Piedmont. Grows 12 to 30 inches, blue flowers in late summer; sun to part sun in moist, silty loam; a few sources.

Scutellaria lateriflora (Mad–dog skullcap) – wet woods, stream banks and moist pastures, FACW+; statewide. Grows 12 to 30 inches, with blue flowers in late summer; sun to part sun in moist silty loam; many sources.

Scutellaria leonardii (Small skullcap) – open woodlands and bluffs, shores, limestone glades, gravel and sand prairies; scattered statewide, mostly southeast (Piedmont). Grows to 4 inches in dry to mesic soils with purple flowers in late spring. Prefers shallow soils with sand or gravel, generally dry conditions; good for sunny rock gardens, but intolerant of taller plant competition; a few sources.

Scutellaria serrata (Showy skullcap) – very rare in floodplains and rocky, humusy woodlands; mostly southeast (Piedmont, Atlantic Coastal Plain). Endangered. Grows 1 to 2 feet, blue to violet flowers in late spring; prefers rich, well–drained soil in part shade; ideal in groups for moist to dry woodland or shade gardens; a few sources.

Sedum ternatum (Woodland stonecrop) – rocky banks, cliffs and woodlands, as well as damp sites along stream banks, bluff bases and stony ledges. Mostly southwest (Southern Allegheny Plateau); scattered elsewhere. Grows 3 to 6 inches, white flowers in early spring; average, medium, well–drained soils in full sun to part shade, pH 5 to 7; many sources.

Senna hebecarpa (Northern wild senna) – moist open woods, wetland edges, floodplains, and along roadsides, FAC; mostly southeast (Piedmont), also statewide except northern and western Allegheny plateaus. Grows 3 to 6 feet, yellow flowers in summer; part sun to part shade in moist, rich sandy loam, pH 5.5 to 7; many sources.

Senna marilandica (Southern wild senna) – rare in dry open woods, openings and thickets; FAC+, mostly south. Grows 3 to 6 feet, yellow flowers in summer; well–drained sandy to clay medium moisture loams in full sun; many sources.

Silene caroliniana ssp. pensylvanica (Fire pink) – open, typically gravelly to rocky, usually deciduous woodlands; statewide, except northern and western Allegheny plateaus. Grows 9 to 12 inches, pink flowers in spring; average, dry to medium moisture, well–drained soils in full sun to part shade. Prefers sunny sites in dryish sandy or gravelly soils with some part afternoon shade; a few sources.

Silene nivea (Snowy campion) – mesic to moist alluvial woodlands and thickets, FAC; widely scattered statewide. Grows up to 8 to 12 inches, with white flowers in summer; sun to part sun in sandy, well–drained loam; a few sources.

Silene stellata (Starry campion) – wooded slopes, barrens and roadside banks; statewide except Northern Glaciated and Unglaciated Allegheny Plateaus. Grows 12 to 36 inches, white flowers in summer; part sun to part shade in dry to moist sandy loam. pH 5 to 7; several sources.

Silene virginica (Fire pink) – moist deciduous woodland slopes and bluffs; mostly west (Southern Allegheny Plateau). Grows 12 to 18 inches with red flowers in late spring; well drained, dry to medium moisture, average soil in full sun to part shade; prefers moist, sandy to clay soils with excellent drainage in part shade; many sources.

Silphium asteriscus var. trifoliatum (Whorled rosinweed) – prairies, dry thickets and meadows, roadsides and along railways, mostly southwest (Southern Allegheny Plateau). Grows 4 to 6 feet, yellow flowers in late summer. Prefers dry, prairie habitats in full sun. AKA *Silphium trifoliatum var. trifoliatum*; a few sources.

Sisyrinchium albidum (White blue–eyed–grass) – very rare in prairies, rich open woods and open slopes, often on thin sandy to rocky soil. Listed as extirpated, but some doubt as to whether continental range should include Pennsylvania. Grows 1 to 3 feet, white flowers in late spring; prefers full to part sun on dry, sandy to gravelly well drained soil; a few sources.

Sisyrinchium angustifolium (Blue–eyed grass) – meadows, flood plains, moist fields, and mesic open woods; statewide. Grows up to 15 inches, with pale blue flowers in early summer; sun to part shade in moist sandy loam, pH 5 to 7; many sources.

Sisyrinchium atlanticum (Eastern blue–eyed–grass) – Very rare in thin woods, open fields and coastal dunes that are sandy and dry to moist. Mostly southeast (Atlantic Coastal Plain); endangered. Grows 1 to 3 feet in sun on moist, slightly acidic sandy, peaty, rich loamy soil; a few sources.

Sisyrinchium montanum var. crebrum (Blue–eyed grass) – dry to mesic open woods, roadsides and fields, FACW–; mostly northeast (Northern Glaciated Allegheny Plateau), scattered elsewhere. Grows up to 20 inches, with violet flowers in early summer; sun to part shade in dry to moist sandy loam; several sources.

Sium suave (Water–parsnip) – swamps, bogs, wet meadows, pond margins, OBL; scattered statewide. Grows up to 6 feet, white flowers in late summer; full to part sun in moist to wet rich loams; a few sources.

Solanum carolinense (Horse–nettle) – dry to mesic fields, roadsides, sandy stream banks, UPL; statewide. Grows up to 3 feet, pale violet to white flowers in summer; full to part sun in average sandy loam. Considered a noxious weed in many western states; a few sources.

Solidago altissima (Canada goldenrod) – dry to moist soils in fields and river banks as well as disturbed areas such as roadsides, FACU–; statewide. Grows up to 6 feet, yellow flowers in late summer and fall; sun to part sun in dry, sandy loam; a few sources.

Solidago bicolor (Silver rod) – dry open woods; statewide. Grows up to 40 inches; white flowers in late summer to fall; part shade in dry sandy loam, pH 5 to 6; several sources.

Solidago caesia (Bluestem goldenrod) – dry upland open woods, thickets and clearings, FACU; statewide. Grows 18 to 36 inches, yellow flowers late summer to fall; part sun to shade in dry to moist rich loam, pH 5 to 7; many sources.

Solidago canadensis var. hargeri (Canada goldenrod) – dry to mesic fields and along roadsides, FACU; statewide. Grows up to 6 feet, yellow flowers in late summer into fall; sun to part sun in dry to moist sandy loam; several sources.

Solidago curtisii (Curtis's goldenrod) – rare in mostly Appalachian shaded, mesic thickets and woods; southwest (Southern Allegheny Plateau) and endangered. Grows 2 to 3 feet in rich well–drained soils, part sun to part shade; yellow flowers in late summer; a few sources.

Solidago erecta (Slender goldenrod) – rare in dry woods, disturbed open soils, road embankments; mostly south, endangered. Grows 12 to 24 inches, yellow flowers in early autumn. Grow in well–drained sandy to rocky soils in full sun. AKA *Solidago speciosa var. erecta*; a few sources.

Solidago flexicaulis (Zigzag goldenrod) – moist upland woods and rocky wooded slopes, FACU; statewide. Grows 18 to 36 inches, yellow flowers in late summer through fall; part shade to shade in moist rich loam, pH 5.5 to 7; many sources.

Solidago gigantea var. gigantea (Smooth goldenrod) – moist fields, woods, and floodplains, FACW; statewide. Grows up to 6 feet, yellow flowers in late summer through fall; sun to part sun in dry to moist sandy loam; a few sources.

Solidago juncea (Early goldenrod) – fields, meadows, rocky banks and along roadsides; statewide. Grows up to 4 feet, yellow flowers in late summer to fall; sun to part sun in dry to moist sandy loam, pH 5 to 6; several sources.

Solidago nemoralis (Gray goldenrod) – fields, woods and roadsides in dry sterile soils; statewide. Grows up to 3 feet, yellow flowers late summer to fall; sun to part shade in dry sandy loam; many sources.

Solidago odora ssp. odora (Sweet goldenrod, anise–scented goldenrod) – dry open woods and barrens. Mostly east of Central Appalachians. Grows up to 4 feet, yellow flowers in late summer to fall; sun to part shade in dry to moist sandy loam, pH 4 to 6; several sources.

Solidago patula ssp. patula (Spreading goldenrod) – moist soils in swamp margins, boggy ground, wet meadows, roadside ditches, seeps, and the edges of wet woods, OBL. Statewide, mostly south. Grows up to 6 feet, with yellow flowers in late summer to fall; moist sandy loam in sun to part shade; a few sources.

Solidago rigida (Stiff goldenrod) – rare in dry fields and prairies; UPL, widely scattered, mostly southeast (Piedmont), endangered. Yellow flowers in late summer to fall. Grow in full sun in well–drained, medium to dry moisture average soil; many sources. AKA *Oligoneuron rigidum*.

Solidago roanensis (Mountain goldenrod) – rare in woods and clearings, rock crevices, edges of balds and rocky banks; southwest (Southern Allegheny Plateau and Allegheny Mountains). Grows 12 to 36 inches in sun to part sun in well–drained, rocky soils; a few sources.

Solidago rugosa (Wrinkle–leaf goldenrod) – woods, fields, floodplains and waste ground, FAC; two local varieties, *rugosa* and *villosa*; statewide. Grows up to 4 feet, with yellow flowers in late summer into fall; sun to part shade in moist sandy loam; pH 5.5 to 7; several sources.

Solidago speciosa (Showy goldenrod) – moist meadows and rocky woods and thickets; scattered statewide, especially southeast. Grows up to 6 feet, with yellow flowers from late summer into fall; sun to part shade in dry to moist sandy loam, pH 6 to 7; many sources.

Solidago uliginosa (Bog goldenrod) – bogs and wet areas, fens, marshes, and sometimes in wet woods, OBL; scattered statewide, mostly east and west edges. Grows up to 5 feet, yellow flowers from late summer into fall; sun to part sun in moist, well drained soil; a few sources.

Solidago ulmifolia var. ulmifolia (Elm–leaved goldenrod) – wooded slopes, roadside banks and shale barrens; statewide, especially south. Grows up to 4 feet, with yellow flowers in late summer to fall; sun to part shade in dry rocky sandy loam; a few sources.

Spiranthes casei (Case's ladies'–tresses) – very rare in mesic to dry meadows, barrens open woodlands, outcrops and old fields; mostly north central area (Northern Unglaciated Allegheny Plateau); endangered. Grows 8 to 16 inches, yellowish to greenish–white flowers in late summer; prefers dry to moist; in sandy, acidic, sterile soil in sun to part shade; a few sources.

Spiranthes cernua (Nodding ladies tresses) – wet to dry open sites in fens, marshes, meadows, swales, prairies, open woodlands, riverbanks, shores, ditches, roadsides, and moist old fields, FACW; statewide.

Grows 5 to 15 inches, white flowers in late summer and early fall; sun to part sun in moist silty loam, pH 4.5 to 6.5; a few sources.

Spiranthes vernalis (Spring ladies tresses) – rare in old fields, dry to moist meadows and dune hollows, along roadsides; FAC. Southeast (Piedmont); endangered. White flowers in fall. Grow in full sun to part shade in medium moist, rich well–drained soil; a few sources.

Stachys palustris var. pilosa (Hedge–nettle) – very rare in wet meadows and marshes; scattered in south (Piedmont, Southern Allegheny Plateau). Grows 20 to 40 inches, pink to white flowers in summer; prefers moist to wet rich soils in full sun to part shade; a few sources.

Streptopus amplexifolius (Twisted stalk) – rare in rich, moist, coniferous and deciduous woods, seepy outcrops, often near waterfalls, FAC+; scattered northeast and endangered. Grows up to 36 inches, greenish–white flowers in summer; part shade to shade in rich loam, pH 5 to 6; a few sources.

Streptopus roseus var. perspectus (Rose mandaria) – cool to cold, moist woods and stream banks; Allegheny Mountains and northern plateaus. Grows up to 24 inches, with pink–rose flowers in early summer; part shade to shade in moist rich loam, pH 5 to 6. AKA *Streptopus lanceolatus var lanceolatus*; a few sources.

Symphyotrichum cordifolium (Blue wood aster) – rich, dry or moist woodlands, bluff bases, stream banks and moist ledges; statewide. Grows up to 5 feet, pale blue flowers in late fall; part shade to shade in dry to moist sandy loam, pH 5.6 to 7.5; many sources.

Symphyotrichum drummondii var. drummondii (Hairy heart–leaved aster) – very rare in open deciduous woods, clearings, thickets, stream banks, swamp edges; southwest (Southern Allegheny Plateau); UPL. Grows up to 4 feet, bluish–white flowers in autumn. Prefers wet to dry mesic loamy to rocky soils in part shade; a few sources.

Symphyotrichum ericoides ssp. ericoides (White heath aster) – dry to mesic meadows and fields, FACU. Mostly along the southern Delaware River, scattered elsewhere. Grows 10 to 50 inches, white flowers in fall; sun to part sun in dry sandy loam; many sources.

Symphyotrichum laeve (Smooth blue aster) – dry woods, rocky ledges. Two varieties: *var. laeve*, common in mostly the Central Appalachians and Piedmont, while *var. concinnum* is very rare in the southeast (Piedmont) Mostly south central and eastern counties in Pennsylvania; scattered elsewhere. Grows 10 to 40 inches, pale to dark blue flowers in fall; sun to part shade in dry sandy loam, pH 4 to 7; many sources.

Symphyotrichum lateriflorum (Calico aster) – mesic to moist old fields, edges of woods, rocky woods, and waste ground, FACW–; statewide. Grows 10 to 45 inches, white flowers in autumn; sun to part shade in moist sandy loam; pH 4 to 7, prefers 6.6 to 7; a few sources.

Symphyotrichum novae-angliae (New England aster) – moist prairies, meadows, thickets, low valleys and stream banks, FACW–; statewide. Grows 3 to 6 feet, purple flowers in fall; average, medium, well–drained soil in full sun. Prefers moist, rich soils, pH 5.5 to 7; many sources.

Symphyotrichum novi–belgii var. novi–belgii (New York aster) – rare in meadows, damp thickets, shorelines; FACW+. Southeast (Piedmont, Atlantic Coastal Plain). Grows to 30 inches, white to blue flowers in late summer. Grow in well–drained, moist, average soils in full sun; many sources.

Symphyotrichum oblongifolium (Aromatic aster) – fields, prairies and openings, typically over limestone substrates. Mostly along the Allegheny front and in southwest (Southern Allegheny Plateau). Grows 1 to 3 feet with lavender flowers in late summer; well drained, dry to medium average soils in full sun; prefers sandy soils and tolerates poor soils and drought; many sources.

Symphyotrichum patens (Late purple aster) – dry, sandy, moist, open woods and old fields. Statewide except northern plateaus; most common in southeast (Piedmont). Grows 15 to 45 inches, blue flowers in fall; part shade to shade in dry to moist sandy loam, pH 5 to 6; a few sources.

Symphyotrichum praealtum (Veiny–lined aster) – open woods or thickets, wet prairies and meadows, lake and stream margins and moist banks, and oak savannas; FACW. Scattered statewide. Grows 20 to 60 inches in full to part sun, with blue flowers in autumn. Prefers wet, loamy soils; a few sources.

Symphyotrichum prenanthoides (Zig–zag aster) – swamps, stream banks and low woods, FAC; statewide. Grows 10 to 40 inches, blue to pale purple flowers in early fall; sun to part shade in moist, well–drained soil; a few sources.

Symphyotrichum puniceum var. puniceum (Purple–stemmed aster) – swampy ground of spring–fed meadows, stream banks and moist ditches, FACW; statewide. Grows up to 6 feet, blue flowers in early autumn; average, wet, well–drained soil in full sun. Listed as threatened in Pennsylvania; many sources.

Symphyotrichum shortii (Short's aster) – mesic, open, typically thin oak–hickory woodlands, woods edges, thickets and stream banks, calcareous hummocks, mostly southwest (Southern Allegheny Plateau). Grows 2 to 4 feet, white flowers in autumn, with a preference to partial sun and mesic to slightly dry, circumneutral to slightly alkaline, loamy to rocky woodland soil. Richer soils produce taller plants, which may need support when in bloom; a few sources.

Symphyotrichum undulatum (Heart–leaved aster) – dry woods, sandy slopes and old fields; statewide. Grows 15 to 45 inches, with blue–violet flowers in autumn; sun to part shade in dry sandy loam; a few sources.

Symplocarpus foetidus (Skunk cabbage) – swamps, wet woods, along streams, and other wet low areas, OBL; statewide. Grows 1 to 3 feet, yellow–brown flowers in early spring; part sun to part shade in moist to wet humusy loam; pH 5 to 7; several sources.

Taenidia integerrima (Yellow pimpernel) – rocky upland woods, bluffs, thickets and slopes, as well as prairies and savannahs; statewide, mostly south and scattered elsewhere. Grows 16 to 32 inches, yellow flowers in early summer; part sun in poor, clay, rocky or sandy soils; a few sources.

Tephrosia virginiana (Goat's rue) – dry, sandy acidic woods. Mostly southeast (Central Appalachians and Piedmont) and southwest (Southern Allegheny Plateau). Grows 10 to 30 inches, yellow–white/pinkish purple flowers in summer; part sun to part shade in dry acidic sandy loam; several sources.

Teucrium canadense var. virginicum (Wild germander) – flood plains, lake margins, moist fields and meadows, FACW–; statewide. Grows 18 to 36 inches, purple to pink or cream color flowers in summer; sun to part sun in moist silty loam; a few sources.

Thalictrum dasycarpum (Purple meadow–rue) – very rare in deciduous woodlands along streams, damp thickets, swamps, and wet meadows and prairies; FACW. Reported only in Warren and Forest counties. Grows 3 to 5 feet with purple–white flowers in late spring; well–drained, medium moisture average soils in full sun to part shade; prefers rich humusy and moist soil in dappled light. Intolerant of hot and humid conditions; many sources.

Thalictrum dioicum (Early meadow–rue) – rich, mesic to moist rocky woods, ravines, alluvial terraces, especially on north–facing slopes, FAC; statewide. Grows 10 to 30 inches; greenish to purple flowers in spring; part sun to part shade in moist rich loam, pH 5 to 7; several sources.

Thalictrum pubescens (Tall meadow–rue) – rich mesic upland woods and wet meadows, thickets and stream banks, FACW+; statewide. Grows 2 to 10 feet, white to purplish flowers in summer; part sun to part shade in moist rich loam, pH 5.5 to 7; a few sources.

Thalictrum revolutum (Purple meadow–rue) – dry open woods, brushy banks, thickets and barrens, UPL. Statewide except northern tier; most common southeast (Central Appalachians, Piedmont). Grows 2 to 6 feet, white flowers in early summer; sun to part shade in dry sandy loam; a few sources.

Thalictrum thalictroides (Rue anemone) – rich, moist deciduous upland woods, wooded banks and thickets; statewide except for Allegheny Mountains and Northern Unglaciated Allegheny Plateau. Grows 4 to 12 inches, white flowers, early spring; part shade to shade in rich humus, pH 4 to 7; goes dormant if the soil becomes too dry; many sources.

Thaspium trifoliatum (Meadow–parsnip) – rich woodland slopes, ravines and woods edges. Two varieties: *var. trifoliatum*, mostly southeast (Piedmont) and *var. flavum,* mostly southwest (Southern Allegheny Plateau). Grows 12 to 30 inches, yellow flowers in spring; prefers full sun to part shade in mesic, well–drained soils; a few sources.

Tiarella cordifolia (Foamflower) – moist, rocky deciduous woods and wooded slopes, FAC–; mostly Allegheny plateaus, north and west, sparse in Central Appalachians and Piedmont. Grows 4 to 14 inches, white flowers in spring; part sun to part shade in moist rich loam. pH 5 to 7; many sources.

Tipularia discolor (Cranefly orchid) – rare in deciduous woodlands and stream banks, especially in acidic oak–pine woodlands and depressions under sweet gum canopies; FACU. Mostly southeast (Piedmont). Grows 4 to 10 inches, yellow–green–purple flowers in summer; prefers part sun to part shade in humus rich, well drained soils; a few sources.

Tradescantia ohiensis (Spiderwort, Bluejacket) – rare in fields, thickets, rarely in woodlands, sometimes along streams; FAC. Scattered southeast and west; endangered. Blue flowers in early summer.

Grow in well–drained dry to medium average soil in full sun to part shade; prefers acidic moist sandy soil in full sun; many sources.

Tradescantia virginiana (Spider lily or widows tears) – dry to mesic upland wooded slopes, shale outcrops and moist fields, FACU; scattered south, especially Piedmont; absent in northern Allegheny plateaus. Grows 12 to 36 inches, blue to purple flowers in spring; sun to part shade in moist, well–drained sandy loam. Prefers moist acidic soils, but tolerates poor soils; many sources.

Trautvetteria caroliniensis (Carolina tassel–rue) – rare in bogs, stream banks, wooded seepage slopes, mostly southwest (Southern Allegheny Plateau); FACW–. Grows 18 to 40 inches, white flowers in summer on rich, humusy, mesic to moist loam in part shade; a few sources.

Triadenum virginicum (Marsh St. Johns Wort) – marshes, bogs, swampy woods, stream banks; OBL; statewide, especially Western Glaciated and Northern Glaciated Allegheny Plateaus and Allegheny Mountains, scattered elsewhere. Grows 12 to 24 inches, pink to purple flowers in summer; mesic to moist rich loams in sun to part sun; a few sources.

Trillium cernuum var cernuum (Nodding trillium) – rich, moist, mixed deciduous–coniferous forests and swamps, FACW. Mostly southeast (Piedmont), scattered elsewhere. Grows up to 15 inches, white flowers in spring; part shade to shade in moist rich humus, pH 5 to 6; a few sources.

Trillium cuneatum (Huger's trillium) – rich, often upland woods, especially with limestone soils, along with less calcareous sites, sometimes old fields, ditches, or coal–mine tailings; scattered west and southeast (Piedmont). Yellow, purple, green and brown flowers in early spring. Grows 10 to 12 inches and more in rich, humusy, moist soils in part shade to shade. Similar to *Trillium sessile*, which lacks the height; a few sources.

Trillium erectum var. erectum (Purple trillium) – cool, rich, moist neutral to acidic soils of upland deciduous forests, mixed deciduous–coniferous forests, and coniferous swamp borders, FACU–; statewide, but widely scattered southeast (Central Appalachians, Piedmont). Grows up to 15 inches, maroon flowers, spring; part shade to shade in moist rich loam; pH 4 to 7 but prefers 4.5 to 6; many sources.

Trillium flexipes (Declined trillium) – rich forest floodplains, swampy woods and wooded slopes, typically over limestone; FAC. Scattered throughout south and west (Piedmont, Western Glaciated and Southern

Allegheny Plateaus). Grows 1 to 2 feet, white flowers in spring; prefers part shade to shade in rich, humusy, constantly moist, well–drained soil; a few sources.

Trillium grandiflorum (Large flowered trillium) – rich deciduous or mixed coniferous–deciduous upland woods, floodplains, and along roadsides. Mostly west (Western Glaciated, Southern Allegheny Plateaus, Erie and Ontario Lake Plain), scattered east. Grows up to 15 inches, white flowers becoming pink in spring; part shade to shade in moist rich loam. pH 6 to 7 but prefers 6.0; many sources.

Trillium sessile (Toadshade trillium) – rich woodlands, calcareous, clayey alluvium on floodplains and riverbanks and less fertile soils in high, dry limestone woods, FACU–. Mostly southwest (Southern Allegheny Plateau), scattered elsewhere. Grows up to 12 inches, maroon flowers in spring; part shade to shade in moist rich loam; many sources.

Trillium undulatum (Painted trillium) – deep acidic humus in mixed deciduous–coniferous woods; prefers deep shade except at higher elevations, FACU. Allegheny Mountains and northern Allegheny Plateaus; sparse in Southern Allegheny Plateau, Central Appalachians and Piedmont areas. Grows up to 15 inches, white flowers with rose–purple triangle in late spring; part shade to shade in moist rich loam, pH 4 to 6; several sources.

Triosteum perfoliatum (Horse–gentian, wild coffee) – open rocky woods and thickets, calcareous hillsides, scattered statewide. Grows 2 to 3 feet, purplish–greenish flowers in late spring; prefers light shade to dappled shade in slightly dry to mesic loamy or rocky soil with much organic matter. Fruits can be dried, roasted ground and used as a coffee substitute; a few sources.

Trollius laxus (Spreading globe–flower) – very rare in rich, moist calcareous meadows, swamps and moist, open woods, OBL. Mostly east–central (Hudson Valley and Lower New England Sections), widely scattered elsewhere; endangered. Grows 4 to 20 inches, yellow flowers in spring; part sun to part shade in moist, rich calcareous loam; a few sources.

Typha angustifolia (Narrow–leaved cat–tail) – wet meadows, fens, estuaries, marshes, bogs, ditches, and along lake shores; OBL. Mostly southeast (Piedmont); scattered elsewhere. Grow in moist to wet rich organic soils, including shallow standing water, in full sun; many sources.

Typha latifolia (Common cat–tail) – swamps, marshes, wet shores, ditches, or wet soil, OBL; statewide. Grows 3 to 9 feet and blooms in early summer; rich loams in full sun to part shade in water to 12 inches deep. Because it is an aggressive colonizer, many plant them in underwater containers; many sources.

Urtica dioica ssp. gracilis (Great nettle) – dry to mesic alluvial upland woods, margins of deciduous woodlands, along fencerows and in waste places, FACU. Statewide except sparse in the Allegheny Mountains, Central Appalachians and Blue Ridge Mountains. Grows 3 to 6 feet, greenish flowers in late spring; part sun to part shade in moist, rich sandy loam; many sources.

Utricularia gibba (Humped bladderwort) – rare aquatic; shallow water or exposed peat sand or mud flats, OBL. Scattered statewide, mostly northeast (Northern Glaciated Allegheny Plateau); believed to be extirpated. Yellow flowers in summer. An insectivore; water must be rich in microorganisms for it to survive; grow in full sun; a few sources.

Utricularia purpurea (Purple bladderwort) – aquatic; suspended in lakes and ponds, OBL. Northeastern counties in Pennsylvania. Pink to purple flowers in late summer; full sun in soft, quiet water from shallow to more than 10 feet deep; a few sources.

Utricularia resupinata (Northeastern bladderwort) – Very rare carnivore in shores, shallows, quiet water, muddy–soil swamps; observed adjacent to Lake Erie but believed to be extirpated. A floating perennial up to 4 inches, white to pink flowers in summer. A challenging plant for water gardens; a few sources.

Uvularia grandiflora (Bellwort) – rich, moist, deciduous forests and thickets, and forested floodplains. Mostly southwest (Southern Allegheny Plateau); scattered elsewhere. Yellow flowers in spring. Grow in well–drained medium moisture average soils in part shade to full shade; prefers humusy, moist soil in part shade; many sources.

Uvularia perfoliata (Bellwort) – dry to mesic upland deciduous woods and thickets in acid to neutral soils, FACU; statewide. Grows 6 to 18 inches, yellow flowers in spring; part sun to part shade in moist rich loam, pH 5 to 6; several sources.

Uvularia sessilifolia (Bellwort) – dry woods, moist hardwood coves, thickets and alluvial bottomlands, FACU–; statewide. Grows 6 to 18 inches, yellow flowers in spring; part sun to part shade in dry to moist sandy loam, pH 5 to 6; many sources.

Vallisneria americana var. americana (Tape–grass) – aquatic; streams, lakes, rivers, OBL. Mostly Central Appalachians and northeast (Northern Glaciated Allegheny Plateau), scattered elsewhere. Grows up to 12 inches, produces green flowers; full sun, rich silty loam covered with sand in water 12 inches deep. An important food source for turtles; several sources.

Veratrum virginicum (Bunchflower) – bogs, marshes, wet woods, savannahs, meadows and damp clearings, FACW+. Mostly southeast (Piedmont); scattered elsewhere. Grows up to 7 feet, white flowers in early summer; full sun to part shade in moist to wet sandy to clayey loam; a few sources. AKA *Melanthium virginicum.*

Veratrum viride (False hellebore) – moist to wet woods, stream banks and seeps, FACW+; statewide. Grows up to 4 feet, with green flowers in spring; part sun to part shade in moist, rich loam; a few sources.

Verbena hastata (Blue vervain) – moist to wet meadows, flood plains and wet river bottomlands, stream banks and the edges of sloughs, FACW+; statewide. Grows up to 4 feet, with blue flowers in summer; sun to part sun in moist rich loam; many sources.

Verbena urticifolia (White vervain) – moist meadows, fields, woodland borders, gravelly seeps, abandoned fields and waste ground, especially after site disturbance, FACU; statewide. Grows up to 4 feet, white flowers in summer; part sun in moist to mesic fertile loam; a few sources.

Verbesina alternifolia (Wingstem) – moist slopes and lowlands in woodlands, including alluvial flats along streams; FAC. Mostly south. Grows 4 to 8 feet in full sun to part shade with yellow flowers in late summer. Prefers consistently moist and organically rich soils, but does well in average mesic well–drained soils; a few sources.

Vernonia gigantea var. gigantea (Ironweed) – floodplains, meadows and moist fields, mostly west (Western Glaciated and Southern Allegheny Plateaus); FAC. Grows 3 to 7 feet, purple flowers in late summer; prefers full sun to light shade in mesic to moist fertile, loamy soil. Sunny sites require more moisture than those in shade; a few sources.

Vernonia glauca (Appalachian ironweed) – rare in dry fields, open slopes and marshes; southeast (Piedmont, Atlantic Coastal Plain). Grows to 5 feet in full sun, with deep purple flowers in late summer; requires moist, loamy soil; a few sources.

Vernonia noveboracensis (New York ironweed) – stream banks and in wet fields and pastures, FACW+; statewide except north (northern Allegheny plateaus). Grows up to 6 feet, with brownish–purple flowers in summer; sun to part sun in moist rich loam, pH 5.5 to 7. Prefers rich, moist, slightly acidic soils; many sources.

Veronica americana (American speedwell) – moist riverbanks and stream edges and in ditches, OBL; statewide. Grows 4 to 10 inches, light blue to violet flowers in summer and fall; part shade in moist, humusy loam; a few sources.

Veronicastrum virginicum (Culver's–root) – moist meadows, thickets and swamps, FACU; statewide except north–central (Northern Unglaciated Allegheny Plateau). Grows up to 6 feet, white or pink flowers in summer; sun to part sun in moist rich loam, pH 5.5 to 7. Many sources.

Vicia americana (Purple vetch) – dry to moist, gravelly shores, thickets, meadows, and roadside banks, FAC. Widely scattered, mostly east. Grows up to 3 feet, blue to violet flowers in early summer; sun to part sun in moist rich loam; a few sources.

Viola affinis (LeConte's violet) – rich moist, especially alluvial, woods, FACW; statewide. except north–central counties. Grows up to 16 inches, blue–violet flowers in spring; sun to part shade in moist, sandy loam; a few sources.

Viola bicolor (Field pansy) – fields, dry open woods and floodplain terraces, FACU; mostly south. Grows up to 10 inches, pale blue flowers with yellow centers in spring; sun to part shade in dry to moist rich loam; a few sources.

Viola blanda (Sweet white violet) – moist woods and swamps, FACW; statewide. Grows up to 16 inches, white flowers in spring; sun to part shade in moist rich sandy loam. Prefers humusy, moisture–retentive soils and forms large carpets in the wild by spreading through runners; a few sources.

Viola canadensis (Canada violet) – moist woods and swamps; statewide, but sparse in southeast (Central Appalachians and Piedmont). Grows up to 16 inches, white flowers with yellow centers in spring; part shade to shade in sandy humusy loam, pH 5 to 6.5. Naturalizes by vigorous seeding, not runners; a few sources.

Viola cucullata (Blue marsh violet) – bogs, meadows and swamps, FACW+; statewide. Grows up to 16 inches, pale purple flowers in spring; sun to part shade in moist to wet loam; a few sources.

Viola cucullata x saggitata (Blue marsh violet) – bogs, meadows and swamps; statewide. Grows up to 16 inches, blue to violet flowers in spring; part shade to shade in moist rich loam. AKA *Viola obiqua*; a few sources.

Viola hirsutula (Southern woodland violet) – open forests and forest clearings. Mostly southeast (Piedmont); scattered elsewhere and absent in northern Allegheny plateaus. Grows up to 16 inches, blue to violet flowers in spring; part shade in moist rich humusy loam; a few sources.

Viola labradorica (American dog violet) – moist woods and swamps, FAC; statewide. Grows up to 16 inches, pale blue flowers in spring; part sun to part shade in moist sandy humusy loam, pH 5 to 6.5. Aggressive spreader by runners and seeds; many sources.

Viola lanceolata var. lanceolata (Lance–leaved violet) – moist, sandy shores, flats and bogs, OBL. Statewide, except absent in north (northern Allegheny plateaus). Grows up to 10 inches, white flowers in spring; sun to part shade in moist sandy loam; a few sources.

Viola macloskeyi ssp. pallens (Sweet white violet) – bogs, swamps and wet woods, OBL; statewide. Grows up to 10 inches, white flowers in spring; sun to part shade in moist, humusy loam; a few sources.

Viola pedata (Birdfoot violet) – sandy or rocky barrens and dry forested slopes, UPL; Southeast, including Central Appalachians and Piedmont. Grows up to 16 inches, blue to violet flowers in spring; sun to part shade in dry to moist sandy loam, pH 4 to 7; many sources.

Viola pubescens var. pubescens (Downy yellow violet) – dry to moist open woods and swamps, FACU; statewide. Grows up to 12 inches, yellow flowers in spring; part shade to shade in moist rich loam, pH 5 to 6; several sources.

Viola rotundifolia (Round–leaved violet) – cool moist woods and banks, FAC+; statewide except southwest (Southern Allegheny Plateau) and south central (Central Appalachians, Blue Ridge Mountains). Grows up to 10 inches, yellow flowers in spring; part shade to shade in moist humusy loam; soil should not dry out and prefers cooler climates. Freely self–seeds and can become weedy; a few sources.

Viola sagittata (Ovate–leaved violet, Arrow–leaved violet) – dry woods, fields and edges, FACW; statewide. Two varieties: *ovata* (Ovate–leaved violet) and *sagittata* (Arrow–leaved violet). Grows up to 12 inches, blue–violet flowers in spring; sun to part shade in dry to moist sandy loam; a few sources.

Viola sororia (Common blue violet) – moist woods, swamps, thickets, FAC; statewide. Grows up to 12 inches, blue flowers in spring; part sun to part shade in moist rich loam, pH 7 to 8. No runners, but aggressively spreads by seed; many sources.

Viola striata (Striped violet) – alluvial woods and alkaline swamps, FACW; statewide. Grows up to 12 inches, white flowers in spring; part sun to part shade in moist, rocky silty loam. No runners; spreads by seed; several sources.

Waldsteinia fragarioides (Barren strawberry) – moist rich woods and pastures; statewide, but sparse southeast (Piedmont) and southwest (Southern Allegheny Plateau). Forms a mat to 6 inches in height with yellow flowers in spring; average, medium, well–drained soil in full sun to part shade. Tolerates a wide range of soils, but prefers slightly acidic humusy soil; a few sources.

Wolffia columbiana (Water–meal) – aquatic; quiet waters of lakes, ponds, marshes, ditches and bogs. OBL; widely scattered, statewide. Grow in full sun in moderate to fertile shallow water; plant in silty loam; a few sources.

Zizia aptera (Golden–alexander) – woodlands, wooded slopes, thickets, glades, prairies, clearings and roadsides, FAC; mostly southeast (Central Appalachians, Piedmont), scattered elsewhere and absent in north (northern Allegheny plateaus). Grows 12 to 30 inches, yellow flowers in late spring; part sun to part shade in dry to moist rich loam, pH 5.5 to 7; many sources.

Zizia aurea (Golden–alexander) – moist woods and meadows, thickets, glades and prairies; wooded bottomland, stream banks, floodplains; FAC–; statewide. Grows 12 to 32 inches, yellow flowers in late spring; average, medium moisture, well–drained soils in full sun to part shade; pH 5.5 to 7; many sources.

APPARENTLY UNAVAILABLE

The following 366 species of native plants whose range includes Pennsylvania are apparently unavailable in the commercial marketplace on a national scale:

> *Aconitum reclinatum* (White monkshood)
> *Agrimonia gryposepala* (Agrimony)
> *Agrimonia microcarpa* (Small-fruited agrimony)
> *Agrimonia pubescens* (Downy agrimony)
> *Agrimonia rostellata* (Woodland agrimony)
> *Alopecurus aequalis* (Short-awned foxtail)

Ambrosia psilostachya (Western ragweed)
Amianthium muscaetoxicum (Fly-poison)
Angelica triquinata (Angelica)
Angelica venenosa (Deadly angelica)
Antennaria howellii ssp. canadensis (Howell's pussytoe)
Antennaria solitaria (Solitary pussytoe)
Apocynum florabundum (Dogbane)
Aralia hispida (Bristly sarsaparilla)
Arethusa bulbosa ssp. leptoclados (Dragon's-mouth)
Arnica acaulis (Leopard's-bane)
Asclepias quadrifolia (Four-leaved milkweed)
Asclepias rubra (Red milkweed)
Aureolaria flava var. macrantha (Yellow false-foxglove)
Aureolaria laevigata (False-foxglove)
Boehmeria cylindrica var. cylindrica (False nettle)
Boehmeria cylindrica var. drummondiana (False nettle)
Brickellia eupatorioides (False boneset)
Callitriche heterophylla (Water-starwort)
Callitriche palustris (Water-starwort)
Calystegia sepium (Hedge bindweed)
Calystegia spithamaea ssp. spithamaea (Low bindweed)
Campanula aparinoides (Marsh bellflower)
Cardamine angustata (Toothwort)
Cardamine bulbosa (Bittercress)
Cardamine concatenata (Toothwort)
Cardamine douglassii (Purplecress)
Cardamine rotundifolia (Mountain watercress)
Cerastium arvense var. villosissimum (Serpentine barrens chickweed)
Ceratophyllum muricatum (Hornwort)
Chrysosplenium americanum (Golden saxifrage)
Cicuta bulbifera (Water-hemlock)
Circaea alpina x lutetiana (Enchanter's-nightshade)
Circaea lutetiana ssp. canadensis (Enchanter's-nightshade)
Circaea x laneyi (Enchanter's-nightshade)
Cirsium discolor (Field thistle)
Cirsium pumilum (Pasture thistle)
Coeloglossum viride var. virescens (Frog orchid)
Comandra umbellata (Bastard toadflax)
Commelina virginica (Virginia dayflower)
Conioselinum chinense (Hemlock-parsley)
Corallorhiza maculata (Spotted coralroot)
Corallorhiza odontorhiza (Autumn coralroot)

Corallorhiza trifida (Early coralroot)
Corallorhiza wisteriana (Wister's coralroot)
Cryptogramma stelleri (Slender rockbrake)
Cynoglossum virginianum (Wild comfrey)
Dalibarda repens (Dewdrop)
Decodon verticillatus (Water-willow)
Desmodium canescens (Hoary tick-trefoil)
Desmodium ciliare (Tick-clover)
Desmodium cuspidatum (Tick-clover)
Desmodium laevigatum (Smooth tick-clover)
Desmodium marilandicum (Maryland tick-clover)
Desmodium nudiflorum (Naked-flowered tick-trefoil)
Desmodium nuttallii (Nuttall's tick-trefoil)
Desmodium obtusum (Tick-trefoil)
Desmodium perplexum (Tick-trefoil)
Desmodium rotundifolium (Round-leaved tick-trefoil)
Desmodium viridiflorum (Velvety tick-trefoil)
Doellingeria infirma (Flat-topped white aster)
Elodea nuttallii (Waterweed)
Elodea schweinitzii (Schweinitz's waterweed)
Epifagus virginiana (Beechdrops)
Epilobium ciliatum (Willow-herb)
Epilobium leptophyllum (Willow-herb)
Epilobium palustre (Marsh willow-herb)
Erigenia bulbosa (Harbinger-of-spring)
Eriocaulon aquaticum (Seven-angle pipewort)
Eriocaulon decangulare (Ten-angle pipewort)
Eriocaulon parkeri (Parkers's pipewort)
Eupatorium album (White-bracted eupatorium)
Eupatorium pilosum (Ragged eupatorium)
Euphorbia ipecacuanhae (Wild ipecac)
Eurybia radula (Rough aster)
Eurybia schreberi (Schreber's aster)
Eurybia spectabilis (Showy aster)
Fimbristylis puberula (Hairy fimbry)
Galium asprellum (Rough bedstraw)
Galium circaezans var. circaezans (Wild licorice)
Galium circaezans var. hypomalacum (Wild licorice)
Galium concinnum (Shining bedstraw)
Galium labradoricum (Bog bedstraw)
Galium lanceolatum (Wild licorice)
Galium latifolium (Purple bedstraw)
Galium obtusum (Cleavers)

Galium palustre (Ditch bedstraw)
Galium pilosum (Bedstraw)
Galium tinctorium (Bedstraw)
Galium trifidum (Cleavers)
Galium triflorum (Sweet-scented bedstraw)
Gentiana catesbaei (Coastal plain gentian)
Gentiana linearis (Narrow-leaved gentian)
Gentiana saponaria (Soapwort gentian)
Geranium bicknellii (Cranesbill)
Geranium carolinianum (Wild geranium)
Geum canadense var. canadense (White avens)
Geum virginianum (Cream-colored avens)
Gnaphalium sylvaticum (Woodland cudweed)
Goodyera repens (Lesser rattlesnake-plantain)
Goodyera tesselata (Checkered rattlesnake-plantain)
Gratiola aurea (Goldenpert)
Helianthemum propinquum (Frostweed)
Heteranthera reniformis (Mud-plantain)
Heuchera pubescens (Alum-root)
Hieracium gronovii (Hawkweed)
Hieracium gronovii x venosum (Hawkweed)
Hieracium paniculatum (Hawkweed)
Hieracium scabrum (Hawkweed)
Hieracium traillii (Green's hawkweed)
Hieracium venosum (Rattlesnake-weed)
Hottonia inflata (American featherfoil)
Houstonia canadensis (Fringed bluets)
Hybanthus concolor (Green-violet)
Hydrocotyle ranunculoides (Floating pennywort)
Hydrophyllum macrophyllum (Large-leaved waterleaf)
Hypericum adpressum (Creeping St.John's-wort)
Hypericum boreale (Dwarf St.John's-wort)
Hypericum denticulatum (Coppery St.Johns-wort)
Hypericum dissimulatum (St.John's-wort)
Hypericum ellipticum (Pale St. John's-wort)
Hypericum ellipticum (Pale St. John's-wort)
Hypericum mutilum (Dwarf St. John's-wort)
Hypericum sphaerocarpum (St. John's-wort)
Iodanthus pinnatifidus (Purple-rocket)
Ipomoea pandurata (Man-of-the-earth)
Isoetes appalachiana (Appalachian quillwort)
Isoetes valida (Carolina quillwort)
Isotria medeoloides (Small whorled-pogonia)

Isotria verticillata (Whorled-pogonia)
Lathyrus ochroleucus (Wild pea)
Lechea intermedia (Pinweed)
Lechea minor (Thyme-leaved pinweed)
Lechea pulchella (Pinweed)
Lechea racemulosa (Pinweed)
Lechea villosa (Pinweed)
Lemna obscura (Little water duckweed)
Lemna perpusilla (Duckweed)
Lemna turionifera (Winter duckweed)
Lespedeza angustifolia (Narrow-leaved bush-clover)
Lespedeza intermedia (Bush-clover)
Lespedeza procumbens (Trailing bush-clover)
Lespedeza repens (Creeping bush-clover)
Lespedeza stuevei (Tall bush-clover)
Ligusticum canadense (Lovage)
Linum intercursum (Sandplain wild flax)
Linum medium var. medium (Yellow flax)
Linum medium var. texanum (Yellow flax)
Linum virginianum (Slender yellow flax)
Liparis liliifolia (Lily-leaved twayblade)
Liparis loeselii (Yellow twayblade)
Listera australis (Southern twayblade)
Listera cordata (Heartleaf twayblade)
Listera smallii (Kidney-leaved twayblade)
Lithospermum canescens (Hoary puccoon)
Lithospermum latifolium (American gromwell)
Lobelia dortmanna (Water lobelia)
Lobelia kalmii (Brook lobelia)
Lobelia nuttallii (Nuttall's lobelia)
Ludwigia decurrens (Upright primrose-willow)
Ludwigia polycarpa (False loosestrife)
Ludwigia sphaerocarpa (Spherical-fruited seedbox)
Lycopus rubellus (Gypsy-wort)
Lycopus uniflorus (Bugleweed)
Lycopus uniflorus x virginicus (Water-horehound)
Lycopus virginicus (Bugleweed)
Lysimachia lanceolata (Loosestrife)
Lysimachia producta (Loosestrife)
Malaxis bayardii (Adder's-mouth)
Malaxis monophyllos var. brachypoda (White adder's-mouth)
Malaxis unifolia (Green adder's-mouth)
Megalodonta beckii (Beck's water-marigold)

Melanthium latifolium (Bunchflower)
Melica nitens (Tall melicgrass)
Monotropa hypopithys (Pinesap)
Monotropa uniflora (Indian-pipe)
Montia chamissoi (Chamisso's miner's-lettuce)
Montia chamissoi (Chamisso's miner's-lettuce)
Myriophyllum farwellii (Farwell's water-milfoil)
Myriophyllum heterophyllum (Broad-leaved water-milfoil)
Myriophyllum humile (Water-milfoil)
Myriophyllum sibiricum (Northern water-milfoil)
Myriophyllum tenellum (Slender water-milfoil)
Myriophyllum verticillatum (Whorled water-milfoil)
Nuphar microphylla (Yellow pond-lily)
Nuphar x rubrodisca (Spatterdock)
Nymphoides cordata (Floating-heart)
Obolaria virginica (Pennywort)
Oclemena acuminata (Wood aster)
Oclemena nemoralis (Leafy bog aster)
Oenothera nutans (Evening-primrose)
Oenothera parviflora var. parviflora (Evening-primrose)
Oenothera pilosella (Sundrops)
Onosmodium virginianum (Virginia false gromwell)
Ophioglossum engelmannii (Limestone adder's-tongue)
Orobanche uniflora (Broom-rape)
Orthilia secunda (One-sided shinleaf)
Oxalis acetosella (Northern wood-sorrel)
Oxalis dillenii ssp. filipes (Southern yellow wood-sorrel)
Oxypolis rigidior (Cowbane)
Panax trifolius (Dwarf ginseng)
Paspalum floridanum var. glabratum (Florida beadgrass)
Penthorum sedoides (Ditch stonecrop)
Phemeranthus teretifolius (Round-leaved fameflower)
Phlox ovata (Mountain phlox)
Physalis subglabrata (Ground-cherry)
Physalis virginiana (Virginia ground-cherry)
Plantago rugelii (Rugel's plantain)
Platanthera blephariglottis (White fringed-orchid)
Platanthera cristata (Crested fringed-orchid)
Platanthera flava var. herbiola (Tubercled rein-orchid)
Platanthera grandiflora (Large purple fringed-orchid)
Platanthera hookeri (Hooker's orchid)
Platanthera hyperborea var. huronensis (Tall green bog-orchid)
Platanthera lacera (Ragged fringed-orchid)

Platanthera leucophaea (Eastern prairie fringed-orchid)
Platanthera orbiculata var. macrophylla (Large round-leaved orchid)
Platanthera orbiculata var. orbiculata (Large round-leaved orchid)
Platanthera peramoena (Purple fringeless orchid)
Platanthera psycodes (Purple fringed-orchid)
Podostemum ceratophyllum (Riverweed)
Polygala paucifolia (Bird-on-the-wing)
Polygonum densiflorum (Smartweed)
Polygonum robustius (Large water-smartweed)
Polygonum scandens var. scandens (Climbing false-buckwheat)
Polygonum setaceum (Swamp smartweed)
Polymnia canadensis (Leaf-cup)
Polymnia uvedalia (Bear's-foot)
Potamogeton alpinus (Northern pondweed)
Potamogeton bicupulatus (Pondweed)
Potamogeton confervoides (Tuckerman's pondweed)
Potamogeton diversifolius (Snailseed pondweed)
Potamogeton epihydrus (Ribbonleaf pondweed)
Potamogeton filiformis var. borealis (Threadleaf pondweed)
Potamogeton foliosus (Leafy pondweed)
Potamogeton friesii (Fries' pondweed)
Potamogeton gramineus (Grassy pondweed)
Potamogeton hillii (Hill's pondweed)
Potamogeton illinoensis (Illinois pondweed)
Potamogeton oakesianus (Oakes' pondweed)
Potamogeton obtusifolius (Blunt-leaved pondweed)
Potamogeton pulcher (Heartleaf pondweed)
Potamogeton pusillus (Pondweed)
Potamogeton spirillus (Snailseed pondweed)
Potamogeton strictifolius (Narrow-leaved pondweed)
Potamogeton tennesseensis (Tennessee pondweed)
Potamogeton vaseyi (Vasey's pondweed)
Potamogeton zosteriformis (Flat-stemmed pondweed)
Potentilla canadensis (Cinquefoil)
Potentilla norvegica ssp. monspeliensis (Strawberry-weed)
Prenanthes altissima (Rattlesnake-root)
Prenanthes crepidinea (Rattlesnake-root)
Prenanthes serpentaria (Lion's-foot)
Prenanthes trifoliolata (Gall-of-the-earth)
Proserpinaca palustris var. crebra (Common mermaid-weed)
Proserpinaca pectinata (Comb-leaved mermaid-weed)

Ptilimnium capillaceum (Mock bishop's weed)
Pycnanthemum clinopodioides (Mountain-mint)
Pycnanthemum torrei (Torrey's mountain-mint)
Pycnanthemum verticillatum var. pilosum (Mountain-mint)
Pycnanthemum verticillatum var. verticillatum (Mountain-mint)
Pyrola americana (Wild lily-of-the-valley)
Pyrola chlorantha (Wintergreen)
Ranunculus ambigens (Water-plantain spearwort)
Ranunculus aquatilis var. diffusus (White water-crowfoot)
Ranunculus caricetorum (Marsh buttercup)
Ranunculus flabellaris (Yellow water-crowfoot)
Ranunculus hederaceus (Long-stalked crowfoot)
Ranunculus micranthus (Small-flowered crowfoot)
Rhynchospora alba (White beak-rush)
Rhynchospora capitellata (Beak-rush)
Rumex hastatulus (Heart sorrel)
Sabatia campanulata (Slender marsh-pink)
Sagina procumbens (Bird's-eye)
Sagittaria australis (Appalachian arrowhead)
Sagittaria filiformis (Arrowhead)
Samolus parviflorus (Water pimpernel)
Sanicula marilandica (Black snake root)
Sanicula odorata (Yellow-flowered sanicle)
Sanicula trifoliata (Large-fruited sanicle)
Schizachyrium scoparium var. littorale (Seaside bluestem)
Scutellaria churchilliana (Skullcap)
Scutellaria elliptica var. elliptica (Hairy skullcap)
Scutellaria galericulata (Common skullcap)
Scutellaria nervosa (Skullcap)
Scutellaria saxatilis (Rock skullcap)
Sedum rosea (Roseroot stonecrop)
Sedum telephioides (Allegheny stonecrop)
Senecio anonymus (Appalachian groundsel)
Senecio antennariifolius (Shale-barren ragwort)
Sericocarpus asteroides (White-topped aster)
Sericocarpus linifolius (Narrow-leaved white-topped aster)
Setaria geniculata (Perennial foxtail)
Sida hermaphrodita (Virginia mallow)
Sisyrinchium fuscatum (Sand blue-eyed-grass)
Sisyrinchium mucronatum (Blue-eyed-grass)
Solidago arguta var. arguta (Forest goldenrod)
Solidago hispida (Hairy goldenrod)

Solidago puberula (Downy goldenrod)
Solidago simplex ssp. randii var. racemosa (Sticky goldenrod)
Solidago squarrosa (Ragged goldenrod)
Spiranthes lacera var. gracilis (Southern slender ladies'-tresses)
Spiranthes lacera var. lacera (Northern slender ladies'-tresses)
Spiranthes lucida (Shining ladies'-tresses)
Spiranthes magnicamporum (Great Plains ladies'-tresses)
Spiranthes ochroleuca (Yellow nodding ladies'-tresses)
Spiranthes ovalis var. erostellata (October ladies'-tresses)
Spiranthes romanzoffiana (Hooded ladies'-tresses)
Spiranthes tuberosa (Slender ladies'-tresses)
Spirodela polyrhiza (Greater duckweed)
Stachys hyssopifolia var. ambigua (Hedge-nettle)
Stachys hyssopifolia var. hyssopifolia (Hedge-nettle)
Stachys nuttallii (Nuttall's hedge-nettle)
Stellaria borealis (Northern stitchwort)
Stellaria corei (Chickweed)
Stellaria longifolia (Long-leaved stitchwort)
Stellaria pubera (Great chickweed)
Stenanthium gramineum (Featherbells)
Stylosanthes biflora (Pencil-flower)
Symphyotrichum boreale (Northern bog aster)
Symphyotrichum depauperatum (Serpentine aster)
Symphyotrichum dumosum (Bushy aster)
Symphyotrichum racemosum (Small white aster)
Symphyotrichum urophyllum (Aster)
Taenidia montana (Mountain pimpernel)
Thalictrum coriaceum (Thick-leaved meadow-rue)
Thaspium barbinode (Meadow-parsnip)
Thaspium trifoliatum var. flavum (Meadow-parsnip)
Triadenum fraseri (Marsh St. Johns-wort)
Trichostema brachiatum (False pennyroyal)
Trientalis borealis (Star-flower)
Trifolium virginicum (Kate's-mountain clover)
Triosteum angustifolium (Horse-gentian)
Triosteum aurantiacum var. aurantiacum (Wild-coffee)
Triosteum aurantiacum var. glaucescens (Wild-coffee)
Triphora trianthophora (Nodding pogonia)
Typha x glauca (Cat-tail)
Utricularia cornuta (Horned bladderwort)
Utricularia geminiscapa (Bladderwort)
Utricularia inflata (Inflated bladderwort)

Utricularia intermedia (Flat-leaved bladderwort)
Utricularia macrorhiza (Common bladderwort)
Utricularia minor (Lesser bladderwort)
Verbena simplex (Narrow-leaved vervain)
Veronica scutellata (Marsh speedwell)
Viola palmata (Early blue violet)
Viola primulifolia (Primrose violet)
Viola renifolia (Kidney-leaved violet)
Viola rostrata (Long-spurred violet)
Viola selkirkii (Great-spurred violet)
Viola striata (Striped violet)
Wolffia brasiliensis (Pointed water-meal)
Xyris difformis (Yellow-eyed-grass)
Xyris montana (Yellow-eyed-grass)
Xyris torta (Yellow-eyed-grass)
Zannichellia palustris (Horned pondweed)
Zigadenus glaucus (Camass)
Zosterella dubia (Water star-grass)

FERNS AND FERN ALLIES

Adiantum aleuticum (Aleutian maidenhair) – rare on shaded banks, serpentine barrens, talus slopes, wooded ravines; limited to serpentine barrens in Lancaster County. Fronds 12 to 24 inches; rhizome: clump-forming. Grow in part shade to shade in a moist humusy loam; prefers growing on serpentine rock; a few sources.

Adiantum pedatum (Northern maidenhair) – rich, deciduous woodlands, often on humus-covered talus slopes and moist lime soils, FAC-; statewide. Fronds 12 to 30 inches; rhizome: short creeping. Grow in part shade to shade in moist sandy organic loam, pH 5 to 7; many sources, including many garden centers.

Asplenium platyneuron (Ebony spleenwort) – forest floor or on rocks, often invading masonry and disturbed soils, FACU; statewide. Fronds 8 to 18 inches; rhizome: short creeping to ascending. Grow in part shade to shade in dry to moist sandy clay loam, pH 5 to 7.5; several sources.

Asplenium resiliens (Black-stemmed spleenwort) – rare on limestone cliffs and in sinkholes on calcareous rock; south (Blue Ridge Mountains); endangered. Fronds: several inches; rhizomes: erect. Grow in moist humusy soil over limestone rocks in part shade; a few sources.

Asplenium trichomanes (Maidenhair spleenwort) – acidic rocks such as sandstone, basalt, and granite, very rarely on calcareous rocks; statewide except northwest. Fronds 4 to 7 inches; rhizome: short creeping to ascending. Grow in part shade to shade in dry to moist rocky, humusy loam, pH 4 to 7.5; a few sources.

Athyrium filix-femina (Lady fern) – wooded valleys along streams, on rich wooded slopes and on floors of ravines, swamps, moist meadows and thickets, FAC; statewide. Fronds 12 to 24 inches; rhizome: erect or ascending in clumps. Grow in sun to part shade in moist rich sandy loam, pH 4 to 7; many sources, including many garden centers.

Botrychium virginianum (Rattlesnake fern) – moist shaded forests, wooded slopes and shrubby second growth, rare or absent in arid regions, FACU; statewide. Fronds 6 to 20 inches, rhizome: erect, subterranean. Grow in part shade to shade in moist rich sandy loam, pH 4 to 6; a few sources.

Camptosorus rhizophyllus (Walking fern) – shaded, usually moss-covered boulders and ledges, usually on limestone or other basic rocks, but occasionally on sandstone or other acidic rocks, rarely on fallen tree trunks; statewide except northwest. Fronds 4 to 10 inches; rhizome: ascending. Grow in part shade to shade in dry to moist calcareous loam, pH 6.5 to 7.5; a few sources.

Cheilanthes lanosa (Hairy lip fern) – rocky slopes and ledges, on a variety of substrates including limestone and granite; mostly east, scattered elsewhere. Fronds 6 to 16 inches; rhizome: short creeping. Grow in part sun to shade in dry sandy loam, pH 5 to 6; a few sources.

Cystopteris bulbifera (Bublet bladder fern) – typically moist calcareous cliffs, but also grows on rock in dense woods and occasionally occurs terrestrially in northern swamps, FAC. Statewide except west central. Fronds 18 to 36 inches; rhizome: short creeping. Grow in part shade to shade in moist calcareous loam, pH 6.5 to 7.5; a few sources.

Cystopteris fragilis (Fragile fern) – commonly on cliff faces, also in thin alkaline soil over rock, FACU; scattered statewide, especially in Central Appalachians and northeast. Fronds 5 to 16 inches; rhizome: compact. Grow in part shade to shade in moist to wet garden soil; a few sources.

Dennstaedtia punctilobula (Hay scented fern) – rocky slopes, meadows, woods, stream banks, and roadsides, in acid soils; statewide. Fronds 15 to 30 inches, rhizome: very long-creeping. Grow in sun to part shade in dry, well drained sandy and acidic loam, pH 4 to 6. Aggressive spreader; forms vast colonies, especially where deer pressure is high because deer ignore it; many sources.

Deparia acrostichoides (Silvery glade fern) – along stream edges, river banks and damp woods, often on shaly slopes, FAC; statewide. Fronds to 40 inches; rhizome: short creeping. Grow in part sun to shade in moist acidic sandy loam, pH 5 to 7 but prefers 5 to 5.7; a few sources.

Diphasiastrum tristachyum (Deep-rooted running-pine) – sterile, acidic soils in open coniferous forests and oak forests, sandy barrens and clearings; statewide except for central counties just east of the Allegheny Front. Stems 6 to 12 inches; rhizome: short creeping. Grow in part shade to shade in moist acidic humusy loam; a few sources.

Diplazium pycnocarpon (Narrow-leaved glade fern) – wooded glades and alluvial thickets, neutral soil, but not in ridge and valley provinces, FAC. Statewide except central higher elevations. Fronds 18 to 40 inches; rhizome: short creeping. Grow in part shade in moist organic circumneutral garden loam; a few sources.

Dryopteris carthusiana (Spinose wood fern) – swampy woods, moist wooded slopes, stream banks, and conifer plantations, FAC+; statewide. Fronds 12 to 36 inches; rhizome: ascending crown. Grow in part sun to shade in moist organic loam; many sources.

Dryopteris celsa (Log fern) – rare seepage slopes, hammocks and on logs in swamps, OBL; mostly southeast (Piedmont, Atlantic Coastal Plain). Fronds to 50 inches; rhizomes: medium to short creeping. Grow in average, mesic to wet soils in part shade to full shade. Prefers acidic, humusy, moist soils in high shade, sheltered from wind; a few sources.

Dryopteris clintoniana (Clinton's wood fern) – deep humus in swampy woods, especially maple swamps. Prefers wet mucky woods, thickets, FACW+; mostly northeast, scattered elsewhere. Fronds 24 to 48 inches; rhizome: short creeping. Grow in part shade to shade in moist to wet rich silty loam, pH 4 to 6; a few sources.

Dryopteris cristata (Crested shield fern) – swamps, swampy woods, or open shrubby wetlands; prefers wet mucky woods, thickets, FACW+; statewide. Fronds 12 to 36 inches, rhizome: short creeping. Grow in part shade to shade in moist rich silty loam, pH 4 to 6; a few sources.

Dryopteris goldiana (Goldie's wood fern) – dense, moist woods, especially ravines, limey seeps, or at the edge of swamps, in deep humus, FAC+. Mostly southeast (Piedmont); scattered elsewhere. Fronds 36 to 48 inches, rhizome: short creeping. Grow in part shade to shade in moist rich humusy loam, pH 4 to 7; many sources.

Dryopteris intermedia (Evergreen wood fern) – moist rocky woods, especially hemlock hardwoods, ravines, and edges of swamps, FACU; statewide. Fronds 18 to 36 inches. Rhizome: erect crown Grow in part shade to shade in moist organic loam, pH 4.5 to 7.5; a few sources.

Dryopteris marginalis (Marginal wood fern) – rocky, wooded slopes and ravines, edges of woods, stream banks and road banks, and rock walls, FACU-; statewide. Fronds 18 to 30 inches, rhizome: erect crown. Grow in part sun to shade in moist rich sandy loam, pH 5 to 6; many sources, including many garden centers.

Equisetum arvense (Field horsetail) – moist roadsides, riverbanks, fields, marshes, pastures, and tundra, FAC; statewide. Stems 8 to 18 inches, rhizome: long creeping. Grow in sun to part sun in moist rich sandy loam; a few sources.

Equisetum fluviatile (Water horsetail) – standing water; in ponds, ditches, marshes, swales, edges of rivers and lakes, OBL. Mostly northeast (Northern Glaciated Allegheny Plateau); scattered elsewhere. Stems 24 to 26 inches; rhizome: short creeping. Grow in sun to part sun in ponds and pond edges or frequently inundated or poorly drained low area with a base of silty loam; a few sources.

Equisetum hyemale var. affine (Scouring-rush) – riverbanks, lakeshores and woodlands; moist sandy and gravelly slopes; stream banks, embankments and roadsides, FACW. Mostly southeast (Piedmont), west (Southern Allegheny Plateau) and south-central (Allegheny Mountains). Stems 14 to 48 inches; rhizome: creeping. Grow in sun to part shade in rich moist sandy loam. Can be difficult to control because of deep rhizomes; many sources.

Equisetum sylvaticum (Woodland horsetail) – moist open woods and wet meadows, FACW. Statewide, except southwest. Stems 10 to 30 inches. Rhizome: creeping. Grow in sun to part shade in moist sandy clay loam; a few sources.

Gymnocarpium dryopteris (Common oak fern) – cool, coniferous and mixed woods and at base of shale talus slopes often in pockets of humus, UPL. Mostly northeast (Northern Glaciated Allegheny Plateau); scattered elsewhere. Fronds 9 to 12 inches; rhizome: wide or long creeping. Grow in part shade to shade in moist rocky humus; a few sources.

Lycopodium annotinum (Bristly clubmoss) – swampy or cool shaded often moist coniferous forests, mountain forests, and exposed grassy or rocky sites, FAC. Mostly north (northern Allegheny plateaus); south-central (Allegheny Mountains); scattered elsewhere. Stems 2 to 10 inches; rhizome: long creeping. Grow in part sun to shade in mesic to moist rich acidic humus; a few sources.

Lycopodium clavatum (Common clubmoss) – bogs, open woods and rocky barrens, FAC. Stems 2 to 10 inches; rhizome: long creeping; statewide. Grow in part sun to part shade in mesic rich acidic humus; a few sources.

Lycopodium obscurum (Flat branched ground-pine) – rich hardwood forests and successional shrubby areas, FACU; statewide. Stems 8 to 10 inches; rhizome: long-creeping. Grow in part shade to shade in mesic to moist rich acidic humus; a few sources.

Lygodium palmatum (Climbing fern or Hartford fern) – rare in moist thickets, barrens, swamp edges, open woods, acidic, poorly drained and peaty soil, FACW. Scattered statewide, especially northeast. Twining, climbing to 15 feet; rhizome: short creeping. Grow in full shade in acidic, peaty sandy loam, pH 4 to 7. Can be difficult to grow; a few sources.

Matteuccia struthiopteris (Ostrich fern) – rich humus on rocky stream banks, moist alluvial flats, floodplains, mucky swamps and rich woods, FACW. Mostly north (northern Allegheny plateaus); scattered elsewhere. Fronds 24 to 72 inches; rhizome: erect, but with wide-reaching stolons. Grow in part sun to shade in moist organic loams; pH 5 to 7.5. Dramatic vase-like habit; forms extensive colonies via multiple stolons; many sources.

Onoclea sensibilis (Sensitive fern) – open swamps, thickets, marshes, or low woods, in muddy soil in sunny wet meadows or shaded stream bank locations, often forming thick stands, FACW; statewide. Fronds 12 to 36 inches; rhizome: short creeping. Grow in part sun to shade in moist silty humusy loams, pH 4.5 to 7.5 but prefers acidic soil; many sources, including better garden centers.

Osmunda cinnamomea (Cinnamon fern) – swamps, stream banks, roadsides, Moist areas, acidic soils, frequently in vernal seeps, ponds and swamps, FACW; statewide. Fronds 30 to 60 inches; rhizome: erect with occasional offshoots. Grow in part sun to part shade in moist acidic organic humusy to silty soils, pH 5.5 to 7; many sources.

Osmunda claytoniana (Interrupted fern) – oozy mud swamps, bogs, and stream banks; also, rich, mesic woods and open woods and shaded roadsides, FAC; statewide. Fronds 24 to 48 inches; rhizome: erect with occasional offshoots. Grow in part sun to part shade in rich mesic to moist silty loam, pH 4 to 6; many sources.

Osmunda regalis (Royal fern) – swamps, bogs, bluffs, stream banks in moist acidic soils, OBL; statewide. Fronds 24 to 60 inches; rhizome: erect with occasional offshoots. Grow in part sun to part shade in moist to wet silty organic loam, pH 4 to 6; many sources.

Pellaea atropurpurea (Purple cliffbrake) – dry soils adjacent to dolomite glades and crevices of limestone and dolomite outcrops, bluffs, boulders and sink holes. Mostly southeast (Central Appalachians, Piedmont); scattered elsewhere. Fronds 8 to 20 inches; rhizome: short creeping. Grow in part sun to part shade in dry to mesic sandy loam, pH 5.5 to 7.5 but prefers 6.5 to 7.5; a few sources.

Phegopteris connectilis (Long beech fern or narrow beech fern) – cool shade, woods in moist loose humus, strongly to moderately acid soil, or on rocks in shaded rock crevices. Mostly northeast (Northern Glaciated Allegheny Plateau); scattered elsewhere. Fronds 8 to 18 inches; rhizome: medium creeping. Grow in part shade to shade in mesic to moist rocky sandy humusy loam, pH 4 to 6; a few sources.

Phegopteris hexagonoptera (Broad beech fern) – moist woods, usually in full shade, often in moderately acid soils, FAC; statewide. Fronds 12 to 24 inches, rhizome: long creeping. Grow in part shade to shade in moist acidic garden loam; a few sources.

Polypodium virginianum (Common polypody) – rocks, boulders, cliffs, ledges, rocky woods; on a variety of substrates; statewide. Fronds 4 to 14 inches; rhizome: sort to medium creeping. Grow in part shade to shade in moist rich loam, pH 4 to 6; a few sources.

Polystichum acrostichoides (Christmas fern) – forest floors and shady, rocky slopes in organically rich, dry to medium wet, well-drained soil, FACU-; statewide. Fronds 12 to 24 inches; rhizome: multiple crowns. Grow in part shade to shade in dry to moist sandy rich loam, pH 4 to 7; many sources, including most garden centers.

Polystichum braunii (Braun's holly fern) – moist places in boreal forests; interior moist forests; cool rocky shaded ravines. Scattered northeast (Northern Glaciated Allegheny Plateau). Fronds 8 to 36 inches; rhizome: clump-forming. Grow in part shade to shade on cool sites in peaty, humusy moist loam; a few sources.

Pteridium aquilinum (Northern bracken fern) – sunny to partly shaded dry areas with infertile soil in barrens, pastures, and open woodlands in moderately to strong acid soil, abundant, forming large colonies, FACU; statewide. Fronds 18 to 50 inches; rhizome: very long creeping. Grow in sun to part shade in dry to mesic sterile sandy loam, pH 4 to 5. Unpalatable to deer; aggressive spreader and forms large colonies; a few sources.

Selaginella apoda (Meadow spikemoss) – swamps, meadows, marshes, pastures, damp lawns, open woods, and stream banks, in basic to acidic soil, FACW. Mostly southeast (Central Appalachians, Piedmont) and west (Southern Allegheny Plateau); scattered elsewhere. Mat forming, low creeping multi-branched rhizome. Grow in part sun to part shade in moist to wet rich loam; a few sources.

Thelypteris noveboracensis (New York fern) – terrestrial in moist woods, especially near swamps, streams, and in vernal seeps of ravines, often in slightly disturbed secondary forests, frequently forming large colonies; prefers dry oak, beech, maple and birch woods, FAC; statewide. Fronds 12 to 24 inches; rhizome: long creeping. Grow in high shade in mesic to moist humus rich sandy loam, pH 4 to 6. Aggressive spreader and can become invasive, forming huge woodland colonies. Reported to be ignored by deer, hence the carpeting; a few sources. AKA *Parathelypteris noveboracensis*; several sources.

Thelypteris palustris var. pubescens (Marsh fern) – swamps, bogs, and marshes in soft rich muddy soil, also along riverbanks and roadside ditches, and in wet woods, FACW; statewide. Fronds 18 to 30 inches; rhizome: long creeping. Grow in part sun to part shade in moist to wet rich silty loam, pH 4 to 7 but prefers 4.5 to 6.5; several sources.

Woodsia ilvensis (Rusty woodsia) – sunny cliffs and rocky slopes, usually in contact with rock; found on variety of substrates. South central (Central Appalachians) and northeast (Northern Glaciated Allegheny Plateau); scattered elsewhere. Fronds 3 to 8 inches; rhizome: erect to ascending. Grow in part sun to part shade in moist to wet acidic garden soil, pH 5 to 6; a few sources.

Woodsia obtusa (Blunt lobed woodsia) – cliffs and rocky slopes (rarely terrestrial); found on a variety of substrates including both granite and limestone. Mostly southeast (Central Appalachians, Piedmont); scattered elsewhere. Fronds 5 to 15 inches; rhizome: short creeping or ascending. Grow in part sun to part shade in dry to mesic sandy humusy loam, pH 5 to 7.5; a few sources.

Woodwardia areolata (Netted chain fern) – acidic bogs, seeps, and wet woods, FACW. Mostly southeast (Piedmont, Atlantic Coastal Plain); scattered elsewhere. Fronds 12 to 24 inches, rhizome: long-creeping. Grow in part sun to part shade in moist to wet rich loam; a few sources.

Woodwardia virginica (Virginia chain fern) – acidic swamps, marshes, bogs, and roadside ditches over noncalcareous substrates, OBL. Mostly northeast (Northern Glaciated Allegheny Plateau); scattered elsewhere. Fronds 18 to 24 inches; rhizome: long creeping. Grow in high shade to dappled shade in acidic moist to wet garden soil; a few sources.

APPARENTLY UNAVAILABLE

A total of 43 fern and fern ally species do not appear to be commercially available:

       Asplenium montanum (Mountain spleenwort)
       Asplenium ruta-muraria (Wall rue spleenwort)
       Asplenium trichomanes (Maidenhair spleenwort)
       Asplenium x ebenoides (Scott's spleenwort)

Botrychium dissectum (Cut-leaved grape-fern)
Botrychium lanceolatum (Triangle moonwort)
Botrychium matricariifolium (Daisy-leaved moonwort)
Botrychium multifidum (Leathery grape fern)
Botrychium oneidense (Blunt-lobed grape fern)
Botrychium simplex (Least moonwort)
Cystopteris protrusa (Protruding bladder fern)
Cystopteris tenuis (Fragile fern)
Cystopteris x laurentiana (Laurentian bladder fern)
Diphasiastrum digitatum (Deep-rooted running-pine)
Diphasiastrum digitatum x tristachyum (Ground-pine)
Dryopteris intermedia x marginalis (Hybrid wood-fern)
Dryopteris x boottii (Boott's hybrid wood fern)
Dryopteris x dowellii (Dowell's wood-fern)
Dryopteris x pittsfordensis (Pittsford wood-fern)
Dryopteris x slossonae (Boot's hybrid wood fern)
Dryopteris x triploidea (Triploid hybrid wood fern)
Dryopteris x uliginosa (Braun's wood fern)
Equisetum variegatum (Variegated horsetail)
Equisetum x ferrissi (Intermediate scouring-rush)
Equisetum x litorale (Shore horsetail)
Gymnocarpium appalachianum (Appalachian oak-fern)
Huperzia lucidula (Shining firmoss)
Huperzia porophila (Sandstone-loving firmoss)
Isoetes echinospora (Spiny-spored quillwort)
Isoetes engelmannii (Engelmann's quillwort)
Isoetes riparia (Shore quillwort)
Isoetes x dodgei (Dodge's quillwort)
Lycopodiella alopecuroides (Foxtail bog clubmoss)
Lycopodiella appressa (Appressed bog clubmoss)
Lycopodiella inundata (Northern bog clubmoss)
Lycopodiella margueritae (Marguerite's clubmoss)
Lycopodium dendroideum (Round-branch ground-pine)
Ophioglossum pusillum (Northern adder's-tongue)
Pellaea glabella var. glabella (Smooth cliffbrake)
Polypodium appalachianum (Appalachian polypody)
Polystichum x potteri (Shield-fern)
Thelypteris simulata (Massachusetts fern)
Trichomanes intricatum (Filmy fern)

GRASSES, SEDGES AND RUSHES

Agrostis hyemalis (Hairgrass or Winter bentgrass) – dry or moist soil in woods and fields, bogs, meadows, and along roadsides, FAC. Mostly southeast far west; scattered elsewhere. Grows 12 to 32 inches; sun to part shade in dry to moist sandy loam; a few sources.

Agrostis perennans (Autumn bentgrass) – woods, thickets, open areas, and on stream banks, FACU; statewide. Grows 20 to 40 inches; part sun to part shade in moist silty loam; a few sources.

Agrostis scabra (Fly–away grass) – meadows, shrublands, woodlands, marshes, and stream and lake margins, FAC; statewide, especially northeast. Grows 12 to 32 inches; sun to part sun in dry to moist sandy loam; a few sources.

Ammophila breviligulata (American beachgrass) – Very rare on beaches and sand dunes on the Atlantic coast and along the Great Lakes; considered important in stabilizing dunes; extreme southeast (Coastal Plain) and northwest (Erie and Ontario Lake Plain). Grows 1 to 3 feet in full sun, dry to mesic conditions and on very sandy soil; a few sources.

Andropogon gerardii (Big bluestem) – stream banks, roadsides, moist meadows, and prairies, FAC–; statewide. Grows 3 to 10 feet; sun to part sun in average, dry to medium, well to drained soils in full sun, prefers dry, infertile soil; many sources.

Andropogon glomeratus (Broom–sedge) – Moist meadows, swales and swamps, FACW+. Mostly southeast, especially Piedmont and Coastal Plain. Grows 2 to 5 feet in full sun in moist to wet, relatively sterile soils; poor drainage is helpful; a few sources.

Andropogon virginicus (Broom sedge or bluestem) – old fields, hillsides, and waste grounds, FACU; statewide except Allegheny Mountains and Northern Unglaciated Allegheny Plateau. Grows 20 to 60 inches; sun to part sun in dry to moist sandy to medium loams; many sources.

Aristida purpurascens (Arrow–feather) – Rare in glades, fields, and pine savannahs in sandy or clay soils, FAC. Southeast, especially

Piedmont. Grows 15 to 30 inches in dry, sandy soils in full sun, but tolerates some shade; a few sources.

Bouteloua curtipendula (Side–oats grama) – rare in prairies, fields, forest openings, open rocky slopes; widely scattered (mostly Central Appalachians, Piedmont). Clump–forming; grows to 3 feet in dry to medium moisture average soils in full sun; tolerates many soils from well–drained sandy loams to heavy clays; many sources.

Brachyelytrum erectum (Bearded shorthusk) – moist to dry de-ciduous woods and thickets, occasionally over limestone bedrock; statewide. Grows 20 to 40 inches; part shade, in mesic soil containing loam, sandy loam, or some rocky material; a few sources.

Bromus altissimus (Bromegrass) – shaded or open woods, along stream banks, and on alluvial plains and slopes, FACW; statewide. Also known as *Bromus latigumus*; part sun to part shade in moist, sandy loam; a few sources.

Bromus ciliatus (Fringed brome) – damp meadows, thickets, woods and stream banks, FACW. Mostly northeast (Northern Glaciated Al-legheny Plateau), scattered elsewhere. Grows 24 to 60 inches; sun to part shade in rich sandy loam; a few sources.

Bromus kalmii (Bromegrass) – sandy, gravelly, or limestone soils in open woods and calcareous fens, FACU. Scattered statewide, mostly east. Grows 20 to 40 inches; part sun to part shade in dry to moist rocky sandy loam; several sources.

Bromus pubescens (Canada brome) – shaded, moist, often upland de-ciduous woods; statewide. Grows 24 to 60 inches; part shade to shade in dry to moist sandy loam; a few sources.

Calamagrostis canadensis (Canada bluejoint) – wet meadows, bogs, and swamps; two varieties, *canadensis* (more common) and *macou-niana*, FACW; statewide. Grows 24 to 60 inches; sun to part sun in rich moist loam; many sources.

Carex alata (Broad–winged sedge) – Rare in sedge meadows, bog margins, swampy woods, often on hummocks; reported on both acidic and calcareous soils, OBL. Mostly northwest (Erie Lake Plain and Western Glaciated Allegheny Plateau). Grows 1.5 to 2 feet in full sun to part shade; prefers peaty, moist to wet soils and may go dormant in summer if soil is not consistently moist. Good for water or bog gardens, or in wet soils adjacent to streams and ponds; a few sources.

Carex albursina (White bear sedge) – On steep slopes and around limestone escarpments in moist beech–maple and mixed deciduous forests; occasionally under oaks or oak–hickory; UPL. Scattered statewide. Grows 12 inches in light to medium shade and moist to slightly dry sites with some organic matter and some protection from wind; a few sources.

Carex annectens (Yellowfruit sedge) – dry to moist, often calcareous soils in open habitats and wet meadows, FACW; statewide. Grows 16 to 40 inches; sun to part sun in dry to moist sandy loam; a few sources.

Carex appalachica (Appalachian sedge) – dry to mesic deciduous or mixed forests, usually on sandy or rocky soils. Mostly east, scattered elsewhere except Central Appalachians. Grows 8 to 24 inches; part sun to part shade in dry to moist rocky sandy loam; a few sources.

Carex aquatilis (Water sedge) – Rare in shallow water along shores and in marshes, commonly over neutral to calcareous substrates, OBL. Widely scattered statewide. Grows 1 to 3 feet in sun to part shade, typically in wet soil to standing water; good for wetland restoration projects; a few sources.

Carex argyrantha (Hay sedge) – dry and rocky (especially sandstone) woods and clearings; statewide. Grows 12 to 40 inches; part shade to shade in dry rocky sandy loam; a few sources.

Carex atherodes (Awned sedge) – Rare in wet prairies and meadows, marshes, wet thickets, and open sites near streams, ponds and lakes, sometimes in water up to 20 inches deep, OBL. Widely scattered statewide; endangered. Grows 12 to 40 inches in sun to part shade in rich, consistently moist to wet sites; a few sources.

Carex atlantica ssp. capillacea (Prickly bog sedge) – swamps, bogs, and along shores, OBL; mostly southeast (Piedmont), scattered elsewhere. Grows 4 to 40 inches; part sun to part shade in moist silty loam; a few sources.

Carex aurea (Golden–fruited sedge) – Rare in open to shaded moist habitats, typically meadows and seepage slopes and most often on calcareous soils, FACW. Mostly northwest (Erie and Ontario Lake Plain); endangered. Grows up to 20 inches and prefers part shade and moist alkaline soils; a few sources.

Carex baileyi (Bailey's sedge) – sandy, peaty, or gravelly pond, lake, and stream shores, meadows, swamps, seeps, ditches, usually in acidic soils, OBL; statewide except southeast (Central Appalachians and Piedmont). Grows 8 to 28 inches; part sun to part shade in moist to wet rich silty loam; a few sources.

Carex bebbii (Bebb's sedge) – rare in wet places with calcareous or neutral soils, gravelly lakeshores, stream banks, meadows and forest seeps, OBL; northwest (Erie and Ontario Lake Plain) and east (Hudson Valley Section). Grows 8 to 32 inches; sun to part shade in moist rich loam; many sources.

Carex bicknellii (Bicknell's sedge) – rare in dry woods, thickets, fields and barrens. Mostly east (Piedmont, Delaware River Valley). Grows 12 to 48 inches; sun to part shade in dry to mesic sandy loam; a few sources.

Carex blanda (Eastern woodland sedge) – swamps, bottomlands and mesic to dry woods, including lawns, roadsides and stream banks, FAC; statewide, mostly southeast (Piedmont and Central Appalachians). Grows 6 to 24 inches; sun to part shade in dry to mesic rich sandy loam; a few sources.

Carex brevior (Sedge) – prairies, meadows, open woods, dry road banks, often in calcareous or neutral soils. Mostly southeast (Piedmont). Grows 12 to 40 inches; sun to part shade in dry to mesic rich sandy loam; several sources.

Carex bromoides (Brome–like sedge) – wet hardwood forests, wooded floodplains and swamps, occasionally wet meadows and marsh edges, FACW; statewide. Grows 10 to 32 inches; part sun to part shade in moist, rich humusy loam; a few sources.

Carex bushii (Sedge) – dry to moist upland woods, thickets, and fields, FACW. Mostly southeast (Piedmont, Central Appalachians); scattered elsewhere. Grows 10 to 36 inches; medium to moist soils in full sun to part shade; a few sources.

Carex buxbaumii (Bauxbaum's sedge) – calcareous swamps, swales, wet meadows, marshes, and fens, OBL. Mostly southeast (Piedmont); widely scattered elsewhere. Grows 10 to 40 inches; sun to part sun in moist to wet silty loam, circumneutral soils; a few sources.

Carex cephalophora (Oval–leaf sedge) – dry to wet to mesic deciduous or mixed forests, thickets, but rarely open grassy habitats, FACU; statewide. Grows 12 to 32 inches; part sun to part shade in dry, mesic to wet rich sandy loam; a few sources.

Carex comosa (Longhair sedge) – swamps and wet thickets, stream, pond and lakeshores, depressions in wet meadows, marshes, often in shallow water or on emergent stumps, floating logs, and floating mats of vegetation, OBL; mostly northwest (Western Glaciated Allegheny Plateau), northeast (Northern Glaciated Allegheny Plateau) and southeast (Piedmont, Central Appalachians). Grows 20 to 48 inches; sun to part sun in wet, silty, loam and sometimes standing water; many sources.

Carex conjuncta (Soft fox sedge) – Openings in floodplain forests, seasonally wet meadows, swales, thickets and upper borders of tidal marshes, FACW. Scattered statewide, but most common in the southeast (Piedmont). Grows up to 3 feet in full sun to light shade in moist, fertile, loamy soils; a few sources.

Carex conoidea (Open field sedge) – moist meadows and prairies, shores of lakes, ponds, and rivers, usually in acidic sands or loams, FACU; mostly southeast (Piedmont), scattered elsewhere. Grows 5 to 30 inches; sun to part sun in moist, rich organic loam; a few sources.

Carex crawfordii (Crawford's sedge) – Rare in standing water, moist to wet sites and open, sandy, somewhat dry disturbed areas, FAC. Scattered north (northern Allegheny plateaus) endangered. Grows 10 to 20 inches in sun to part sun in wet to mesic, well–drained soils; a few sources.

Carex crinita var. brevicrinis (Sedge) – rare in wet meadows, marshes, bogs, floodplain forests, swamps and edges of streams, lakes and ponds, OBL; widely scattered, especially southeast (Piedmont); endangered. Grows 3 to 4 feet in moist to wet, well–drained rich soils in sun to part shade; prefers part shade; many sources.

Carex crinita var. crinita (Fringed sedge or Short–hair sedge) – swamps, floodplain forests, wet meadows, marshes, bogs, stream edges, margins of lakes and ponds and roadside ditches, OBL; statewide. Grows 28 to 60 inches; sun to part shade in moist to wet silty organic loam; many sources.

Carex cristatella (Crested sedge) – moist to wet meadows, marshes, thickets, stream banks, and ditches, FACW. Mostly southeast (Piedmont), scattered elsewhere. Grows 12 to 40 inches; sun to part sun in moist to wet silty organic loam; a few sources.

Carex davisii (Davis' sedge) – rich deciduous floodplain forests and forest margins, usually along streams, meadows, fields and thickets; often on calcareous soils, FAC–; southeast, especially Piedmont. Grows 12 to 36 inches; sun to part shade in rich humus; a few sources.

Carex deweyana var. deweyana (Dewey sedge) – wet to mesic to dry to mesic forests, and forest edges, FACU. Northern tier, especially Northern Glaciated Allegheny Plateau. Grows 8 to 40 inches; part sun to part shade in rich rocky loam; a few sources.

Carex diandra (Lesser panicled sedge) – rare on bog hummocks and pond margins, OBL. Extreme northeast and northwest (glaciated plateaus). Grows 12 to 30 inches; sun to part sun on pond edges in wet, organic loam; a few sources.

Carex eburnea (Ebony sedge) – rare in conifer or mixed forests, sometimes fens, stable dunes, alvars (exposed limestone pavement) and calcareous cliffs, FACU. Scattered, mostly central and northwest (Alleghenies and Erie Lake Plain).Grows 6 to 8 inches in sun to part shade to shade with soft, thread–like foliage in spherical shapes to make a fine groundcover for woodlands and rock gardens. Grow in dry, calcareous soils; a few sources.

Carex echinata var. echinata (Prickly sedge) – bogs, swamps, peaty or sandy shores of streams or lakes, wet meadows, usually in acidic soils, OBL; mostly east, scattered elsewhere. Grows 4 to 36 inches; sun to part sun in moist to wet silty loam; a few sources.

Carex emoryi (Sedge) – stream banks, swales, marshes, seepy areas and fens, OBL. Scattered statewide. Grows 12 to 40 inches; sun to part shade in moist to wet rich sandy loam; a few sources.

Carex flava (Yellow sedge) – moist to wet habitats, such as open meadows, fens, partially shaded shrub peaty wetlands and swamps, on lime to rich soils, OBL; mostly northeast (Northern Glaciated Allegheny Plateau) and northwest (Western Glaciated Allegheny Plateau). Grows 4 to 32 inches; sun to part sun in moist to wet rich loam; a few sources.

Carex folliculata (Northern long sedge) – wet forests, bogs, seeps, wet meadows, marsh edges, stream banks, lakeshores, in acidic, sandy, or peaty soils, OBL; statewide. Grows 12 to 48 inches; part sun to shade in moist to wet rich humusy soils; a few sources.

Carex frankii (Frank's sedge) – moist to wet meadows and woodlands, stream banks, ditches, low marshy ground, often calcareous, OBL; mostly south. Grows up to 2 feet with leaves up to 1/3 inch wide in full sun (preferred) to part shade in a wet to moist silty to loamy soil; temporary flooding is tolerated, making it ideal for erosion control and rain gardens; a few sources.

Carex geyeri (Geyer's sedge) – rare in dry mountain and subalpine grasslands, burns and open conifer woodlands, common in the western U.S. but isolated in central Pennsylvania and consequently technically listed as endangered. Grows 6 to 12 inches on well–drained rocky, gravelly or sandy soils in sun to part sun; a few sources.

Carex glaucodea (Blue sedge) – mesic to wet deciduous forests or seasonally moist prairies, usually in clays or loams; mostly southeast (Piedmont), scattered southwest and northeast. Grows 4 to 20 inches; part sun to part shade in clayey to sandy loams; a few sources.

Carex gracillima (Graceful sedge) – mesic to dry deciduous forests, including edges and openings, mixed conifer to hardwood forests, coniferous swamps, thickets, meadows, and along roadsides, FACU; statewide. Grows 8 to 40 inches; part shade in dry to mesic sandy loam; a few sources.

Carex granularis (Limestone meadow sedge) – meadows, fens, glades, or shores, moist woods, and bottomland swamps, especially along streams usually in clayey or sandy to clay soils, FACW+. Throughout Pennsylvania, except northern tier counties. Two varieties *granularis* and *haleana* (mostly southeast) Grows 8 to 36 inches; part sun to part shade in moist to wet rich silty loam; a few sources.

Carex grayi (Sedge) – wet to mesic deciduous forests and openings, typically on fine alluvial or lacustrine deposits, and river bottoms, FACW+. Mostly southeast (Piedmont); scattered statewide. Grows 18 to 30 inches in fertile, moist soil in full sun, especially at or near water; tolerates light shade; many sources.

Carex grisea (Wood Gray sedge) – dry to moist rich deciduous woodlands, meadows, swales and ditches, FAC. Scattered statewide, especially southeast. Grows 8 to 30 inches; part shade in rich moist organic loam; a few sources.

Carex gynandra (Nodding sedge) – swamps, floodplain forests, wet meadows, marshes, bogs, stream edges, margins of lakes and ponds and roadside ditches, OBL; statewide. Grows 30 to 60 inches; part sun to part shade in moist to wet silty loam; a few sources.

Carex hirsutella (Fuzzy wuzzy sedge) – meadows and dry to mesic woods in neutral to basic soils; statewide. Grows 10 to 30 inches; sun to part shade in dry to mesic sandy loam; a few sources.

Carex hirtifolia (Hairy sedge) – mesic to dry thickets, lowland forests and forested slopes; mostly southeast (Piedmont) and scattered elsewhere. Grows 12 to 32 inches; part sun to part shade in mesic to dry soil containing loam, clay to loam, or some rocky material. Above average tolerance of dry conditions; a few sources.

Carex hyalinolepis (Shoreline sedge) – Very rare along streams, lakes and ponds and in swamps and wet meadows, often on clay soils with seasonal saturation, OBL. Extreme southeast (Atlantic Coastal

Plain). Grows up to 4 feet in full to part sun on moist to wet clay to silt loams; a few sources.

Carex hystericina (Bottlebrush sedge) – swamps, moist meadows and fens, seeps and edges of lakes, ponds and streams, mostly in calcareous soils, OBL. Mostly southeast (Piedmont, Central Appalachians) and northwest (Western Glaciated Allegheny Plateau). Grows 8 to 40 inches; sun to part sun in moist to wet rich silty loam; many sources.

Carex interior (Inland sedge) – wet meadows and prairies, fens, swamps, river and lakeshores, seeps; usually in calcareous soils, OBL. Scattered statewide, especially northwest, southeast. Grows 8 to 40 inches; sun to part sun in moist to wet, rich silty circumneutral loam; a few sources.

Carex intumescens (Great bladder sedge) – dry to wet forests and openings, thickets, and wet meadows, FACW+; statewide. Grows 6 to 32 inches; part shade to shade in dry to mesic acidic humus; a few sources.

Carex jamesii (Sedge) – rich mesic floodplains, slopes, ravines and hardwood forests, typically on lime–rich substrates; UPL; mostly south. Grows 2 to 4 inches on wet to mesic circumneutral to slightly alkaline soils; a few sources.

Carex lacustris (Hairy sedge) – swamps, wet thickets, marsh edges, meadows, fens and shores of lakes, ponds and streams, OBL; scattered statewide except southwest. Grows 10 to 50 inches; sun to part sun in moist to wet silty loam; several sources.

Carex lasiocarpa (Wooly fruit sedge) – wet meadows, stream banks, fens and bogs, lakeshores, especially in very wet sites and sometimes forming floating mats, OBL; mostly northeast (Northern Glaciated Allegheny Plateau) and scattered elsewhere. Grows 10 to 50 inches; sun to part sun in moist to wet silty or peaty loam; a few sources.

Carex laxiculmis var. laxiculmis (Spreading sedge) – wet, low, deciduous or mixed deciduous and evergreen forests; stream edges and springs, and seeps, especially on clay soils; statewide. Grows 4 to 40 inches; part shade to shade in mesic to moist humusy sandy loam; a few sources.

Carex laxiflora (Broad looseflower sedge) – higher elevations of dry to moist deciduous or mixed deciduous to evergreen forests, FACU; statewide. Grows 5 to 25 inches; part shade to shade in mesic to moist humusy sandy loam; a few sources.

Carex lupuliformis (False hop sedge) – rare in calcareous marshes, wet woods, sometimes in shallow water, FACW; scattered statewide. Grows 20 to 48 inches; full sun to part shade in silty rich soils continually moist to wet; a few sources.

Carex lupulina (Hop sedge) – wet mixed to deciduous swampy forests and openings and wet meadows, OBL; statewide. Grows 10 to 50 inches; part sun to part shade in moist to wet rich silty loam; a few sources.

Carex lurida (Shallow sedge) – pond, lake and stream shores, marshes and wet meadows, seeps and swampy forests, usually in sandy acidic soils, OBL; statewide. Grows 10 to 50 inches; sun to part sun in moist to wet rich silty loam; several sources.

Carex molesta (Troublesome sedge) – dry to wet, frequently heavy, calcareous soils in fields, bottomlands and along roadsides. Mostly southeast (Piedmont) and scattered elsewhere. Grows 15 to 45 inches; sun to part shade in dry to wet, clayey to silty loam; a few sources.

Carex muehlenbergii (Muehlenberg's sedge) – sandy, dry savannahs and open forests; mostly east, scattered elsewhere. Grows 10 to 40 inches; sun to part shade in dry sandy loam; a few sources.

Carex normalis (Greater straw sedge) – generally wet woods, thickets, meadows and along roadsides, FACU; statewide. Grows 10 to 50 inches; sun to part shade in moist to mesic sandy clay loam; a few sources.

Carex pedunculata (Longstalk sedge) – rich, rocky, wooded slopes or swampy woods. Scattered statewide except southwest (Southern Allegheny Plateau) and southeast (Central Appalachians). Grows 2 to 12 inches; part shade to shade in moist to dry sandy loams; a few sources.

Carex pellita (Woolly sedge) – swamps, moist meadows, and along shores of lakes and ponds, OBL. Mostly southeast (Piedmont); scattered elsewhere. Grows 12 to 40 inches; full sun to part in moist to wet rich loams; a few sources.

Carex pensylvanica (Pennsylvania sedge) – well to drained, acidic but mineral–rich sandy, rocky, and loamy soils in deciduous forests, edges and openings; statewide. Grows 4 to 16 inches; part shade to shade in dry to mesic sandy rocky loam. Colonizes by rhizomes; many sources.

Carex plantaginea (Plantain sedge) – rich, moist, deciduous or mixed deciduous to evergreen forests, on slopes along streams or along edges of moist depressions. Mostly north (northern Allegheny Plateaus) and southwest (Allegheny Mountains); scattered elsewhere. Grows 8 to 24 inches; part shade in consistently moist organic loams; many sources.

Carex platyphylla (Broad–leaf sedge) – rocky or gravelly slopes in rich, moist deciduous forests, usually on limestone, shale, or calcareous metamorphic rocks, often on clay soils; statewide. Grows 6 to 16 inches; part sun to shade in moist, rich sandy humus; a few sources.

Carex prairea (Prairie sedge) – rare in calcareous fens and marshes, FACW; widely scattered, mostly northwest (Western Glaciated Allegheny Plateau). Grows 20 to 40 inches; sun to part sun in moist rich silty loam. A few sources.

Carex projecta (Necklace sedge) – moist to wet meadows, low spots in deciduous and mixed forests, thickets, stream banks and lake shores, FACW; statewide. Grows 20 to 30 inches; part sun to part shade in moist to wet rich loam; a few sources.

Carex pseudocyperus (Cyperus–like sedge) – wet thickets; shores of lakes, streams and ponds; marshes, wet meadows, sometimes in shallow water or on floating mats of vegetation or logs or on emergent stumps, OBL; mostly northwest (Erie and Ontario Lake Plain), endangered. Grows 2 to 3 feet in full sun on very wet soil to standing water; a few sources.

Carex radiata (Eastern star sedge) – wet to mesic mixed and deciduous forests in usually seasonally wet areas; statewide. Grows 10 to 30 inches; part sun to part shade in mesic to wet to mesic loam; a few sources.

Carex retrorsa (Backward sedge) – rare on lake and pond shores, stream banks, marshes, swamps, wet meadows and thickets, FACW; scattered, mostly north. Grows 12 to 36 inches; shade to part shade in moist to wet organic loam; a few sources.

Carex rosea (Rosy sedge) – dry and mesic deciduous and mixed forests; statewide. Grows 10 to 35 inches; part sun to part shade in dry to mesic sandy loam; a few sources.

Carex scoparia (Broom sedge) – dry to wet open habitats, often on sandy, acidic soils, FACW; statewide. Grows 10 to 40 inches; sun to part sun in dry to wet acidic, sandy loam; several sources.

Carex shortiana (Short's sedge) – thickets and swampy woods, open wet ground including spring–fed meadows, prairie swales, pond margins and ditches, as well as the rich woods of toe slopes, FAC. South central and southwest (Southern Allegheny Plateau, Allegheny Mountains, Northern Ridge and Valley). Most often in calcareous soils.

Grows 12 inches in full to part sun in fertile, moist loamy soils; a few sources.

Carex sparganioides (Bur reed sedge) – dry and mesic deciduous and mixed forests on neutral or basic soils, FACU; statewide. Grows 15 to 40 inches; part sun to part shade in dry to moist humusy loam; a few sources.

Carex sprengelii (Sprengli's sedge) – dry to mesic hardwood and mixed conifer forests and openings, floodplain forests and riverbanks, lakeshores, limestone river bluffs, frequent on calcareous soils, FACU; mostly east (Delaware River Valley). Grows 10 to 40 inches; sun to part shade in dry to mesic rich sandy and alluvial loam; several sources.

Carex squarrosa (Squarrose sedge) – wet woods, swamps, forest edges and moist meadows, FACW. Mostly southeast (Piedmont), scattered south. Grows 18 to 24 inches in full sun to part shade; prefers loamy soils containing silt, sand or gravel and tolerates temporary shallow standing water, making it ideal for rain gardens; a few sources.

Carex sterilis (Atlantic sedge) – white to cedar swamps, wet calcareous prairies, fens and meadows, calcareous seeps, lake and river shores, and wet sunny limestone outcrops, OBL; mostly southeast (Piedmont), widely scattered elsewhere. Grows 1 to 3 inches; full sun to part sun in wet to moist circumneutral sandy loams; a few sources.

Carex stipata var. stipata (Owl fruit sedge) – soils that are periodically saturated or inundated in wet meadows, swamps, marshes, and alluvial bottomlands; statewide. Grows 15 to 40 inches; sun to part sun in moist to wet rich silty and alluvial loam; a few sources.

Carex stricta (Tussock sedge or Upright sedge) – lake shores, bogs, marshes and wet meadows, OBL. Mostly southeast (Piedmont), scattered elsewhere. Grows 6 to 44 inches; sun to part sun in moist to wet rich silty or alluvial loam; many sources.

Carex swanii (Swann's sedge) – mesic to dry forests and scrublands, FACU; statewide. Grows 10 to 20 inches; part sun to part shade in mesic to dry sandy loam; a few sources.

Carex tenera var. tenera (Quill sedge) – moist to dry meadows and open forests, FAC. Scattered statewide except southwest. Grows 10 to 35 inches; part sun to part shade in mesic to wet sandy loam; a few sources.

Carex tribuloides var. tribuloides (Blunt broom sedge) – open floodplain forests, moist to wet grasslands, ditches, stream banks and wet thickets, FACW+; statewide. Grows 20 to 40 inches; sun to part shade in wet to moist gravelly, sandy, peaty or loamy soils; a few sources.

Carex trichocarpa (Hairy fruit sedge) – wet thickets and meadows, near streams and rivers, and in openings in bottomlands, OBL; statewide except southwest. Grows 20 to 50 inches; sun to part sun in moist rich loam; a few sources.

Carex tuckermanii (Tuckerman's sedge) – rare in deciduous swamp forests, thickets, often along streams or pond shores and wet meadows, OBL; mostly northwest (Western Glaciated and Southern Allegheny Plateaus). Grows 16 to 40 inches; sun to part shade in moist to wet silty loam; a few sources.

Carex typhina (Cat–tail sedge) – rare in calcareous wet woods, swales and swamps, FACW+. Scattered statewide and endangered. Grows 12 inches in full sun to part shade in medium to fine–textured, moist to wet soils; a few sources.

Carex utriculata (Northwest territory sedge) – pond and lake shorelines, swamps, marshes, meadows, fens, bogs and wet thickets, OBL. Mostly northeast (Northern Glaciated Allegheny Plateau); scattered elsewhere except southwest. Grows 16 to 40 inches; sun to part sun in moist rich loam; a few sources.

Carex vesicaria (Blister sedge) – stream, pond and lake shores; marshes, bogs, wet meadows, low wet areas in forests, wet thickets and swamps, frequently on sites inundated in spring and dry during summer, OBL; scattered statewide. Grows 5 to 40 inches; sun to part sun in mesic to moist rich sandy loam; a few sources.

Carex virescens (Ribbed sedge) – deciduous forests and banks ranging from mesic to dry; statewide, especially southeast (Piedmont). Grows 15 to 40 inches; part sun to part shade in mesic to dry sandy loam; a few sources.

Carex viridula var. viridula (Green sedge) – rare in open, seasonally moist habitats such as shorelines that are acidic and sandy to organic, fens or calcareous runnels in limestone barrens, OBL. Extreme northwest (Erie and Ontario Lake Plain), endangered. Grows 12 to 30 inches in full to part sun in wet sandy alkaline soils; a few sources.

Carex vulpinoidea var. vulpinoidea (Fox sedge) – marshes, ditches and wet meadows periodically inundated or saturated, OBL; statewide. Grows 16 to 40 inches; sun to part sun in moist to wet silty loam; many sources.

Carex woodii (Pretty sedge) – dry, calcareous woodland slopes; UPL. Mostly southwest (Southern Allegheny Plateau, Allegheny Mountains); scattered west. Grows 6 to 12 inches in average to dry circumneutral soils, part sun to shade; a good choice for no–mow lawn; a few sources.

Chasmanthium latifolium (Northern sea–oats or Indian wood oats) – rare in rich alluvial woods or rocky slopes along streams and on moist bluffs and stream banks, FACU; scattered in south. Grows 20 to 40 inches; part sun to part shade in dry to moist rich sandy loam, pH 5 to 7; many sources.

Chasmanthium laxum (Slender sea–oats) – sandy, moist soils, FAC. Mostly southeast (Atlantic Coastal Plain); endangered. Grows 1 to 3 feet in full sun to part shade on circumneutral, moist pebbly to sandy loam; moderately drought tolerant; a few sources.

Cinna arundinacea (Wood reedgrass) – moist woodlands and swamps, depressions, along streams, and in floodplain and upland woods; less frequent in wet meadows, marshes, and disturbed sites, FACU; statewide. Grows 40 to 60 inches; part sun to part shade in moist to wet humusy loam; a few sources.

Cyperus esculentus (Yellow nutsedge) – low areas of upland prairies and fields, stream edges and pond margins, FACU; statewide. Grows 12 to 40 inches; sun to part sun in moist, rich sandy loams; a few sources.

Cyperus schweinitzii (Schweinitz's flatsedge) – rare in sandy openings in woods, sand dunes, sand bars and along stream banks and lake shores, FACU; mostly southeast (Piedmont). Grows up to 12 inches in full sun on dry, very sandy soil; a few sources.

Danthonia spicata (Poverty grass) – dry rocky, sandy, or mineral soils, usually in open sunny places; statewide. Grows 8 to 24 inches; sun to part shade in dry to mesic sandy loam; a few sources.

Deschampsia flexuosa (Common hairgrass) – dry and generally rocky slopes and in woods and thickets, often on disturbed sites; mostly east, south central. Grows 12 to 40 inches; part sun to part shade in dry to mesic sandy loam; a few sources.

Dichanthelium leibergii (Leiberg's panic grass) – very rare on limestone outcrops and sandy woodlands, FACU. Reported only in Centre County and believed to be extirpated. Grows 1 to 2 feet in sandy, calcareous soils in sun to part sun; AKA *Panicum leibergii;* a few sources.

Dichanthelium oligosanthes (Heller's rosette grass) – loamy, clayey soil of thickets, especially along the Delaware River, FACU. Mostly southeast (Piedmont, Delaware River Valley); widely scattered elsewhere. Grows 10 to 30 inches; part sun in dry to moist clay loam; a few sources. AKA *Panicum oligosanthes var. oligosanthes*

Distichlis spicata *(*Seashore saltgrass) – Very rare in brackish marshes and coastal salt flats and adjacent forests and desert scrub habitats, often in dense monotypic stands as clonal colonies, FACW+; mostly southeast (Piedmont). Grows up to 12 inches in full sun, prefers wet, calcareous and saline soils; a few sources.

Dulichium arundinaceum (Three–way sedge) – open wet places, lake and pond margins, marshes, swamps, bogs and stream shores, OBL; statewide. Can reach 48 inches; part shade in moist to wet sandy to clay loam; several sources.

Echinochloa muricata (Barnyard grass) – moist ground, alluvial shores and often on disturbed sites, FACW+; statewide. Grows 4 to 24 inches; sun to part sun in rich silty loam; a few sources.

Eleocharis acicularis (Needle spike–rush) – bare, wet soil or in lakes, ponds, vernal pools, meadows, springs and disturbed places, OBL; statewide. Can reach 3 feet; sun to part sun in shallow ponds and pools; several sources.

Eleocharis erythropoda (Bald spike–rush) – non–calcareous or calcareous fresh or brackish shores, marshes, wet meadows, fens, stream banks and swales, OBL; statewide, especially southeast (Piedmont). Can reach 3 feet; full sun in wet to mesic sandy loam, prefers pH of 7 to 8; a few sources.

Eleocharis palustris (Creeping spike–rush) – large colonies at lake and stream margins, bogs, swamps and marshy swales; statewide, especially east. Can reach 50 inches; sun to part sun in ponds, rain gardens and retention basins up to 40 inches deep; can be inundated for up to 4 months; a few sources.

Eleocharis parvula *(*Dwarf spike–rush) – brackish or saline tidal marshes, shores, swamps, ponds, mud flats and ditches, OBL; mostly southeast (Piedmont), endangered. Grows up to 12 inches in full sun; commonly sold as a saline aquarium plant; a few sources.

Eleocharis quadrangulata (Four–angled spike–rush) – rare in shallow waters of lake and pond edges, swamps, marshes, OBL; mostly southeast (Piedmont), west (Southern Allegheny Plateau), endangered. Grows to 3 feet in sun to part sun in silty loams in or adjacent to standing water; a few sources.

Eleocharis rostellata (Beaked spike–rush) – rare in very wet calcareous fens, springs and shores, OBL; scattered west (Southern Allegheny Plateau), endangered. Grows 1 to 3 feet in sun to part sun on somewhat nutrient–poor alkaline silt loams; a few sources.

Elymus canadensis var. canadensis (Canada wild–rye) – alluvial shores and thickets, especially near larger rivers and tributaries, FACU+; statewide, especially southeast (Delaware River Valley). Can reach 36 inches; sun to part sun in silty alluvial loam; many sources.

Elymus hystrix (Bottlebrush grass) – dry to moist soils in open woods and thickets, especially on base to rich slopes and small stream terraces; statewide. Grows 24 to 36 inches; part sun to part shade in moist loam; several sources.

Elymus riparius (Riverbank wild–rye) – moist, generally alluvial and often sandy soils in woods and thickets, usually along larger streams and occasionally along upland ditches, FACW; statewide. Grows 40 to 60 inches; part sun to part shade in mesic to moist alluvial sandy loam; several sources.

Elymus trachycaulus (Slender wheatgrass) – generally open or moderately open areas, but sometimes in forests, FACU; mostly northeast (Northern Glaciated Allegheny Plateau) and widely scattered southwest. Grows 15 to 40 inches; sun to part shade in dry to moist sandy loam; a few sources.

Elymus villosus (Wild rye) – moist to moderately dry, generally rocky soils in woods and thickets, especially in calcareous or other base to rich soils; also frequent on drier, sandy soils or damper, alluvial soils in glaciated regions, FACU–; statewide. Grows 20 to 40 inches; part sun to part shade in dry to moist sandy or alluvial loam; several sources.

Elymus virginicus (Virginia wild rye) – moist–damp or rather dry soil, mostly on bottomland or fertile uplands, in open woods, thickets, tall forbs, or weedy sites, FACW–; statewide. Grows 20 to 50 inches; part sun to part shade in sandy, organic loam, pH 5 to 7; many sources.

Eragrostis spectabilis (Purple lovegrass) – dry sandy fields, woods margins, roadsides, usually in sandy to clay loam soils; UPL. Mostly east; widely scattered west. Grows 12 to 24 inches; sun to part sun in dry to moist sandy to clay loams; many sources.

Eriophorum virginicum (Tawny cotton–grass) – bogs and peaty meadows and swamps, OBL. Statewide, scattered in southwest. Grows 1 to 3 feet; full sun in wet, rich silty soil; a few sources.

Festuca paradoxa (Cluster fescue) – very rare in prairies, open woods, thickets, and low open ground, FAC. Scattered statewide, endangered. Grows to 4 feet in wet, wet–mesic and mesic soils in sun to part sun; a few sources.

Festuca subverticillata (Nodding fescue) – moist to dry deciduous or mixed forests with organic rocky soils, FACU; statewide. Grows 24 to 48 inches; part sun to part shade in moist, organic, rocky, sandy loam; a few sources.

Glyceria borealis (Northern mannagrass) – edges and muddy shores of freshwater streams, lakes, and ponds, OBL. Mostly northeast (Northern Glaciated Allegheny Plateau); scattered elsewhere. Can reach 40 inches; sun to part sun in moist to wet silty loam; a few sources.

Glyceria canadensis (Rattlesnake mannagrass) – bogs, swamps, wet woods and marshes near lakes, OBL; statewide. Can reach 36 inches; sun to part sun in moist to wet silty loam; several sources.

Glyceria grandis (American mannagrass) – wet woods and meadows, stream banks, swamps, and in the water of streams, ditches and ponds. Mostly north (northern Allegheny plateaus); scattered south. Can reach 48 inches; sun to part sun in moist to wet silty loam; several sources.

Glyceria melicaria (Slender mannagrass) – swamps, bogs and wet soils, OBL; statewide. Grows 20 to 40 inches; sun to part sun in moist to wet silty loam; a few sources.

Glyceria septentrionalis (Floating mannagrass) – very wet meadows, floodplain forests, swamps, pond and lake margins and in the shallow water of stream margins, OBL. Mostly west and south, especially southeast (Piedmont). Grows 3 to 6 feet in full to part sun and wet conditions; preferred soils combine some organic material with loam, clay or sand and shallow water is tolerated; may spread aggressively; a few sources.

Glyceria striata (Fowl mannagrass) – bogs, along lakes and streams, and in other wet places, OBL; statewide. Grows 20 to 40 inches; sun to part sun in moist to wet silty loam; many sources.

Hesperostipa spartea (Needlegrass, porcupine grass) – very rare in dry prairies and open woodlands, as well as roadsides. Reported only in Lackawanna County. Grows 3 to 6 feet on dry rocky or sandy soils in sun to part sun, generally circumneutral soils; a few sources.

Hierochloe odorata (Vanilla sweetgrass) – very rare in moist meadows or river shores. Grows 18 to 36 inches, FACW; endangered reported only in Wayne, Butler, Erie and Allegheny counties. Grows 12 to 20 inches sun to part sun in moist, organic sandy loam; many sources.

Juncus acuminatus (Sharp–fruited rush) – wet meadows, swamps, marshes, stream banks, shores, ditches, and near springs on rock outcrops, OBL; statewide. Grows 8 to 30 inches; full sun in rich loam, wet to shallow water; a few sources.

Juncus arcticus var. littoralis (Baltic rush) – rare along streams, and in wet meadows, fens and marshes, often slightly alkaline soils, FACW+; scattered statewide. Grows 12 to 36 inches in calcareous silty loams, including standing water; a few sources.

Juncus articulatus (Jointed rush) – swamps and mud flats; wet ground in ditches, lake and stream margins, generally in calcareous soils; mostly northwest (Western Glaciated Allegheny Plateau); scattered elsewhere. Grows 4 to 20 inches; full sun in rich loam, wet to shallow water; a few sources.

Juncus biflorus (Grass rush) – rare in moist, open woods, gravel pits and ditches and boggy fields, FACW. Mostly southeast (Piedmont); scattered south. Grows 12 to 36 inches in silty loams, including standing water; a few sources.

Juncus bufonius (Toad rush) – moist soils in meadows, along lakeshores or stream banks, ditches, or roadsides, frequent in drawdown areas; usually in open sites and often becoming weedy, FACW; statewide. Grows 6 to 20 inches, sun to part sun in moist to wet rich loam; a few sources.

Juncus canadensis (Canada rush) – swamps, marshes, bogs, swales, fens, lake and pond shores; prefers calcareous soils, OBL. Scattered statewide. Grows 12 to 48 inches; full sun in moist to wet rich loams; a few sources.

Juncus dudleyi (Dudley's rush) – exposed or shaded sites, usually moist areas such as along stream banks, ditches, around springs. Scattered statewide. Grows 12 to 32 inches; sun to part shade in sandy to clayey loam; a few sources.

Juncus effusus var. pylaei (Soft rush) – swamps and marshes, and moist to saturated meadows, FACW+; statewide. Can reach 36 inches; sun to part sun in mesic to moist sandy, rich loam; many sources.

Juncus filiformis (Thread rush) – rare on moist to wet soil along stream banks, pools, lakes or in meadow depressions; rarely in bogs. Mostly glaciated plateau area of Monroe County; scattered elsewhere. Grows 6 to 12 inches; sun to part sun in moist to wet sandy rich loam; a few sources.

Juncus gerardii (Blackfoot rush) – rare, can form extensive colonies in exposed estuary and coastal meadows and salt marshes just above line of high–tide line; also inland on waste ground, ballast and moist roadsides where de–icing salts are used. Mostly southeast (Atlantic Coastal Plain), scattered south. Grows 12 to 28 inches in full sun on wet, often salty, silt loams; a few sources.

Juncus greenei (Greene's rush) – very rare on dry sandy well–drained sites near lake shores, in sand dunes or pinelands; Monroe and Pike counties. Grows 10 to 30 inches; sun to part sun in dry sandy loam; a few sources.

Juncus marginatus var. marginatus (Grass–leaved rush) – bogs, shores, marshes and ditches in moist to wet clayey, peaty or sandy soils, FACW; statewide. Grows 10 to 20 inches; sun to part sun in rich, moist to wet sandy, peaty or clay loam; a few sources.

Juncus nodosus (Knotted rush) – moist to wet fields, swamps, fens, marshes, swales, bogs in sandy often calcareous soils, OBL. Widely scattered, mostly northwest and east. Grows 6 to 18 inches; sun to part sun in moist to wet sandy circumneutral soils; a few sources.

Juncus tenuis (Path rush) – moist to dry and sometimes heavily compacted soil of woods, fields, waste ground and paths, FAC–; statewide. Grows 4 to 32 inches; sun to part shade in dry to moist loam; many sources.

Juncus torreyi (Torrey's rush) – rare in calcareous wet meadows and swamps, sometimes on clay soils, and on wet sandy shores and the edges of sloughs and slightly alkaline watercourses, FACW; widely scattered statewide; endangered. Grows 18 to 30 inches in full sun in calcareous, moist to wet silty to clay loams; many sources.

Koeleria macrantha (Junegrass) – very rare in generally sandy upland or high prairie sites, woods openings and open rocky slopes that are cool, semi–arid and somewhat infertile; a cool–season grass that goes dormant in late summer. Reported only as Bradford County;

listed as extirpated. Grows to 18 inches in rocky or sandy soils in full sun. AKA *Celeriac macrantha;* many sources.

Leersia oryzoides (Rice cutgrass) – clayey to sandy heavy wet soils in meadows and bogs, frequently in standing water, OBL; statewide. Grows 30 to 80 inches; full sun in moist to wet mucky to sandy loams; many sources.

Leersia virginica (Cutgrass) – damp to wet woods, often along streams, FACW; statewide. Grows 20 to 50 inches; part sun to part shade in moist, rich sandy loam; a few sources.

Luzula acuminata var. acuminata (Hairy woodrush) – meadows, hillsides and open woods, FAC; statewide, except widely scattered southeast (Piedmont, Central Appalachians). Grows 5 to 15 inches; sun to part sun in rich, sandy loam; a few sources.

Luzula multiflora (Field woodrush) – fields and meadows, clearings, open woods and roadside ditches, FACU; statewide. Can reach 30 inches; sun to part sun in dry to mesic sandy loam, pH 5 to 7; a few sources.

Milium effusum var. cisatlanticum (Milletgrass) – cool rich woods. North (northern Allegheny plateaus); scattered south–central (Allegheny Mountains). Grows 4 to 8 inches; part shade to shade in mesic to moist humusy loam; a few sources.

Milium effusum var. cisatlanticum (Milletgrass) – cool rich woods. Mostly north (glaciated and unglaciated plateaus) and south–central (Allegheny Mountains). Grows 4 to 8 inches; part shade to shade in mesic to moist humusy loam; a few sources.

Muhlenbergia capillaris (Hairgrass, Hair awn muhly) – very rare in dry, exposed ledges, sandy prairies, FACU–. Only in Lancaster County; listed as extirpated. Grows to 3 feet in sandy moist soils in full sun; prized for its stunning pink to lavender floral display in autumn; many sources.

Muhlenbergia frondosa (Wirestem muhly) – thickets, clearings and forest edges and alluvial plains, FAC; statewide. Grows 20 to 40 inches; sun to part shade in moist sandy loam; a few sources.

Muhlenbergia mexicana (Mexican muhly) – bogs, swamps, lake margins, moist prairies and woodlands, FACW. Scattered statewide, mostly east. Grows 20 to 40 inches; sun to part sun in mesic to moist sandy loams; a few sources.

Muhlenbergia glomerata (Spike muhly) – marshes, bogs, fens, meadows, lake shores and stream banks, prefers calcareous soils, FACW; statewide, mostly east. Grows 12 to 36 inches; sun to part sun in moist, rich sandy loam; a few sources.

Muhlenbergia schreberi (Dropseed or Nimblewill) – dry to mesic woodlands and prairies, river banks and ravines, often in sandy to rocky soil, FAC; statewide. Can reach 36 inches; sun to part shade in dry to moist sandy loam; can be invasive; a few sources.

Panicum anceps (Panic grass) – low, sandy, moist soils in forests or in shaded, grassy pasturelands, pine savannahs, borders of flood–plain swamps, mesic woodlands, roadsides, and upland pine–hardwood forests, FAC. Mostly southeast (Piedmont and Atlantic Coastal Plain.) Grows 2 to 4 feet in full to part sun on moist to wet sandy loams, but can adapt to waterlogged and very well–drained sites; a few sources.

Panicum capillare (Witchgrass) – fields, pastures, roadsides, waste places and ditches, FAC–; statewide. Grows 20 to 40 inches; sun to part sun in dry to moist sandy to clayey loam; a few sources.

Panicum clandestinum (Deer–tongue grass) – clearings and edges in damp, sandy woodlands and thickets, FAC+; statewide. Grows 30 to 50 inches; part sun to part shade in moist sandy loam; a few sources.

Panicum dichotomiflorum (Smooth panic grass) – dry to moist open woods, meadows, bogs, swamps, edges of lakes and ponds, FACW–; statewide. Grows 12 to 24 inches; part sun to part shade in dry to moist sandy loam; a few sources.

Panicum rigidulum (Long–leaved panic grass) – rare in swamps, wet woodlands and flood–plain forests, wet pine savannahs, marshy shores of rivers, ponds, and lakes; rarely in dry sites, OBL. Scattered southeast (Piedmont). Grows to 4 feet in sun to part shade in moist, rich soils; AKA *Panicum longifolium;* a few sources.

Panicum rigidulum (Panic grass) – marshy shorelines of rivers, lakes and ponds, swamps, wet pine savannahs, floodplain forests and wet low woods; rarely in dry sites, FACW+; mostly southeast (Piedmont, Atlantic Coastal Plain); scattered elsewhere. Grows 20 to 40 inches; sun to part sun in moist to wet silty loam; a few sources.

Panicum virgatum (Switchgrass) – dry slopes of open oak or pine woodlands, river banks, marshes, but especially mesic to wet tall grass prairies, FAC. Scattered statewide, especially in Delaware River Valley. Can reach 6 feet; full sun to part shade in average, medium to

wet soils. Prefers moist, sandy or clay soils in full sun. Tends to lose co-
lumnar form and flop in rich soils and too much shade; many sources.

Phalaris arundinacea (Reed canary–grass) – dry to wet, well to
drained soil, especially in marshes, swamps, FACW; statewide. Grows
10 to 30 inches; full sun to part shade in dry to wet sandy rich loam;
several sources.

Phragmites australis var. americana (Common reed) – marshes,
lake shores, swales and ditches in wet, muddy ground, FACW. Mostly
southeast (Atlantic Coastal Plain, Piedmont) and northwest (Erie and
Ontario Lake Plain, Western Glaciated Allegheny Plateau), scattered
elsewhere. Grows 3 to 12 feet; full sun in moist to wet muddy loams. A
very aggressive spreader and considered invasive; a few sources.

Poa palustris (Fowl bluegrass) – wet meadows, shores, thickets, riparian and upland areas, FACW. Mostly north and east, scattered
elsewhere. Grows 20 to 50 inches; sun to part sun in moist to wet silty
loam; several sources.

Poa saltuensis (Old–pasture bluegrass) – dry to mesic rich open woodlands and thickets in thin soils over limestone. Mostly north (Northern
and Western Glaciated Allegheny Plateaus), scattered south–central
(Allegheny Mountains). Grows 20 to 50 inches; part sun to part shade
in circumneutral dry to mesic loam; a few sources.

Schizachyrium scoparium var. scoparium (Little bluestem) – old
fields, roadsides and open woods, FACU. Mostly southeast (Piedmont);
scattered elsewhere except north (northern Allegheny plateaus). Grows
20 to 45 inches; sun to part shade in dry to moist sandy loam; many
sources.

Schoenoplectus acutus (Great bulrush) – rare in freshwater marshes,
fens, lakes and ponds, slow streams, commonly emergent in water up
to 5 feet, OBL. Mostly west (Erie and Ontario Lake Plain, Southern
Allegheny Plateau); endangered. Grows 3 to 6 feet in sun in wet soil
to standing water; alkaline tolerant and valuable for shoreline protection; a few sources.

Schoenoplectus purshianus (Bulrush) – lake shores, ponds and
ditches, often emergent with relatively little water to level fluctuations,
OBL. Mostly southeast (Piedmont); scattered elsewhere. Can reach 36
inches; sun to part sun in sandy soils, shallow standing water; a few
sources.

Schoenoplectus tabernaemontani (Great bulrush) – fens, marshes,
bogs, lakes, stream banks and sandbars, often emergent in water to 3

feet deep, OBL; statewide. Grows 18 to 30 inches; sun to part sun in sandy to silty soils, shallow standing water; a few sources.

Scirpus atrocinctus (Blackish wool–grass) – moist to wet meadows, marshes, ditches and swales, FACW+; mostly northeast (Northern Glaciated Allegheny Plateau); scattered elsewhere. Grows 10 to 25 inches; sun to part sun in moist to wet rich silty loam; a few sources.

Scirpus atrovirens (Black bulrush) – marshes, moist meadows, swales, shores and ditches, FACW+; statewide. Grows 20 to 30 inches; sun to part sun in moist to wet rich silty loam; many sources.

Scirpus cyperinus (Wool–grass) – marshes, wet meadows and swales, FACW+; statewide. Grows 30 to 60 inches; sun to part sun in moist to wet rich loam, including shallow water; many sources.

Scirpus expansus (Wood bulrush) – marshes, wet meadows and swales, OBL. Scattered statewide, mostly east. Grows 12 to 30 inches; full sun in wet silty loam, including standing water; a few sources.

Scirpus microcarpus (Panicled bulrush – marshes, moist meadows, swales and ditches, OBL. Scattered statewide, mostly north and east. Grows 12 to 30 inches; full sun in wet silty loam, including standing water; a few sources.

Scirpus pendulus (Rufous bulrush) – marshes, moist meadows and ditches, often associated with calcareous substrates; mostly south, scattered elsewhere. Grows 12 to 30 inches; full sun in wet silty circumneutral loam, including standing water; a few sources.

Scirpus polyphyllus (Leafy bulrush) – swampy places and along streams, usually shaded by trees, OBL; statewide. Grows 12 to 30 inches; part shade in wet rich sandy loam, including standing water; a few sources.

Sorghastrum nutans (Indian–grass) – prairies, woodlands and savannahs, including scrublands, FACU. Mostly southeast (Piedmont); scattered elsewhere except northern tier. Grows 3 to 6 feet; sun to part sun in dry to mesic sandy loam; many sources.

Sparganium americanum (Bur–reed) – lake and pond shores and shallow, neutral to alkaline waters, sometimes forming large stands, OBL; statewide. Grows 20 to 50 inches; sun to part sun in sandy to silty moist to wet loams, including standing water; a few sources.

Sparganium androcladum (Branching bur–reed) – rare on shores and quiet, circumneutral, shallow waters and wet meadows, OBL. Scattered statewide; endangered. Grows to 4 feet in a variety of wet to constantly moist soils and part shade to shade; can grow in water; a few sources.

Sparganium eurycarpum (Bur–reed) – shores, ditches, low marshes, neutral to alkaline water on gravel, sand or mud, occasionally among boulders on wave to washed shorelines, OBL. Scattered statewide, especially southeast (Piedmont) and northwest (Western Glaciated Allegheny Plateau). Grows 20 to 50 inches; full sun in silty to sandy loam on pond edges or in standing water; many sources.

Sparganium fluctuans (Bur–reed) – cold, still, acidic to neutral low–nutrient waters up to 6 feet deep; sometimes covers the surface with strap to shaped leaves, OBL; northeast (Northern Glaciated Allegheny Plateau). Can reach 6 feet; full sun in standing water on silty to sandy loam; a few sources.

Spartina patens (Salt–meadow grass) – saline to brackish marshes, low dunes and sandy beaches, marsh ridges and tidal flats ranging from normal high tide to about 15 feet above sea level, FACW+. Mostly southeast (Atlantic Coastal Plain). Grows 1 to 4 feet in full sun in a wide range of soils from coarse sands to silty clay sediments with pHs ranging from very acidic to very alkaline; a few sources.

Spartina pectinata (Freshwater cordgrass) – marshes, sloughs and floodplains, especially those that are ice–scoured, OBL. Scattered statewide, especially Delaware and Susquehanna River Valleys. Grows 3 to 6 feet; sun to part sun in moist to wet silty and alluvial loam; many sources.

Sphenopholis obtusata (Slender wedgegrass) – forests, marsh edges and prairies on dry open sites, FAC–. Two varieties: *var. major* is statewide, mostly southeast (Piedmont); *var. obtusata*, mostly southeast (Piedmont); a hybrid, *x pensylvanica* is very rare on moist slopes and wet woods, scattered south. Grows 10 to 25 inches; sun to part sun in dry to mesic sandy loam; a few sources.

Sporobolus heterolepis (Prairie dropseed) – rare in mesic prairies, well–drained moraines, rock outcrops, glades, pine savannahs and barrens, lightly grazed pastures, UPL; reported in Lancaster and Chester counties, and endangered. Grows 2 to 3 feet in well–drained, dry to medium average soils in full sun; prefers rocky, dry soils. Tolerant of drought, but slow to establish; many sources.

Tridens flavus (Purpletop) – meadows, fields, roadsides and open woods, FACU. Mostly southeast (Central Appalachians, Piedmont), scattered elsewhere. Grows 40 to 50 inches; sun to part sun in dry sandy to clay loam; a few sources.

Tripsacum dactyloides (Gammagrass) – Rare in swamps and wet shorelines, FACW; mostly southeast (Piedmont). Grows 4 to 8 feet in full sun to part shade, in average, mesic and well–drained soil; does well in shady locations near water; a few sources.

Trisetum spicatum (Oatgrass) – very rare forests, moist meadows, rock ledges and scree fields, FACU. Endangered; reported only in Mercer and Lehigh Counties. Grows 4 to 20 inches; sun to part sun in dry sandy and rocky soils. AKA *Aira spicata*; a few sources.

Vulpia octoflora var. glauca (Six–weeks fescue) – open woodlands and clearings, savannahs, meadows, roadsides in dry and sterile soil; UPL. Mostly southeast (Piedmont), widely scattered elsewhere. Grows 4 to 16 inches; sun to part sun in dry to mesic infertile sandy loams; a few sources.

APPARENTLY UNAVAILABLE

The following 212 species of native graminoids include Pennsylvania in their range, but do not appear to be commercially available:

Agrostis altissima (Tall bentgrass)
Andropogon gyrans (Elliott's beardgrass)
Aristida dichotoma var. dichotoma (Povertygrass)
Bulbostylis capillaris (Sandrush)
Calamagrostis cinnoides (Reedgrass)
Calamagrostis porteri (Porter's reedgrass)
Carex adusta (Crowded sedge)
Carex aestivalis (Sedge)
Carex aestivalis x gracillima (Sedge)
Carex aggregata (Sedge)
Carex albicans (Sedge)
Carex albolutescens (Sedge)
Carex amphibola var. rigida (Sedge)
Carex backii (Back's sedge)
Carex barrattii (Barratt's sedge)
Carex brunnescens (Sedge)
Carex bullata (Bull Sedge)
Carex canescens var. canescens (Sedge)
Carex canescens var. disjuncta (Sedge)
Carex careyana (Carey's sedge)
Carex caroliniana (Sedge)
Carex cephaloidea (Sedge)
Carex chordorrhiza (Creeping sedge)
Carex collinsii (Collin's sedge)
Carex communis (Sedge)

Carex cryptolepis (Northeastern sedge)
Carex cumulata (Sedge)
Carex davisii (Sedge)
Carex debilis var. debilis (Sedge)
Carex debilis var. pubera (Sedge)
Carex debilis var. rudgei (Sedge)
Carex digitalis (Sedge)
Carex disperma (Soft–leaved sedge)
Carex emmonsii (Sedge)
Carex festucacea (Sedge)
Carex foenea (Fernald's hay sedge)
Carex formosa (Handsome sedge)
Carex garberi (Elk sedge)
Carex gracilescens (Sedge)
Carex grisea (Sedge)
Carex haydenii (Cloud sedge)
Carex hirtifolia (Sedge)
Carex hitchcockiana (Sedge)
Carex laevivaginata (Sedge)
Carex leavenworthii (Sedge)
Carex leptalea (Sedge)
Carex leptonervia (Sedge)
Carex limosa (Mud sedge)
Carex longii (Long's sedge)
Carex lucorum (Sedge)
Carex meadii (Mead's sedge)
Carex mesochorea (Midland sedge)
Carex mitchelliana (Mitchell's sedge)
Carex nigromarginata (Sedge)
Carex novae–angliae (Sedge)
Carex oligocarpa (Sedge)
Carex oligosperma (Few–seeded sedge)
Carex ormostachya (Spike sedge)
Carex pallescens (Sedge)
Carex pauciflora (Few–flowered sedge)
Carex paupercula (Bog sedge)
Carex planispicata (Sedge)
Carex polymorpha (Variable sedge)
Carex prasina (Sedge)
Carex retroflexa (Sedge)
Carex retrorsa (Backward sedge)
Carex richardsonii (sedge)
Carex sartwellii (Sartwell's sedge)

Carex scabrata (Sedge)
Carex schweinitzii (Schweinitz' sedge)
Carex seorsa (Sedge)
Carex siccata (Sedge)
Carex straminea (Sedge)
Carex striatula (Sedge)
Carex styloflexa (Sedge)
Carex tonsa var. rugosperma (Sedge)
Carex torta (Sedge)
Carex trisperma (Sedge)
Carex umbellata (Sedge)
Carex vestita (Sedge)
Carex wiegandii (Wiegand's sedge)
Carex willdenovii (Sedge)
Carex x florabundum (Wood's sedge)
Cinna latifolia (Drooping woodreed)
Cladium mariscoides (Twig–rush)
Critesion jubatum (Foxtail–barley)
Cymophyllus fraserianus (Fraser's sedge)
Cyperus bipartitus (Umbrella sedge)
Cyperus dentatus (Umbrella sedge)
Cyperus diandrus (Umbrella sedge)
Cyperus flavescens (Umbrella sedge)
Cyperus houghtonii (Houghton's flatsedge)
Cyperus lancastriensis (Umbrella sedge)
Cyperus lupulinus (Umbrella sedge)
Cyperus plukenetii (Plukenet's flatsedge)
Cyperus refractus (Reflexed flatsedge)
Cyperus retrofractus (Rough flatsedge)
Cyperus retrorsus (Retrorse flatsedge)
Cyperus squarrosus (Umbrella sedge)
Cyperus strigosus (False nutsedge)
Deschampsia cespitosa (Tufted hairgrass)
Eleocharis compressa var. compressa (Flat–stemmed spike–rush)
Eleocharis elliptica (Slender spike–rush)
Eleocharis intermedia (Matted spike–rush)
Eleocharis obtusa var. obtusa (Wright's spike–rush)
Eleocharis olivacea (Capitate spike–rush)
Eleocharis pauciflora var. fernaldii (Spike–rush)
Eleocharis robbinsii (Robbins' spike–rush)
Eleocharis tenuis var. pseudoptera (Slender spike–rush)
Eleocharis tenuis var. tenuis (Spike–rush)

Eleocharis tenuis var. verrucosa (Slender spike–rush)
Eleocharis tricostata (Three–ribbed spike–rush)
Eleocharis tuberculosa (Long–tubercled spike–rush)
Elytrigia pungens (Saltmarsh wheatgrass)
Eragrostis capillaris (Lacegrass)
Eragrostis frankii (Lovegrass)
Eragrostis hypnoides (Creeping lovegrass)
Eragrostis pectinacea (Carolina lovegrass)
Erianthus giganteus (Giant beardgrass)
Eriophorum gracile (Slender cotton–grass)
Eriophorum tenellum (Rough cotton–grass)
Eriophorum vaginatum ssp. spissum (Cotton–grass)
Eriophorum viridicarinatum (Thin–leaved cotton–grass)
Glyceria acutiflora (Mannagrass)
Glyceria borealis (Northern mannagrass)
Glyceria canadensis x grandis (Rattlesnake grass)
Glyceria obtusa (Coastal mannagrass)
Juncus brachycephalus (Small–headed rush)
Juncus brevicaudatus (Narrow–panicled rush)
Juncus debilis (Weak rush)
Juncus dichotomus (Forked rush)
Juncus gymnocarpus (Coville's rush)
Juncus militaris (Bayonet rush)
Juncus pelocarpus (Brown–fruited rush)
Juncus scirpoides (Sedge rush)
Juncus secundus (Rush)
Juncus subcaudatus (Rush)
Leptoloma cognatum (Fall witchgrass)
Luzula bulbosa (Woodrush)
Luzula echinata (Common woodrush)
Muhlenbergia sobolifera (Creeping muhly)
Muhlenbergia sylvatica (Muhly)
Muhlenbergia tenuiflora (Muhly)
Muhlenbergia uniflora (Fall dropseed muhly)
Oryzopsis asperifolia (Spreading ricegrass)
Oryzopsis pungens (Slender mountain ricegrass)
Oryzopsis racemosa (Ricegrass)
Panicum acuminatum (Panic grass)
Panicum annulum (Annulus panic grass)
Panicum bicknellii (Bicknell's panicgrass)
Panicum boreale (Northern panic grass)
Panicum boscii (Panic grass)
Panicum clandestinum (Deer–tongue grass)

Panicum columbianum (Panic grass)
Panicum commutatum (Panic grass)
Panicum depauperatum (Poverty panic grass)
Panicum dichotomum (Panic grass)
Panicum gattingeri (Witchgrass)
Panicum latifolium (Panic grass)
Panicum linearifolium (Panic grass)
Panicum lucidum (Shining panic grass)
Panicum meridionale (Panic grass)
Panicum microcarpon (Panic grass)
Panicum philadelphicum (Panic grass)
Panicum polyanthes (Panic grass)
Panicum recognitum (Fernald's panic grass)
Panicum scoparium (Velvety panic grass)
Panicum sphaerocarpon (Panic grass)
Panicum spretum (Panic grass)
Panicum stipitatum (Panic grass)
Panicum verrucosum (Panic grass)
Panicum villosissimum (Long–haired panic grass)
Panicum xanthophysum (Slender panic grass)
Panicum yadkinense (Yadkin River panic grass)
Paspalum laeve var. circulare (Field beadgrass)
Paspalum laeve var. laeve (Field beadgrass)
Paspalum laeve var. pilosum (Field beadgrass)
Paspalum setaceum var. muhlenbergii (Slender beadgrass)
Paspalum setaceum (Slender beadgrass)
Piptochaetium avenaceum (Black oatgrass)
Poa alsodes (Woodland bluegrass)
Poa autumnalis (Autumn bluegrass)
Poa cuspidata (Bluegrass)
Poa languida (Woodland bluegrass)
Poa paludigena (Bog bluegrass)
Rhynchospora fusca (Brown beak–rush)
Rhynchospora gracilenta (Beak–rush)
Scheuchzeria palustris (Pod–grass)
Schizachne purpurascens (Grass)
Schoenoplectus fluviatilis (River bulrush)
Schoenoplectus heterochaetus (Slender bulrush)
Schoenoplectus pungens (Chairmaker's rush)
Schoenoplectus smithii (Smith's bulrush)
Schoenoplectus subterminalis (Water bulrush)
Schoenoplectus torreyi (Torrey's bulrush)
Scirpus ancistrochaetus (Northeastern bulrush)

Scirpus hattorianus (Bulrush)
Scirpus pedicellatus (Wool–grass)
Scleria minor (Small nut–rush)
Scleria pauciflora (Few–flowered nut–rush)
Scleria triglomerata (Whip–grass)
Sparganium angustifolium (Bur–reed)
Sparganium chlorocarpum (Bur–reed)
Sparganium minimum (Small bur–reed)
Sphenopholis pensylvanica (Swamp–oats)
Sporobolus asper (Dropseed)
Sporobolus clandestinus (Rough dropseed)
Sporobolus vaginiflorus (Poverty grass)
Torreyochloa pallida var. fernaldii (Pale meadowgrass)
Torreyochloa pallida var. pallida (Pale meadowgrass)
Trichophorum planifolium (Club–rush)
Triglochin palustre (Marsh arrow–grass)

WOODY AND HERBACEOUS VINES

Not listed is *Toxicodendron radicans* (eastern poison ivy), considered by most to be unsuitable for landscape planting. Those involved in accurate site restoration will find poison ivy is occasionally available in the commercial marketplace.

Adlumia fungosa (Allegheny-vine) - moist coves, rocky woods, ledges, alluvial slopes, and thickets; statewide. Climbing, to 10 feet. White flowers, summer to fall. Grow in part shade to shade in moist humusy loam; a few sources.

Apios americana (Ground-nut) - moist to wet woods and floodplains, statewide; FACW. Twining, to 10 feet; pink flowers in summer. Sun to part shade in moist sandy loam; a few sources.

Aristolochia macrophylla (Dutchman's pipe) - rare on rugged rocky slopes and in rich, often dissected, upland forests; scattered southwest (Southern Allegheny Plateau). Grows 20 to 30 feet in rich, well drained, moist soil in full sun to part shade; does not tolerate dry soils. To control growth, cut back in late winter; a few sources.

Celastrus scandens (American bittersweet) - dry fields, rocky ledges, woods, hedgerows, statewide; FACU-. Dioecious, twining, to 12-16 feet, greenish-white flowers in early summer. Grow in lean to average soils with regular moisture in full sun; suckers at the roots to form large colonies and can strangle trees and shrubs; many sources.

Clematis occidentalis (Purple clematis) - rare in open woods, banks, gravelly embankments, rocky woods, slopes and cliffs, mostly southeast (Piedmont). Climbing or trailing woody vine to 10 feet; violet flowers in late spring. Grow in part shade to shade in circumneutral mesic sandy to rocky soils; a few sources.

Clematis viorna (Leather-flower) - rare on stream banks and wooded cliffs and thickets, scattered south; endangered. Grows to 35 feet with red to purple flowers in early summer; grow in moist, rich, well drained loam; a few sources.

Clematis virginiana (Virgin's-bower) - stream edges, wet roadsides, fencerows, and other moist, disturbed, wooded or open sites, statewide; FAC. Climbing or trailing woody vine to 15 feet. White flowers in summer. Grow in sun to shade; prefers moist soils in part shade; many sources.

Clitoria mariana (Butterfly pea) - rare in dry, open thickets and open ground, scattered southeast (Piedmont); endangered. Grows 3 to 4 feet in well drained, sandy soils in full to part sun; a few sources

Dioscorea quaternata (Fourleaf yam) - Rich, rocky woods, thickets, talus slopes, mostly south-central and southwest (Central Appalachians, Allegheny Mountains, Southern Allegheny Plateau); FACU. Grow in moist, sandy loams in sun to part shade; a few sources.

Dioscorea villosa (Wild yam) - woods, thickets, rocky slopes; FAC+; statewide. Twining vine to 15 feet; greenish-yellow flowers, early summer. Grow in part shade to shade in dry to moist rocky loam; several sources.

Echinocystis lobata (Prickly cucumber) - moist alluvial soil on stream banks and woods edges; FAC, statewide. Annual vine with 16-20 foot stems; white flowers in summer. Grow in sun to part sun in moist sandy loam. Inedible fruit; a few sources.

Humulus lupulus var. lupuloides (Brewer's hops) - moist alluvial soil, woods edges, thickets and waste ground; FACU; statewide. Twining vine to 30 feet. Greenish flowers in summer. Grow in sun to part sun in moist sandy loam. Used to flavor beer; several sources.

Lonicera dioica var. dioica (Mountain honeysuckle) - rocky moist woods and thickets; FACU; mostly southeast (Piedmont), scattered elsewhere. Climbing woody vine or shrub, 3 to 6 feet; red to purple flowers in late spring. Grow in part sun to part shade in dry to moist circumneutral sandy loam; a few sources.

Lonicera hirsuta (Hairy honeysuckle) - rare in moist woods, swamps and rocky thickets; FAC; widely scattered northeast (Northern Glaciated Allegheny Plateau) and northwest (Western Glaciated Allegheny Plateau) and endangered. Climbing woody vine, to 10 feet; orange-yellow flowers in spring. Grow in part sun to part shade in dry to moist sandy loam; a few sources.

Lonicera sempervirens (Trumpet honeysuckle) - roadsides, woods, thickets; FACU; mostly southeast (Piedmont), widely scattered elsewhere. Woody vine, 10 to 20 feet; red-orange flowers in summer, red fruit in fall. Grow in sun to part sun in moist loamy well drained soil. Tolerates shade, but will flower less; very popular with hummingbirds; several sources.

Menispermum canadense (Moonseed) - deciduous woods and thickets, along streams, bluffs and rocky hillsides, fencerows, mostly south, scattered north; FACU. Shade tolerant woody twining vine, 5 to

30 feet; whitish flowers in early fall. Grow in part sun to part shade in moist sandy loam; a few sources.

Parthenocissus inserta (Grape woodbine) - alluvial thickets, ravines, woodlands, fields, scattered throughout. Woody twining vine, 30 to 50 feet. Green-white flowers in summer followed by blue-black berries attractive to birds. Grow in average, mesic, well-drained soil in full sun to part shade; tolerates full shade and a wide range of soil and climate conditions and is good for erosion control; several sources.

Parthenocissus quinquefolia (Virginia-creeper) - open woods, fields, clearings, stream banks; FACU. Woody tendril vine, 30 to 50 feet. White flowers in spring, with fruit in late fall. Grow in average, medium, well-drained soil in full sun to part shade. Tolerates full shade and a wide range of soil and environmental conditions. Often mistaken for poison ivy, but harmless; many sources.

Passiflora lutea (Passion-flower) - rare in rocky, moist woods and thickets; southwest (Southern Allegheny Plateau) and endangered. Grows 12 to 15 feet with white flowers in summer; prefers moist, well-drained limestone sandy loam; a few sources.

Persicaria arifolia (Halberd-leaf tearthumb) - shaded swamps, ponds, tidal marshes along rivers, wet ravines in forests; OBL; statewide, especially southeast (Piedmont). Annual vine; white to pink flowers in summer. Grow in moist to wet rich loams in sun to part shade; a few sources. AKA *Polygonum arifolium.*

Smilax herbacea (Carrion-flower) - higher elevations in rich woods and floodplains, alluvial thickets, and meadows, often in calcareous soils, statewide; FAC. Climbing vine, 3 to 10 feet greenish-yellow flowers in early summer. Grow in part shade to shade in moist average soil; a few sources.

Smilax hispida (Bristly greenbrier) - swamps, moist woods thickets and roadsides, statewide. Climbing vine, 20 to 40 feet. Greenish yellow flowers late spring. Grow in moist loams in full sun to part shade. Tolerates wet soils; a few sources.

Vitis aestivalis (Summer grape) - open forests, woodlands, woodland borders and thickets; climbs nearly all hardwood and conifer tree species that grow in its range, statewide; FACU. Climbing vine, 15 to 30 feet; yellowish green flowers in spring, fruit in fall. Grow in deep, loamy, medium moisture, well-drained soils in full sun; a few sources.

Vitis riparia (Frost grape) - riverbanks and in alluvial thickets, statewide; FACW. Climbing vine, 30 to 70 feet; yellow-green flowers in

May, fruit in late fall. Grow in sun to shade in moist, rich soil; several sources.

Wisteria frutescens (American wisteria) - rare in alluvial woodland and river bank thickets, widely scattered statewide, FACW-. Grows 25 to 30 feet with white to purple flowers in early summer; sun to shade in acidic to circumneutral loam soil, preferably with south to southwest position and sheltered from cold winds and early morning sun. Prefers a rich soil, but gardeners believe that results in excessive leaf growth; a few sources.

APPARENTLY UNAVAILABLE

A total of 23 herbaceous and woody vines do not appear to be commercially available:

>*Calystegia sepium* (Hedge bindweed)
>*Calystegia silvatica ssp. fraterniflora* (Bindweed)
>*Calystegia spithamaea ssp. purshiana* (Low bindweed)
>*Calystegia spithamaea ssp. stans* (Low bindweed)
>*Cynanchum laeve* (Smooth sallow-wort)
>*Desmodium humifusum* (Tick-trefoil)
>*Galactia regularis* (Eastern milk-pea)
>*Galactia volubilis* (Downy milk-pea)
>*Matelea obliqua* (Anglepod)
>*Mikania scandens* (Climbing hempweed)
>*Phaseolus polystachios* (Wild bean)
>*Polygonum cilinode* (Fringed bindweed)
>*Polygonum scandens var. cristatum* (Climbing false-buckwheat)
>*Smilax glauca* (Catbrier)
>*Smilax pseudochina* (False chinaroot)
>*Smilax pulverulenta* (Carrion-flower)
>*Strophostyles umbellata* (Wild bean)
>*Toxicodendron radicans* (Poison-ivy)
>*Toxicodendron rydbergii* (Giant poison-ivy)
>*Vitis cinerea var. baileyana* (Possum grape)
>*Vitis labrusca* (Fox grape)
>*Vitis novae-angliae* (New England grape)
>*Vitis vulpina* (Frost grape)

APPENDIX: STARTING POINTS

Native perennials that are widely available in the commercial marketplace are common for elemental reasons: they are easy to grow and popular for landscaping. With limited resources, they serve as excellent starting points and require of us only two considerations:

Honest appraisal of the light characteristics of a planting site.

A check of the habitat requirements of the potential addition to the soil conditions (and if the habitat needs adjustment to suit - especially in moisture and drainage).

The following lists are categorized by light and all species should be easy to find. Some plants will appear in more than one section; i.e., a species that grows well in both part sun and part shade.

Groups include:

Full sun sites - unobstructed sunlight throughout the entire day

Sunny sites - at least six to eight hours of direct sun daily

Part sun sites - sunlight for a little over half the day, especially midday to afternoon, but also light shade coming from a high, thin canopy

Part shade sites - sunlight for a little less than half the day, especially in the morning but also including moving pools of sunlight (dappled shade)

Shady sites - completely shaded or with occasional dappled sunlight

Each group includes *forbs* - that is, flowering herbaceous species other than grasses; ferns and fern allies; *graminoids* - grasses, sedges and rushes; vines, both woody and herbaceous; and woody perennials - trees and shrubs.

Full Sun Sites

FORBS

Anaphalis margaritacea
Angelica atropurpurea
Asclepias incarnata
Asclepias syriaca
Baptisia australis
Chamerion angustifolium
Conoclinium coelestinum
Desmodium canadense
Doellingeria umbellata
Eupatorium rugosum
Filipendula rubra
Helianthus occidentalis
Heliopsis helianthoides
Hibiscus moscheutos
Lathyrus japonicus
Lilium superbum
Monarda didyma
Monarda punctata
Nelumbo lutea
Parthenium integrifolium
Penstemon digitalis
Pontederia cordata
Potentilla arguta
Ratibida pinnata
Rudbeckia fulgida
Rudbeckia hirta
Ruellia humilis
Sagittaria latifolia
Salvia lyrata
Saururus cernuus
Sedum ternatum
Senna marilandica
Silene virginica
Solidago rigida
Symphyotrichum novae-angliae
Symphyotrichum novi-belgii
Symphyotrichum oblongifolium
Symphyotrichum puniceum
Tradescantia ohiensis
Typha angustifolia
Typha latifolia
Zizia aurea

GRASSES, SEDGES, RUSHES

Andropogon gerardii
Andropogon virginicus
Bouteloua curtipendula
Calamagrostis canadensis
Carex bebbii
Carex comosa
Carex crinita var crinita
Carex grayi
Carex hystericina
Carex stricta
Elymus hystrix
Eragrostis spectabilis
Hierochloe odorata
Juncus effusus
Juncus tenuis
Juncus torreyi
Koeleria macrantha
Leersia oryzoides
Muhlenbergia capillaries
Panicum virgatum
Schizachyrium scoparium
Scirpus cyperinus
Sorghastrum nutans
Sparganium eurycarpum
Spartina pectinata

VINES

Celastrus scandens
Clematis virginiana
Lonicera sempervirens
Parthenocissus quinquefolia

Full Sun Sites

TREES, SHRUBS

Abies balsamea
Acer negundo
Acer rubrum
Acer saccharinum
Acer saccharum
Aesculus glabra
Amelanchier canadensis
Amelanchier laevis
Amorpha fruticosa
Arctostaphylos uva-ursi
Asimina triloba
Betula nigra
Betula papyrifera
Calycanthus floridus
Carya ovata
Ceanothus americanus
Celtis occidentalis
Cephalanthus occidentalis
Cercis canadensis
Chionanthus virginicus
Comptonia peregrina
Cornus alternifolia
Cornus florida
Cornus racemosa
Corylus americana
Crataegus crus-galli
Diospyros virginiana
Fagus grandifolia
Fraxinus americana
Fraxinus pennsylvanica
Gymnocladus dioicus
Juglans cinerea
Juglans nigra
Juniperus virginiana
Lindera benzoin
Liquidambar styraciflua
Liriodendron tulipifera
Magnolia acuminata
Magnolia virginiana
Myrica pensylvanica
Nyssa sylvatica

Ostrya virginiana
Oxydendrum arboreum
Photinia melanocarpa
Photinia pyrifolia
Physocarpus opulifolius
Picea mariana
Picea rubens
Pinus resinosa
Pinus strobus
Platanus occidentalis
Populus tremuloides
Prunus americana
Prunus maritima
Prunus serotina
Quercus alba
Quercus bicolor
Quercus coccinea
Quercus imbricaria
Quercus macrocarpa
Quercus palustris
Quercus phellos
Quercus rubra
Rhus glabra
Rhus typhina
Robinia pseudoacacia
Rosa carolina
Rosa palustris
Rosa virginiana
Salix nigra
Sambucus canadensis
Sassafras albidum
Sorbus americana
Spiraea alba
Spiraea tomentosa
Tilia americana
Tsuga canadensis
Ulmus americana
Viburnum opulus
Viburnum prunifolium
Viburnum trilobum

Sunny Sites

FORBS

Agastache nepetoides
Agastache scrophulariifolia
Allium cernuum
Anaphalis margaritacea
Anemone canadensis
Anemone cylindrica
Anemone virginiana
Angelica atropurpurea
Asclepias incarnata
Asclepias syriaca
Asclepias tuberosa
Asclepias verticillata
Astragalus canadensis
Baptisia australis
Caltha palustris
Chamerion angustifolium
Chelone glabra
Claytonia virginica
Conoclinium coelestinum
Desmodium canadense
Eupatorium fistulosum
Eupatorium maculatum
Eupatorium perfoliatum
Eupatorium purpureum
Eupatorium rugosum
Eurybia macrophylla
Filipendula rubra
Gentiana andrewsii
Gentiana clausa
Helenium autumnale
Heliopsis helianthoides
Hibiscus moscheutos
Hypericum pyramidatum
Iris cristata
Iris versicolor
Lathyrus japonicus
Lespedeza capitata
Liatris spicata
Lilium superbum
Lobelia cardinalis
Lobelia inflata

Lobelia siphilitica
Lupinus perennis
Mimulus ringens
Monarda didyma
Monarda fistulosa
Nelumbo lutea
Opuntia humifusa
Packera aurea
Parthenium integrifolium
Penstemon digitalis
Phlox paniculata
Phlox pilosa
Pontederia cordata
Potentilla arguta
Pycnanthemum virginianum
Ratibida pinnata
Rudbeckia fulgida
Rudbeckia hirta
Rudbeckia laciniata
Rudbeckia triloba
Ruellia humilis
Sagittaria latifolia
Salvia lyrata
Saururus cernuus
Scutellaria lateriflora
Sedum ternatum
Senna marilandica
Silene virginica
Sisyrinchium angustifolium
Solidago canadensis
Solidago nemoralis
Solidago rigida
Solidago speciosa
Symphyotrichum ericoides
Symphyotrichum laeve
Symphyotrichum novae-angliae
Symphyotrichum novi-belgii
Symphyotrichum oblongifolium
Symphyotrichum puniceum
Tradescantia ohiensis
Tradescantia virginiana

Continued

Sunny Sites

FORBS

Typha angustifolia
Typha latifolia
Verbena hastata
Vernonia noveboracensis

Veronicastrum virginicum
Viola pedata
Zizia aurea

FERNS, FERN ALLIES

Athyrium filix-femina
Dennstaedtia punctilobula

Equisetum hyemale

GRASSES, SEDGES, RUSHES

Andropogon gerardii
Andropogon virginicus
Bouteloua curtipendula
Calamagrostis canadensis
Carex bebbii
Carex comosa
Carex crinita var crinita
Carex grayi
Carex hystericina
Carex stricta
Carex vulpinoidea
Elymus canadensis
Elymus hystrix
Eragrostis spectabilis

Hierochloe odorata
Juncus effusus
Juncus tenuis
Juncus torreyi
Koeleria macrantha
Leersia oryzoides
Muhlenbergia capillaries
Panicum virgatum
Schizachyrium scoparium
Scirpus atrovirens
Scirpus cyperinus
Sorghastrum nutans
Sparganium eurycarpum
Spartina pectinata

TREES, SHRUBS

Abies balsamea
Acer negundo
Acer rubrum
Acer saccharinum
Acer saccharum
Aesculus glabra
Amelanchier canadensis
Amelanchier laevis
Amorpha fruticosa
Arctostaphylos uva-ursi

Asimina triloba
Betula nigra
Betula papyrifera
Calycanthus floridus
Carya ovata
Ceanothus americanus
Celtis occidentalis
Cephalanthus occidentalis
Cercis canadensis
Chionanthus virginicus

Continued

Sunny Sites

TREES, SHRUBS

Comptonia peregrina
Cornus alternifolia
Cornus florida
Cornus racemosa
Corylus americana
Crataegus crus-galli
Diospyros virginiana
Fagus grandifolia
Fraxinus americana
Ilex verticillata
Juglans cinerea
Juglans nigra
Juniperus virginiana
Larix laricina
Lindera benzoin
Liquidambar styraciflua
Liriodendron tulipifera
Magnolia acuminata
Magnolia virginiana
Myrica pensylvanica
Nyssa sylvatica
Ostrya virginiana
Oxydendrum arboreum
Photinia melanocarpa
Photinia pyrifolia
Physocarpus opulifolius
Picea mariana
Picea rubens
Pinus resinosa
Pinus strobus
Platanus occidentalis
Populus tremuloides
Prunus americana
Prunus maritima
Prunus serotina

Prunus virginiana
Quercus alba
Quercus bicolor
Quercus coccinea
Quercus imbricaria
Quercus macrocarpa
Quercus palustris
Quercus phellos
Quercus rubra
Rhus glabra
Rhus typhina
Robinia pseudoacacia
Rosa carolina
Rosa palustris
Rosa virginiana
Salix discolor
Salix exigua
Salix nigra
Sambucus canadensis
Sambucus racemosa
Sassafras albidum
Sorbus americana
Spiraea alba
Spiraea tomentosa
Symphoricarpos albus
Symphoricarpos orbiculatus
Tilia americana
Tsuga canadensis
Ulmus americana
Vaccinium macrocarpon
Viburnum cassinoides
Viburnum dentatum
Viburnum opulus
Viburnum prunifolium
Viburnum trilobum

VINES

Celastrus scandens
Clematis virginiana
Humulus lupulus var. lupuloides

Lonicera sempervirens
Parthenocissus quinquefolia

Part Sun Sites

FORBS

Actaea rubra
Agastache scrophulariifolia
Allium cernuum
Allium tricoccum
Anaphalis margaritacea
Anemone canadensis
Anemone cylindrica
Anemone virginiana
Angelica atropurpurea
Aquilegia canadensis
Aralia racemosa
Asclepias incarnata
Asclepias syriaca
Asclepias tuberosa
Asclepias verticillata
Astragalus canadensis
Baptisia australis
Caltha palustris
Caulophyllum thalictroides
Chamerion angustifolium
Chelone glabra
Claytonia virginica
Conoclinium coelestinum
Desmodium canadense
Erythronium americanum
Eupatorium fistulosum
Eupatorium maculatum
Eupatorium perfoliatum
Eupatorium purpureum
Eupatorium rugosum
Eurybia macrophylla
Filipendula rubra
Fragaria vesca
Fragaria virginiana
Gentiana andrewsii
Gentiana clausa
Geranium maculatum
Helenium autumnale
Heliopsis helianthoides
Heuchera americana

Hibiscus moscheutos
Hypericum pyramidatum
Iris cristata
Iris versicolor
Lathyrus japonicus
Lespedeza capitata
Liatris spicata
Lilium superbum
Lobelia cardinalis
Lobelia inflata
Lobelia siphilitica
Lupinus perennis
Mertensia virginica
Mimulus ringens
Monarda didyma
Monarda fistulosa
Nelumbo lutea
Opuntia humifusa
Packera aurea
Penstemon digitalis
Phlox paniculata
Phlox pilosa
Physostegia virginiana
Potentilla arguta
Pycnanthemum virginianum
Rudbeckia fulgida
Rudbeckia laciniata
Rudbeckia triloba
Ruellia humilis
Salvia lyrata
Saururus cernuus
Scutellaria lateriflora
Sedum ternatum
Senna hebecarpa
Silene virginica
Sisyrinchium angustifolium
Solidago caesia
Solidago canadensis
Solidago nemoralis
Solidago speciosa

Continued

Part Sun Sites

FORBS

Symphyotrichum ericoides
Symphyotrichum laeve
Thalictrum dasycarpum
Tiarella cordifolia
Tradescantia virginiana
Urtica dioica
Uvularia sessilifolia
Verbena hastata
Vernonia noveboracensis
Veronicastrum virginicum
Viola labradorica
Viola pedata
Viola sororia
Zizia aptera
Zizia aurea

GRASSES, SEDGES, RUSHES

Calamagrostis canadensis
Carex bebbii
Carex comosa
Carex crinita var crinita
Carex hystericina
Carex stricta
Carex vulpinoidea
Chasmanthium latifolium
Elymus canadensis
Elymus hystrix
Elymus riparius
Elymus virginicus
Eragrostis spectabilis
Hierochloe odorata
Juncus effusus
Juncus tenuis
Schizachyrium scoparium
Scirpus atrovirens
Scirpus cyperinus
Sorghastrum nutans
Sparganium americanum

FERNS, FERN ALLIES

Athyrium filix-femina
Dennstaedtia punctilobula
Dryopteris carthusiana
Dryopteris marginalis
Equisetum hyemale
Matteuccia struthiopteris
Onoclea sensibilis
Osmunda cinnamomea
Osmunda claytoniana
Osmunda regalis
Thelypteris noveboracensis
Thelypteris palustris

TREES, SHRUBS

Abies balsamea
Acer negundo
Acer rubrum
Acer saccharinum
Acer saccharum
Aesculus glabra
Amelanchier canadensis
Amelanchier laevis
Amorpha fruticosa
Arctostaphylos uva-ursi
Asimina triloba
Betula nigra
Betula papyrifera
Calycanthus floridus
Carya ovata
Ceanothus americanus

Continued

Part Sun Sites

TREES, SHRUBS

Celtis occidentalis
Cephalanthus occidentalis
Cercis canadensis
Chimaphila maculata
Chionanthus virginicus
Clethra alnifolia
Comptonia peregrina
Cornus alternifolia
Cornus florida
Cornus racemosa
Corylus americana
Crataegus crus-galli
Diospyros virginiana
Fagus grandifolia
Fraxinus americana
Ilex verticillata
Juglans nigra
Kalmia latifolia
Larix laricina
Lindera benzoin
Liquidambar styraciflua
Magnolia acuminata
Magnolia virginiana
Myrica pensylvanica
Nyssa sylvatica
Ostrya virginiana
Oxydendrum arboreum
Photinia melanocarpa
Photinia pyrifolia
Physocarpus opulifolius
Picea mariana
Picea rubens
Pinus resinosa
Pinus strobus
Platanus occidentalis
Populus tremuloides
Prunus americana
Prunus serotina
Prunus virginiana
Ptelea trifoliata
Quercus alba
Quercus bicolor
Quercus coccinea

Quercus imbricaria
Quercus macrocarpa
Quercus palustris
Quercus phellos
Quercus rubra
Rhododendron calendulaceum
Rhododendron maximum
Rhododendron periclymenoides
Rhododendron prinophyllum
Rhododendron viscosum
Rhus glabra
Rhus typhina
Robinia pseudoacacia
Rosa carolina
Rosa palustris
Rosa virginiana
Salix discolor
Salix exigua
Salix nigra
Sambucus canadensis
Sambucus racemosa
Sassafras albidum
Sorbus americana
Spiraea tomentosa
Symphoricarpos albus
Symphoricarpos orbiculatus
Tilia americana
Tsuga canadensis
Ulmus americana
Vaccinium corymbosum
Vaccinium macrocarpon
Viburnum cassinoides
Viburnum dentatum
Viburnum lentago
Viburnum opulus
Viburnum trilobum

VINES

Clematis virginiana
Humulus lupulus var. lupuloides
Lonicera sempervirens
Parthenocissus quinquefolia

Part Shade Sites

FORBS

Actaea pachypoda
Actaea racemosa
Actaea rubra
Allium tricoccum
Anaphalis margaritacea
Anemone canadensis
Anemone cylindrica
Anemone virginiana
Angelica atropurpurea
Aquilegia canadensis
Aralia racemosa
Arisaema triphyllum
Aruncus dioicus
Asarum canadense
Asclepias tuberosa
Asclepias verticillata
Baptisia australis
Caltha palustris
Caulophyllum thalictroides
Chamerion angustifolium
Chelone glabra
Claytonia virginica
Clintonia umbellulata
Cornus canadensis
Desmodium canadense
Dicentra cucullaria
Dicentra eximia
Dodecatheon meadia
Eupatorium rugosum
Eurybia divaricata
Eurybia macrophylla
Filipendula rubra
Fragaria vesca
Fragaria virginiana
Gentiana andrewsii
Gentiana clausa
Geranium maculatum
Gillenia trifoliata
Goodyera pubescens
Heliopsis helianthoides

Heuchera americana
Hydrastis canadensis
Iris cristata
Jeffersonia diphylla
Lilium superbum
Maianthemum canadense
Maianthemum racemosum
Mertensia virginica
Mitchella repens
Mitella diphylla
Packera aurea
Panax quinquefolius
Phlox divaricata
Phlox stolonifera
Physostegia virginiana
Podophyllum peltatum
Polemonium reptans
Polygonatum biflorum
Polygonatum pubescens
Pycnanthemum virginianum
Rudbeckia laciniata
Ruellia humilis
Sanguinaria canadensis
Saururus cernuus
Sedum ternatum
Senna hebecarpa
Silene virginica
Sisyrinchium angustifolium
Solidago caesia
Solidago flexicaulis
Solidago nemoralis
Solidago speciosa
Symphyotrichum cordifolium
Symphyotrichum laeve
Thalictrum dasycarpum
Thalictrum thalictroides
Tiarella cordifolia
Trillium erectum
Trillium grandiflorum
Trillium sessile

Continued

Part Shade Sites

FORBS

Urtica dioica
Uvularia grandiflora
Uvularia sessilifolia
Viola labradorica

Viola pedata
Viola sororia
Zizia aptera
Zizia aurea

FERNS, FERN ALLIES

Adiantum pedatum
Asplenium platyneuron
Athyrium filix-femina
Dennstaedtia punctilobula
Dryopteris carthusiana
Dryopteris goldiana
Dryopteris marginalis
Equisetum hyemale

Matteuccia struthiopteris
Onoclea sensibilis
Osmunda cinnamomea
Osmunda claytoniana
Osmunda regalis
Polystichum acrostichoides
Thelypteris noveboracensis
Thelypteris palustris

GRASSES, SEDGES, RUSHES

Carex bebbii
Carex crinita
Carex crinita var crinita
Carex pensylvanica
Carex plantaginea
Chasmanthium latifolium

Elymus hystrix
Elymus riparius
Elymus virginicus
Schizachyrium scoparium
Sparganium americanum

TREES, SHRUBS

Abies balsamea
Acer negundo
Acer rubrum
Acer saccharinum
Acer saccharum
Aesculus glabra
Amelanchier canadensis
Amelanchier laevis
Amorpha fruticosa
Arctostaphylos uva-ursi
Asimina triloba
Betula nigra

Betula papyrifera
Calycanthus floridus
Carpinus caroliniana
Carya ovata
Ceanothus americanus
Cephalanthus occidentalis
Chimaphila maculata
Chionanthus virginicus
Clethra alnifolia
Comptonia peregrina
Cornus alternifolia
Cornus amomum

Continued

— Part Shade Sites —

TREES, SHRUBS

Cornus florida
Cornus racemosa
Cornus sericea
Corylus americana
Diervilla lonicera
Diospyros virginiana
Fagus grandifolia
Fraxinus americana
Gaultheria procumbens
Hamamelis virginiana
Hydrangea arborescens
Ilex verticillata
Kalmia latifolia
Lindera benzoin
Liquidambar styraciflua
Magnolia acuminata
Magnolia virginiana
Nyssa sylvatica
Ostrya virginiana
Oxydendrum arboreum
Physocarpus opulifolius
Picea mariana
Picea rubens
Populus tremuloides
Prunus americana
Prunus serotina
Prunus virginiana
Ptelea trifoliata
Quercus rubra

Rhododendron calendulaceum
Rhododendron maximum
Rhododendron periclymenoides
Rhododendron prinophyllum
Rhododendron viscosum
Rhus glabra
Rhus typhina
Robinia pseudoacacia
Rosa palustris
Salix exigua
Salix nigra
Sambucus canadensis
Sambucus racemosa
Sassafras albidum
Sorbus americana
Sorbus decora
Symphoricarpos albus
Symphoricarpos orbiculatus
Tilia americana
Tsuga canadensis
Vaccinium corymbosum
Vaccinium macrocarpon
Viburnum cassinoides
Viburnum dentatum
Viburnum lentago
Viburnum opulus
Viburnum prunifolium
Viburnum trilobum

VINES

Clematis virginiana

Parthenocissus quinquefolia

Shady Sites

FORBS

Actaea pachypoda
Actaea racemosa
Arisaema triphyllum
Asarum canadense
Clintonia umbellulata
Cornus canadensis
Dicentra cucullaria
Dicentra eximia
Eurybia divaricata
Gillenia trifoliata
Goodyera pubescens
Jeffersonia diphylla
Maianthemum canadense
Maianthemum racemosum
Mertensia virginica
Mitchella repens
Mitella diphylla

Panax quinquefolius
Phlox divaricata ssp. divaricata
Phlox stolonifera
Podophyllum peltatum
Polemonium reptans
Polygonatum biflorum
Polygonatum pubescens
Sanguinaria canadensis
Solidago caesia
Solidago flexicaulis
Symphyotrichum cordifolium
Thalictrum dasycarpum
Thalictrum thalictroides
Trillium erectum
Trillium grandiflorum
Trillium sessile
Uvularia grandiflora

FERNS, FERN ALLIES

Adiantum pedatum
Asplenium platyneuron
Athyrium filix-femina
Dryopteris carthusiana
Dryopteris goldiana

Dryopteris marginalis
Equisetum hyemale
Matteuccia struthiopteris
Onoclea sensibilis
Polystichum acrostichoides

TREES, SHRUBS

Betula papyrifera
Carpinus caroliniana
Chimaphila maculata
Cornus amomum ssp. amomum
Diervilla lonicera
Gaultheria procumbens
Hamamelis virginiana
Lindera benzoin
Picea mariana
Prunus virginiana
Ptelea trifoliata

Sorbus decora
Tsuga canadensis
Viburnum dentatum

SEDGES

Carex pensylvanica

VINES

Clematis virginiana
Parthenocissus quinquefolia

APPENDIX: PROTECTED SPECIES

A total of 539 species of native plants are considered protected in Pennsylvania because they are rare, threatened, endangered or extirpated (i.e., gone in the state). As with any native species, they should never be collected from the wild. However, many are propagated by legitimate nurseries and are to varying degrees commercially available. Including them in the home landscape is a positive environmental step.

EXTIRPATED

Acalypha deamii (Two-seeded copperleaf)

Aeschynomene virginica (Sensitive joint-vetch)

Agalinis obtusifolia (Blue-ridge false-foxglove)

Agrostis perennans (Tall bentgrass)

Arctostaphylos uva-ursi (Bearberry manzanita)

Asclepias rubra (Red milkweed)

Berberis canadensis (American barberry)

Buchnera americana (Bluehearts)

Carex adusta (Crowded sedge)

Carex backii (Rocky Mountain sedge)

Carex barrattii (Barratt's sedge)

Carex chordorrhiza (Creeping sedge)

Carex hyalinolepis (Shore-line sedge)

Carex sartwellii (Sartwell's sedge)

Carex siccata (Fernald's hay sedge)

Chamaecyparis thyoides (Atlantic white cedar)

Commelina erecta (Slender day-flower)

Commelina virginica (Virginia day-flower)

Coreopsis rosea (Pink tickseed)

Crassula aquatica (Water pigmy-weed)

Croton willldenowii (Elliptical rushfoil)

Cynoglossum virginianum var. boreale (Northern hound's-tongue)

Cyperus polystachyos (Many-spiked flatsedge)

Cyperus retrorsus (Retrorse flatsedge)

Cypripedium candidum (Small white lady's-slipper)

Desmodium sessilifolium (Sessile-leaved tick-trefoil)

Dichanthelium leibergii (Leiberg's panic-grass)

Dichanthelium ovale var. addisonii (Cloaked panic-grass)

Distichlis spicata (Sea-shore salt-grass)

Draba reptans (Carolina whitlow-grass)

Echinacea laevigata (Smooth coneflower)

Eleocharis tricostata (Three-ribbed spike-rush)

Eleocharis tuberculosa (Long-tubercled spike-rush)

Elodea schweinitzii (Schweinitz's waterweed)

Eriocaulon decangulare (Ten-angle pipewort)

Eriocaulon parkeri (Parker's pipewort)

Eryngium aquaticum (Marsh eryngo)

Eupatorium album (White thoroughwort)

Eupatorium leucolepis (White-bracted thoroughwort)

Fimbristylis puberula (Hairy fimbry)

Galactia regularis (Eastern milk-pea)

Galactia volubilis (Downy milk-pea)

Gentiana alba (Yellow gentian)

Gentiana catesbaei (Elliott's gentian)

Gentianopsis virgata (Lesser fringed gentian)

Gymnocarpium × *heterosporum* (Oak fern)

Gymnopogon ambiguus (Broad-leaved beardgrass)

Helianthus angustifolius (Swamp sunflower)

Hordeum pusillum (Little barley)

Hottonia inflata (American featherfoil)

Houstonia serpyllifolia (Creeping bluets)

Huperzia selago (Mountain clubmoss)

Hydrocotyle umbellata (Many-flowered pennywort)

Hypericum adpressum (Creeping St. John's-wort)

Hypericum crux-andreae (St. Peter's-wort)

Hypericum denticulatum (Coppery St. John's-wort)

Hypericum drummondii (Nits-and-lice)

Hypericum gymnanthum (Clasping-leaved St. John's-wort)

Ilex glabra (Ink-berry)

Itea virginica (Virginia willow)

Juncus greenei (Greene's rush)

Koeleria macrantha (Junegrass)

Leiophyllum buxifolium (Sand-myrtle)

Lemna obscura (Little water duckweed)

Lemna valdiviana (Pale duckweed)

Lespedeza stuevei (Tall bushclover)

Limosella australis (Awl-shaped mudwort)

Lobelia nuttallii (Nuttall's lobelia)

Ludwigia sphaerocarpa (Spherical-fruited seedbox)

Lycopodium sabinifolium (Fir clubmoss)

Micranthemum micranthemoides (Nuttall's mud-flower)

Muhlenbergia capillaris (Short muhly)

Onosmodium virginianum (Virginia false-gromwell)

Ophioglossum vulgatum (Southeastern adder's tongue)

Packera plattensis (Prairie ragwort)

Parthenium integrifolium (American fever-few)

Paspalum floridanum (Florida beadgrass)

Phoradendron leucarpum (Christmas mistletoe)

Piptochaetium avenaceum (Black oatgrass)

Platanthera cristata (Crested yellow orchid)

Platanthera leucophaea (Prairie white-fringed orchid)

Polygala lutea (Yellow milkwort)

Polygonum ramosissimum (Bushy knotweed)

Populus heterophylla (Swamp cottonwood)

Potamogeton alpinus (Northern pondweed)

Prenanthes racemosa (Glaucous rattlesnake-root)

Proserpinaca pectinata (Comb-leaved mermaid-weed)

Ptilimnium capillaceum (Mock bishop-weed)

Pycnanthemum verticillatum var. *pilosum* (Hairy mountain-mint)

Ranunculus flammula (Creeping spearwort)

Ranunculus hederaceus (Long-stalked crowfoot)

Ratibida pinnata (Prairie coneflower)

Rhododendron calendulaceum (Flame azalea)

Rhynchospora fusca (Brown beaked-rush)

Rhynchospora gracilenta (Beaked-rush)

Ruellia caroliniensis (Carolina petunia)

Rumex hastatulus (Heart sorrel)

Sabatia campanulata (Slender marsh pink)

Saccharum giganteum (Sugarcane plumegrass)

Sagittaria filiformis (Arrow-head)

Schoenoplectus heterochaetus (Slender bullrush)

Sisyrinchium albidum (Blue-eyed-grass)

Sisyrinchium fuscatum (Sand blue-eyed grass)

Smilax pseudochina (Long-stalked greenbrier)

Sparganium natans (Small bur-reed)

Spiraea virginiana (Virginia spiraea)

Spiranthes magnicamporum (Ladies'-tresses)

Spiranthes tuberosa (Slender ladies'-tresses)

Stachys hyssopifolia (Hyssop hedge-nettle)

Stuckenia filiformis ssp. filiformis (Threadleaf pondweed)

Trifolium reflexum (Buffalo clover)

Triglochin palustris (Marsh arrowgrass)

Utricularia gibba (Fibrous bladderwort)

Utricularia resupinata (Northeastern bladderwort)

Viola renifolia (Kidney-leaved white violet)

Viola tripartita (Three-parted violet)

ENDANGERED

Aconitum reclinatum (White monkshood)

Acorus americanus (Sweet flag)

Agalinis auriculata (Eared false-foxglove)

Agalinis paupercula (Small-flowered false foxglove)

Aletris farinosa (Colic-root)

Alisma triviale (Broad-leaved water plantain)

Alnus viridis (Mountain alder)

Amelanchier bartramiana (Oblong-fruited serviceberry)

Amelanchier humilis (Low serviceberry)

Amelanchier obovalis (Coastal Plain serviceberry)

Amelanchier sanguinea (Roundleaf serviceberry)

Anemone cylindrica (Long-fruited anemone)

Antennaria solitaria (Single-head pussytoes)

Arabis hirsuta (Hairy rock-cress)

Arabis missouriensis (Missouri rock-cress)

Arethusa bulbosa (Swamp-pink)

Arnica acaulis (Leopard's-bane)

Artemisia campestris (Beach wormwood)

Asclepias variegata (White milkweed)

Asplenium bradleyi (Bradley's spleenwort)

Asplenium resiliens (Black-stalked spleenwort)

Astragalus neglectus (Cooper's milk-vetch)

Bidens beckii (Beck's water-marigold)

Bidens bidentoides (Swamp beggar-ticks)

Boltonia asteroides (Aster-like boltonia)

Camassia scilloides (Wild hyacinth)

Carex atherodes (Awned sedge)

Carex aurea (Golden-fruited sedge)

Carex bebbii (Bebb's sedge)

Carex bicknellii (Bicknell's sedge)

Carex bullata (Bull sedge)

Carex careyana (Carey's sedge)

Carex crawfordii (Crawford's sedge)

Carex crinita (Short hair sedge)

Carex cryptolepis (Northeastern sedge)

Carex eburnea (Ebony sedge)

Carex formosa (Handsome sedge)

Carex garberi (Elk sedge)

Carex geyeri (Geyer's sedge)

Carex meadii (Mead's sedge)

Carex mitchelliana (Mitchell's sedge)

Carex pauciflora (Few-flowered sedge)

Carex pseudocyperus (Cyperus-like sedge)

Carex retrorsa (Backward sedge)

Carex richardsonii (Richardson's sedge)

Carex schweinitzii (Schweinitz's sedge)

Carex sterilis (Atlantic sedge)

Carex typhina (Cattail sedge)

Carex viridula (Green sedge)

Cerastium arvense ssp. velutinum (Mouse-ear chickweed)

Chasmanthium laxum (Slender sea-oats)

Chenopodium foggii (Fogg's goosefoot)

Chrysogonum virginianum (Green-and-gold)

Chrysopsis mariana (Maryland golden aster)

Cirsium horridulum (Horrible thistle)

Cladium mariscoides (Twig rush)

Clematis viorna (Vase-vine leather-flower)

Clethra acuminata (Mountain pepper-bush)

Clitoria mariana (Butterfly-pea)

Conioselinum chinense (Hemlock-parsley)

Corallorhiza wisteriana (Wister's coral-root)

Corydalis aurea (Golden corydalis)

Cryptogramma stelleri (Slender rock-brake)

Cymophyllus fraserianus (Fraser's sedge)

Cynanchum laeve (Smooth swallow-wort)

Cyperus diandrus (Umbrella flatsedge)

Cyperus houghtonii (Houghton's flatsedge)

Cyperus refractus (Reflexed flatsedge)

Cypripedium parviflorum (Small yellow lady's-slipper)

Cystopteris laurentiana (Laurentian bladder fern)

Dasiphora fruticosa ssp. floribunda (Shrubby cinquefoil)

Delphinium exaltatum (Tall larkspur)

Diarrhena obovata (American beakgrain)

Dicentra eximia (Wild bleeding-hearts)

Dichanthelium dichotomum var. dichotomum (Annulus panic-grass)

Panicum lucidum (Shining panic-grass)

Dichanthelium laxiflorum (Panic-
grass)
*Dichanthelium oligosanthes var.
scribnerianum* (Velvety panic-
grass)
*Dichanthelium sabulorum var.
patulum* (Panic-grass)
Dichanthelium spretum (Acuminate
dichanthelium)
Dichanthelium xanthophysum
(Slender panic-grass)
Dodecatheon meadia (Common
shooting-star)
Dryopteris campyloptera (Mountain
wood fern)
Dryopteris celsa (Log fern)
Echinochloa walteri (Walter's
barnyard-grass)
Elatine americana (Long-stemmed
water-wort)
Eleocharis compressa (Flat-stemmed
spike-rush)
Eleocharis elliptica (Slender spike-
rush)
Eleocharis geniculata (Capitate
spike-rush)
Eleocharis obtusa (Spike-rush)
Eleocharis parvula (Dwarf spike-
rush)
Eleocharis quadrangulata (Four-
angled spike-rush)
Eleocharis quinqueflora (Few-
flowered spike-rush)
Eleocharis rostellata (Beaked spike-
rush)
Eleocharis tenuis var. verrucosa
(Slender spike-rush)
Elephantopus carolinianus
(Elephant's foot)
Epilobium strictum (Downey willow-
herb)
Equisetum × ferrissii (Scouring
rush)
Equisetum variegatum (Variegated
horsetail)
Eriophorum gracile (Slender cotton-
grass)

Eriophorum tenellum (Rough cotton-
grass)
Euphorbia ipecacuanhae (Wild
ipecac)
Euphorbia purpurea (Glade spurge)
Euphorbia spathulata (Blunt-leaved
spurge)
Eurybia spectabilis (Low showy
aster)
Festuca paradoxa (Cluster fescue)
Frasera caroliniensis (American
columbo)
Fraxinus profunda (Pumpkin ash)
Galium labradoricum (Labrador
marsh bedstraw)
Gaylussacia brachycera (Box
huckleberry)
Gaylussacia dumosa (Dwarf
huckleberry)
Gentiana saponaria (Soapwort
gentian)
Gentiana villosa (Striped gentian)
Geranium bicknellii (Cranesbill)
Glyceria obtusa (Blunt manna-
grass)
Gratiola aurea (Golden-pert)
Gymnocarpium appalachianum
(Appalachian oak fern)
Helianthemum bicknellii (Bicknell's
hoary rockrose)
Heteranthera multiflora
(Multiflowered mud-plantain)
Hieracium greenii (Maryland
hawkweed)
Hierochloe odorata (Vanilla sweet-
grass)
Huperzia porophila (Rock clubmoss)
Hydrophyllum macrophyllum
(Large-leafed water-leaf)
Iodanthus pinnatifidus (Purple
rocket)
Iris cristata (Crested dwarf iris)
Iris prismatica (Slender blue iris)
Iris verna (Dwarf iris)
Iris virginica (Virginia blue flag)
Isotria medeoloides (Small-whorled
pogonia)

Juncus brachycarpus (Short-fruited rush)
Juncus dichotomus (Forked rush)
Juncus militaris (Bayonet rush)
Juncus scirpoides (Scirpus-like rush)
Juncus torreyi (Torrey's rush)
Lathyrus palustris (Marsh pea)
Lespedeza angustifolia (Narrowleaf bush clover)
Ligusticum canadense (Lovage)
Linum intercursum (Sandplain wild flax)
Linum sulcatum (Grooved yellow flax)
Lipocarpha micrantha (Common hemicarpa)
Listera australis (Southern twayblade)
Listera cordata (Heart-leaved twayblade)
Listera smallii (Kidney-leaved twayblade)
Lithospermum caroliniense (Hispid gromwell)
Lithospermum latifolium (American gromwell)
Lobelia kalmii (Brook lobelia)
Lobelia puberula (Downy lobelia)
Lonicera hirsuta (Hairy honeysuckle)
Lonicera oblongifolia (Swamp fly honeysuckle)
Lonicera villosa (Mountain fly honeysuckle)
Ludwigia decurrens (Upright primrose-willow)
Ludwigia polycarpa (False loosestrife seedbox)
Luzula bulbosa (Wood-rush)
Lycopodiella alopecuroides (Foxtail clubmoss)
Lycopus rubellus (Taper-leaved bugle-weed)
Lyonia mariana (Stagger-bush)
Lythrum alatum (Winged loosestrife)

Malaxis brachypoda (White adder's-mouth)
Marshallia grandiflora (Large-flowered marshallia)
Matelea obliqua (Oblique milkvine)
Meehania cordata (Heart-leafed meehania)
Mitella nuda (Naked bishop's-cap)
Monarda punctata (Spotted bee-balm)
Montia chamissoi (Chamisso's miner's-lettuce)
Muhlenbergia uniflora (False dropseed muhly)
Myriophyllum farwellii (Farwell's water-milfoil)
Myriophyllum heterophyllum (Broad-leaved water-milfoil)
Myriophyllum sibiricum (Northern water-milfoil)
Myriophyllum verticillatum (Whorled water-milfoil)
Najas marina (Holly-leaved naiad)
Nelumbo lutea (American lotus)
Oclemena nemoralis (Bog aster)
Oligoneuron rigidum var. rigidum (Stiff goldenrod)
Onosmodium bejariense var. hispidissimum (False gromwell)
Ophioglossum engelmannii (Limestone adder's-tongue)
Packera antennariifolia (Cat's-paw ragwort)
Panicum amarum var. amarulum (Southern sea-beach panic-grass)
Parnassia glauca (Carolina grass-of-parnassus)
Paronychia fastigiata var. nuttallii (Forked chickweed)
Passiflora lutea (Passion-flower)
Paxistima canbyi (Canby's mountain-lover)
Pedicularis lanceolata (Swamp lousewort)
Phlox latifolia (Mountain phlox)
Phlox pilosa (Downy phlox)

Phlox subulata ssp. brittonii (Moss pink)

Phyllanthus caroliniensis (Carolina leaf-flower)

Physalis virginiana (Virginia ground-cherry)

Piptatherum pungens (Slender mountain-ricegrass)

Platanthera dilatata (Leafy white orchid)

Platanthera hookeri (Hooker's orchid)

Platanthera hyperborea (Leafy northern green orchid)

Pluchea odorata (Shrubby camphor-weed)

Poa autumnalis (Autumn bluegrass)

Polemonium vanbruntiae (Jacob's-ladder)

Polygala cruciata (Cross-leaved milkwort)

Polygala curtissii (Curtis's milkwort)

Polygala incarnata (Pink milkwort)

Polygala polygama (Bitter milkwort)

Polygonella articulata (Eastern jointweed)

Polygonum careyi (Carey's smartweed)

Polygonum setaceum (Swamp smartweed)

Polystichum braunii (Braun's holly fern)

Populus balsamifera (Balsam poplar)

Potamogeton friesii (Fries' pondweed)

Potamogeton gramineus (Grassy pondweed)

Potamogeton hillii (Hill's pondweed)

Potamogeton oakesianus (Oakes' pondweed)

Potamogeton obtusifolius (Blunt-leaved pondweed)

Potamogeton praelongus (White-stemmed pondweed)

Potamogeton pulcher (Spotted pondweed)

Potamogeton strictifolius (Narrow-leaved pondweed)

Potamogeton tennesseensis (Tennessee pondweed)

Potamogeton vaseyi (Vasey's pondweed)

Potentilla paradoxa (Bushy cinquefoil)

Prenanthes crepidinea (Rattlesnake-root)

Prunus maritima (Beach plum)

Pycnanthemum pycnanthemoides (Southern mountain-mint)

Pycnanthemum torrei (Torrey's mountain-mint)

Quercus falcata (Southern red oak)

Quercus phellos (Willow oak)

Quercus shumardii (Shumard's oak)

Ranunculus fascicularis (Tufted buttercup)

Ranunculus pusillus (Low spearwort)

Rhamnus lanceolata (Lanceolate buckthorn)

Rhexia mariana (Maryland meadow-beauty)

Rhodiola rosea (Roseroot stonecrop)

Rhododendron atlanticum (Dwarf azalea)

Rhynchospora capillacea (Capillary beaked-rush)

Ribes lacustre (Bristly black currant)

Ribes missouriense (Missouri gooseberry)

Rubus cuneifolius (Sand blackberry)

Ruellia humilis (Fringed-leaved petunia)

Sagittaria calycina var. spongiosa (Long-lobed arrow-head)

Salix candida (Hoary willow)

Salix caroliniana (Carolina willow)

Salix pedicellaris (Bog-willow)

Salix petiolaris (Slender willow)

Samolus valerandi ssp. parviflorus (Pineland pimpernel)

Scheuchzeria palustris (Pod-grass)

Schoenoplectus acutus var. acutus (Hard-stemmed bullrush)

Schoenoplectus smithii (Smith's bullrush)

Schoenoplectus torreyi (Torrey's bullrush)

Scleria minor (Minor nutrush)

Scleria reticularis (Reticulated nutrush)

Scleria verticillata (Whorled nutrush)

Scutellaria saxatilis (Rock skullcap)

Scutellaria serrata (Showy skullcap)

Sericocarpus linifolius (Narrow-leaved white-topped aster)

Shepherdia canadensis (Canada buffalo-berry)

Sibbaldiopsis tridentata (Three-toothed cinquefoil)

Sida hermaphrodita (Sida)

Sisyrinchium atlanticum (Eastern blue-eyed grass)

Solidago arguta (Harris' goldenrod)

Solidago curtisii (Curtis' goldenrod)

Solidago erecta (Slender goldenrod)

Solidago simplex ssp. randii var. racemosa (Sticky goldenrod)

Sorbus decora (Showy mountain-ash)

Sparganium androcladum (Branching bur-reed)

Spiranthes casei (Case's ladies'-tresses)

Spiranthes ovalis (October ladies'-tresses)

Spiranthes romanzoffiana (Hooded ladies'-tresses)

Spiranthes vernalis (Spring ladies'-tresses)

Sporobolus clandestinus (Rough dropseed)

Sporobolus heterolepis (Prairie dropseed)

Stachys cordata (Nuttall's hedge-nettle)

Streptopus amplexifolius (White twisted-stalk)

Stylosanthes biflora (Pencil-flower)

Symphyotrichum boreale (Rush aster)

Taenidia montana (Mountain pimpernel)

Thalictrum coriaceum (Thick-leaved meadow-rue)

Tradescantia ohiensis (Ohio spiderwort)

Trichostema setaceum (Blue-curls)

Trifolium virginicum (Kate's mountain clover)

Triosteum angustifolium (Horse-gentian)

Triphora trianthophora (Nodding pogonia)

Triplasis purpurea (Purple sandgrass)

Tripsacum dactyloides (Gamma grass)

Trisetum spicatum (Narrow false oats)

Trollius laxus (Spreading globe flower)

Utricularia radiata (Floating bladderwort)

Vernonia glauca (Tawny ironweed)

Viburnum nudum (Possum haw viburnum)

Viola brittoniana (Coast violet)

Viola pedatifida (Prairie violet)

Vitis cinerea var. baileyana (Possum grape)

Vitis × novae-angliae (New England grape)

Vitis rupestris (Sand grape)

Zigadenus elegans ssp. glaucus (Death-camas)

THREATENED

Aconitum uncinatum (Blue
monkshood)
Ammannia coccinea (Scarlet
ammannia)
Ammophila breviligulata (America
beachgrass)
Arceuthobium pusillum (Dwarf
mistletoe)
Argentina anserina (Silverweed)
Aristida purpurascens (Arrow
feather)
Bouteloua curtipendula (Tall
gramma)
Carex alata (Broadwinged sedge)
Carex aquatilis (Water sedge)
Carex collinsii (Collin's sedge)
Carex diandra (Lesser pinacled
sedge)
Carex flava (Yellow sedge)
Carex limosa (Mud sedge)
Carex oligosperma (Few seeded
sedge)
Carex polymorpha (Variable sedge)
Carex prairea (Prairie sedge)
Carex tetanica (Wood's sedge)
Carex wiegandii (Wiegand's sedge)
Chamaesyce polygonifolia (Small
sea-side spurge)
Cypripedium reginae (Showy lady's-
slipper)
Digitaria cognata (Fall witchgrass)
Dodecatheon amethystinum
(Jeweled shooting-star)
Dryopteris clintoniana (Clinton's
shield fern)
Eleocharis intermedia (Matted
spike-rush)
Eleocharis robbinsii (Robin's spike-
rush)
Ellisia nyctelea (Ellisia)
Erigenia bulbosa (Harbinger-of-
spring)
Eriophorum viridicarinatum (Thin-
leaved cotton-grass)

Eubotrys racemosa (Swamp dog-
hobble)
Euthamia caroliniana (Grass-leaved
goldenrod)
Fimbristylis annua (Annual fimbry)
Glyceria borealis (Small-floating
manna-grass)
Goodyera tesselata (Checkered
rattlesname-plantain)
Hypericum densiflorum (Bushy St.
John's-wort)
Hypericum majus (Larger Canadian
St. John's-wort)
Ilex opaca (American holly)
Juncus alpinoarticulatus ssp.
nodulosus (Richardson's rush)
Juncus arcticus ssp. littoralis (Baltic
rush)
Juncus biflorus (Grass-leaved rush)
Juncus brachycephalus (Small-
headed rush)
Lathyrus japonicus (Beach peavine)
Lathyrus ochroleucus (Wild-pea)
Linnaea borealis (Twinflower)
Lobelia dortmanna (Water lobelia)
Lycopodiella appressa (Southern bog
clubmoss)
Lysimachia hybrida (Lance-leaved
loosestrife)
Magnolia virginiana (Sweet bay
magnolia)
Melica nitens (Three-flowered
meltic-grass)
Minuartia glabra (Applachian
sandwort)
Myrica gale (Sweet bayberry)
Myriophyllum tenellum (Slender
water-milfoil)
Najas gracillima (Bushy naiad)
Nymphoides cordata (Floating-
heart)
Oenothera argillicola (Shale-barren
evening-primrose)

Panicum philadelphicum
(Tuckerman's panicgrass)
Phemeranthus teretifolius (Round-leaved fame-flower)
Platanthera ciliaris (Yellow fringed-orchid)
Platanthera peramoena (Purple fringeless orchid)
Poa paludigena (Bog bluegrass)
Poa saltuensis (Woodland bluegrass)
Potamogeton confervoides
(Tuckerman's pondweed)
Potamogeton richardsonii (Red-head pondweed)
Prunus alleghaniensis (Allegheny plum)
Ptelea trifoliata (Common hop-tree)
Ranunculus longirostris (Eastern white water-crowfoot)
Ribes triste (Red currant)
Ruellia strepens (Limestone petunia)
Salix serissima (Autumn willow)

Scirpus ancistrochaetus
(Northeastern bullrush)
Scirpus pedicellatus (Stalked bullrush)
Scleria pauciflora (Few-flowered nutrush)
Spiraea betulifolia (Dwarf spiraea)
Symphyotrichum depauperatum
(Serpentine aster)
Symphyotrichum novi-belgii (Long-leaved aster)
Symphyotrichum puniceum (Shining aster)
Utricularia intermedia (Flat-leaved bladderwort)
Utricularia minor (Lesser bladderwort)
Vittaria appalachiana (Appalachian gametophyte fern)
Woodwardia areolata (Netted chain fern)
Xyris (Yellow-eyed-grass)

VULNERABLE

Cypripedium parviflorumvar.
pubescens (Large yellow lady's slipper)

Hydrastis canadensis (Goldenseal)
Panax quinquefolius (Ginseng)

RARE

Actaea podocarpa (Mountain bugbane)
Amaranthus cannabinus
(Waterhemp ragweed)
Andromeda polifolia (Bog-rosemary)
Antennaria virginica (Shale-barren pussytoes)
Aplectrum hyemale (Puttyroot)
Asplenium pinnatifidum (Lobed spleenwort)
Baccharis halimifolia (Eastern baccharis)
Cakile edentula (American sea-rocket)

Carex buxbaumii (Brown sedge)
Carex disperma (Soft-leaved sedge)
Carex lasiocarpa (Slender sedge)
Carex magellanica (Bog sedge)
Cyperus odoratus (Engelmann's flatsedge)
Cyperus schweinitzii (Schweinitz's flatsedge)
Elatine minima (Small waterwort)
Eleocharis olivacea (Capitate spike-rush)
Gaultheria hispidula (Creeping snowberry)

Hylotelephium telephioides
(Allegheny stonecrop)
Juncus filiformis (Thread rush)
Juncus gymnocarpus (Coville's rush)
Ledum groenlandicum (Common
labrador-tea)
Lupinus perennis (Wild blue lupine)
Lygodium palmatum (Hartford fern)
Magnolia tripetala (Umbrella
magnolia)
Malaxis bayardii (Bayard's malaxis)
Menziesia pilosa (Minniebush)
Opuntia humifusa (Prickly-pear
cactus)
Orontium aquaticum (Golden club)
Packera anonyma (Plain ragwort)
Phyla lanceolata (Fog-fruit)
Potamogeton illinoensis (Illinois
pondweed)
Potamogeton robbinsii (Flat-leaved
pondweed)
Potamogeton zosteriformis (Flat-
stem pondweed)
Prunus pumila (Sand cherry)
Pyrularia pubera (Buffalo nut)
Ranunculus trichophyllus (White
water-crowfoot)

Rotala ramosior (Tooth-cup)
Sagittaria subulata (Subulate
arrow-head)
Saxifraga micranthidifolia (Lettice
saxofrage)
Schizachyrium littorale var. littorale
(Seaside bluestem)
Schoenoplectus fluviatilis (River
bullrush)
Solidago roanensis (Tennessee
golden-rod)
Sporobolus cryptandrus (Sand
dropseed)
Tipularia discolor (Crainfly orchid)
Trautvetteria caroliniensis (Carolina
tassel-rue)
Trillium nivale (Snow trillium)
Utricularia purpurea (Purple
bladderwort)
Uvularia puberula (Mountain
bellwort)
Viburnum opulus var. americanum
(Highbush cranberry)
Wolffiella gladiata (Bog mat)
Xyris montana (Yellow-eyed grass)
Zizania aquatica (Indian wild rice)

APPENDIX: INVASIVE, NOXIOUS PLANTS

Source: Pennsylvania Department of Conservation and Natural Resources. For a more extensive list of invasive species, contact DCNR, Bureau of Forestry, P.O. Box 8552, Harrisburg, Pennsylvania 17105-8552)

* An asterisk (*) denotes that a species has cultivars that are not known to be invasive. Cultivars are cultivated varieties of plant species bred for predictable attributes like shorter height, showier flowers, or colored foliage. An example is Norway Maple 'Crimson King' grown for its reddish leaves; this cultivar is not known to be invasive. If you choose to plant a cultivar of an invasive species, ask a professional horticulturist about the cultivar's potential to be invasive.

HERBACEOUS PLANTS

Aegopodium podagraria (Goutweed) – Commonly planted in the past and escaped; spreads aggressively by roots

Alliaria petiolata (Garlic mustard) – Invasive in many states; spreading aggressively in woodlands by seed

Carduus nutans (Musk thistle) – Pennsylvania noxious weed

Cirsium arvense (Canada thistle) – Pennsylvania noxious weed

Cirsium vulgare (Bull thistle) – Pennsylvania noxious weed

Datura stramonium (Jimsonweed) – Sometimes cultivated; spreads by seed, Pennsylvania noxious weed

Galega officinalis (Goatsrue) – Pennsylvania and Federal noxious weed

Heracleum mantegazzianum (Giant hogweed) – Pennsylvania and federal noxious weed, sap can cause burning blisters

Hesperis matronalis (Dame's rocket) – Planted in gardens; escaped and naturalized along roads; spreads by seed

Lythrum salicaria, L. virgatum (Purple loosestife) – Garden escape which has become invasive in many states; Pennsylvania noxious weed

Myriophyllum spicatum (Eurasian water-milfoil) – Invasive in many states; aquatic

Ornithogallum nutans, umbellatum (Star-of-Bethlehem) – Common garden plant which has widely escaped

Pastinaca sativa (Wild parsnip) – Found commonly along roadsides; widespread and abundant; spread by seed

Perilla frutescens (Beefsteak plant) – Garden escape; widespread mostly along roadsides; spread by seed

Polygonum (Falopia) cuspidatum (Japanese knotweed) – Invasive in many states; difficult to control; spreads by roots and seeds

Ranunculus ficaria (Lesser celandine) – Spreads by roots and shoots; can be very aggressive in wetlands

Trapa natans (Water chestnut) – Wetland plant; should not be introduced as it will escape, spread, and naturalize

Grasses

Bromus tectorum (Cheatgrass) – Annual grass; invasive throughout the west; spreads by seed

Microstegium vimineum (Japanese stilt grass) – Annual grass; invasive in many states; spreading through woodlands by seed

* *Miscanthus sinensis* (Maiden grass) – Commonly planted ornamental grass which can escape and spread by seed

Phalaris arundinacea (Reed canary grass) – Aggressive wetland grass; native and introduced strains; widespread and abundant

Phragmites australis (Common reed) – Native and introduced strains; wetland grass which can form huge colonies

Sorghum bicolor ssp. drummondii (Shattercane) – Pennsylvania noxious weed

Sorghum halepense Johnson grass) – Pennsylvania noxious weed; spreads by roots and seeds

Shrubs

* *Berberis thunbergii* (Japanese barberry) – Escaped from cultivation and invasive in many states; spread by birds

Berberis vulgaris (European barberry) – Escaped from cultivation; spread by birds

Elaegnus angustifolia (Russian olive) – Escaped from plantings and invasive in many states; spread by birds

Elaeagnus umbellata (Autumn olive) – Escaped from plantings and invasive in many states; rapidly spread by birds

* *Euonymus alatus* (Winged Euonymus) – Escaped from plantings; invasive in moist forests

Ligustrum obtusifolium (Border privet) – Escaped from cultivation; seeds spread by birds

Ligustrum vulgare (Common privet) – Planted very commonly in the past and escaped; invasive in many states

Lonicera maackii (Amur honeysuckle) – Escaped from plantings; seeds spread by birds

Lonicera morrowii (Morrow's honeysuckle) – Escaped from plantings and invasive in many states; seeds spread by birds

Lonicera morrowii x tatarica (Bell's honeysuckle) – Escaped from cultivation

Lonicera standishii (Standish honeysuckle) – Escaped from plantings; seeds spread by birds

Lonicera tartarica (Tartarian honeysuckle) – Escaped from plantings; seeds spread by birds

Rhamnus catharticus (Common buckthorn) – Becoming a problem in Pennsylvania

Rhamnus frangula (Glossy buckthorn) – Becoming a problem in Pennsylvania

Rubus phoenicolasius (Wineberry) – Common bramble; not cultivated; spread by seed

Rosa multiflora (Multiflora rose) – Invasive in many states; seeds spread by birds; Pennsylvania noxious weed

* *Spiraea japonica* (Japanese spiraea) – Frequently planted; escaped in some areas

* *Viburnum opulus var. opulus* (Guelder rose) – Resembles native Viburnum trilobum which it replaces; both are cultivated and planted

TREES

* *Acer platanoides* (Norway maple) – Commonly planted and escaped; invasive in many states; wind spreads prolific seeds

Acer pseudoplatanus (Sycamore maple) – Escaped from cultivation; wind spreads prolific seeds

Ailanthus altissima (Tree-of-heaven) – Invasive in many states; wind spreads prolific seeds

Paulownia tomentosa (Princess tree) – Prolific seeds fall to start new seedlings

* *Pyrus calleryana* (Callery pear) – Commonly planted street tree; becoming a problem as an escape

Ulmus pumila (Siberian elm) – Escaped from cultivation

VINES

Akebia quinata (Fiveleaf akebia) – Escaped from cultivation

Ampelopsis brevipedunculata (Porcelain-berry) – Escaped from cultivation

Celastrus orbiculatus (Oriental bittersweet) – Escaped from cultivation and invasive in many states; spreading rapidly (by birds)

Lonicera japonica (Japanese honeysuckle) – Invasive in many states

Polygonum perfoliatum (Mile-a-minute vine) – Range expanding; Pennsylvania noxious weed

Pueraria lobata (Kudzu) – Invasive in many states; Pennsylvania noxious weed

APPENDIX: ANNUALS

Although this book focuses on native perennials, a considerable number of annuals are commercially available, generally as seed, for landscaping purposes. Many more are not reported as available on a national search. These lists identify both, all of which include Pennsylvania in their continenal range.

COMMERCIALLY AVAILABLE

Agalinis purpurea (False-foxglove)
Agalinis tenuifolia (Slender false-foxglove)
Amaranthus albus (Tumbleweed)
Ambrosia artemisiifolia (Common ragweed)
Ambrosia trifida (Giant ragweed)
Amphicarpaea bracteata (Hog peanut)
Atriplex patula (Spreading orach)
Aureolaria pedicularia (Cut-leaf false-foxglove)
Bidens cernua (Bur-marigold)
Bidens frondosa (Beggar-ticks)
Blephilia hirsuta (Wood-mint)
Cakile edentula (American sea-rocket)
Campanula americana (Tall bellflower)
Castillea coccinea (Indian paintbrush)
Chamaecrista fasciculata (Partridge-pea)
Chenopodium capitatum (Indian-paint)
Conyza canadensis var. canadensis (Horseweed)
Crotalaria sagittalis (Rattlebox)
Crotalaria sagittalis (Rattlebox)
Cuscuta pentagona (Field dodder)
Cyperus erythrorhizos (Redroot flatsedge)
Dracocephalum parviflorum (Dragonhead)

Echinochloa muricata (Barnyard-grass)
Echinocystis lobata (Prickly cucumber)
Galium aparine (Bedstraw)
Gaura biennis (Gaura)
Gentianella quinquefolia (Stiff gentian)
Gentianopsis crinita (Eastern fringed gentian)
Geranium robertianum (Herb-robert)
Gnaphalium obtusifolium (Fragrant cudweed)
Hedeoma pulegioides (American pennyroyal)
Impatiens capensis (Jewelweed)
Impatiens pallida (Pale jewelweed)
Juncus bufonius (Toad rush)
Lactuca canadensis var. canadensis (Wild lettuce)
Lactuca floridana (Woodland lettuce)
Linum sulcatum (Grooved yellow flax)
Lobelia inflata (Indian-tobacco)
Myosotis laxa (Wild forget-me-not)
Oenothera laciniata (Cut-leaved evening-primrose)
Panicum capillare (Witchgrass)
Panicum dichotomiflorum (Smooth panic grass)
Phacelia purshii (Miami-mist)
Polanisia dodecandra ssp. dodecandra (Clammyweed)

Polygonum arifolium (Halberd-leaf tearthumb)
Polygonum pensylvanicum (Smartweed)
Polygonum punctatum var. confertiflorum (Dotted smartweed)
Polygonum sagittatum (Tearthumb)
Portulaca oleracea (Purslane)
Ranunculus abortivus var. abortivus (Small-flowered crowfoot)
Ranunculus abortivus var. eucyclus (Small-flowered crowfoot)
Ranunculus pensylvanicus (Bristly crowfoot)
Sabatia angularis (Common marsh-pink)
Salvia reflexa (Lance-leaved sage)

Sicyos angulatus (Bur cucumber)
Strophostyles helvola (Wild bean)
Trichostema dichotomum (Blue-curls)
Triodanis perfoliata var. perfoliata (Venus's looking-glass)
Utricularia gibba (Humped bladderwort)
Utricularia subulata (Slender bladderwort)
Verbena urticifolia (White vervain)
Viola bicolor (Field pansy)
Vulpia octoflora var. glauca (Six-weeks fescue)
Xanthium strumarium (Common cocklebur)
Zizania aquatica (Wild-rice)

APPARENTLY UNAVAILABLE ANNUALS

A alypha deamii (Three-seeded mercury)
Acalypha gracilens (Slender mercury)
Acalypha rhomboidea (Three-seeded mercury)
Acalypha virginica (Three-seeded mercury)
Adlumia fungosa (Allegheny vine)
Aeschynomene virginica (Sensitive joint-vetch)
Agalinis auriculata (Eared false-foxglove)
Agalinis decemloba (Blue Ridge false-foxglove)
Agalinis paupercula (Small-flowered false-foxglove)
Alopecurus carolinianus (Carolina foxtail)
Amaranthus cannabinus (Salt-marsh water-hemp)

Amaranthus pumilus (Seabeach amaranth)
Ammannia coccinea (Tooth cup)
Arabis canadensis (Sicklepod)
Arabis laevigata var. burkii (Smooth rockcress)
Arabis lyrata (Lyre-leaved rockcress)
Arabis missouriensis (Missouri rockcress)
Aristida dichotoma var. curtissii (Povertygrass)
Aristida dichotoma var. dichotoma (Povertygrass)
Aristida longispica var. geniculata (Slender threeawn)
Aristida longispica var. longispica (Slender threeawn)
Aristida oligantha (Prairie threeawn)
Atriplex littoralis (Seashore orach)
Atriplex prostrata (Halberd-leaved orach)

Atriplex prostrata (Halberd-leaved orach)
Bartonia paniculata (Screwstem)
Bartonia paniculata (Screwstem)
Bartonia virginica (Bartonia)
Bidens bidentoides (Swamp beggarticks)
Bidens bipinnata (Spanish needles)
Bidens comosa (Beggar-ticks)
Bidens connata (Beggar-ticks)
Bidens discoidea (Small beggarticks)
Bidens laevis (Showy bur-marigold)
Bidens vulgata (Beggar-ticks)
Bulbostylis capillaris (Sandrush)
Callitriche terrestris (Waterstarwort)
Cardamine parviflora var. arenicola (Small-flowered bittercress)
Cardamine pensylvanica (Pennsylvania bittercress)
Cenchrus longispinus (Sandbur)
Cerastium nutans (Nodding chickweed)
Chaerophyllum procumbens (Slender chervil)
Chamaecrista nictitans (Wild sensitive-plant)
Chamaecrista nictitans (Wild sensitive-plant)
Chamaesyce maculata (Spotted spurge)
Chamaesyce nutans (Eyebane)
Chamaesyce polygonifolia (Seaside spurge)
Chamaesyce vermiculata (Hairy spurge)
Chenopodium album var. missouriense (Lamb's quarters)
Chenopodium bushianum (Pigweed)
Chenopodium foggii (Goosefoot)
Chenopodium simplex (Mapleleaved goosefoot)
Chenopodium standleyanum (Woodland goosefoot)
Collinsia verna (Blue-eyed-Mary)

Crassula aquatica (Waterpigmyweed)
Critesion pusillum (Little-barley)
Croton capitatus (Hogwort)
Crotonopsis elliptica (Elliptical rushfoil)
Cuphea viscosissima (Blue waxweed)
Cuphea viscosissima (Blue waxweed)
Cuscuta campestris (Dodder)
Cuscuta cephalanthii (Buttonbush dodder)
Cuscuta cephalanthii (Buttonbush dodder)
Cuscuta compacta (Dodder)
Cuscuta corylii (Hazel dodder)
Cuscuta gronovii var. gronovii (Common dodder)
Cuscuta gronovii var. gronovii (Common dodder)
Cuscuta gronovii var. latiflora (Dodder)
Cuscuta polygonorum (Smartweed dodder)
Cynoglossum boreale (Northern hound's-tongue)
Cyperus acuminatus (Short-pointed flatsedge)
Cyperus bipartitus (Umbrella sedge)
Cyperus compressus (Umbrella sedge)
Cyperus diandrus (Umbrella sedge)
Cyperus engelmannii (Engelmann's flatsedge)
Cyperus filicinus (Umbrella sedge)
Cyperus flavescens (Umbrella sedge)
Cyperus odoratus (Umbrella sedge)
Cyperus polystachyos var. texensis (Many-spiked flatsedge)
Cyperus squarrosus (Umbrella sedge)
Cyperus tenuifolius (Thin-leaved flatsedge)
Digitaria filiformis (Slender crabgrass)

Digitaria serotina (Dwarf crabgrass)
Diodia teres (Rough buttonweed)
Draba reptans (Whitlow-grass)
Echinochloa walteri (Walter's barnyard-grass)
Eclipta prostrata (Yerba-de-tajo)
Elatine americana (American waterwort)
Elatine minima (Small waterwort)
Eleocharis caribaea (Spike-rush)
Eleocharis engelmannii (Spike-rush)
Eleocharis intermedia (Matted spike-rush)
Eleocharis microcarpa (Spike-rush)
Eleocharis obtusa var. obtusa (Wright's spike-rush)
Eleocharis obtusa var. peasei (Spike-rush)
Ellisia nyctelea (Waterpod)
Epifagus virginiana (Beechdrops)
Eragrostis capillaris (Lacegrass)
Eragrostis frankii (Lovegrass)
Eragrostis hypnoides (Creeping lovegrass)
Eragrostis pectinacea (Carolina lovegrass)
Erechtites hieraciifolia (Fireweed)
Erechtites hieraciifolia (Fireweed)
Erigeron annuus (Daisy fleabane)
Erigeron strigosus var. beyrichii (Daisy fleabane)
Erigeron strigosus var. strigosus (Daisy fleabane)
Euphorbia commutata (Wood spurge)
Euphorbia obtusata (Blunt-leaved spurge)
Fimbristylis annua (Annual fimbry)
Fimbristylis autumnalis (Slender fimbry)
Floerkea proserpinacoides (False-mermaid)
Gentianopsis virgata (Narrow-leaved fringed gentian)
Geranium bicknellii (Cranesbill)

Geranium carolinianum (Wild geranium)
Gnaphalium macounii (Fragrant cudweed)
Gnaphalium purpureum var. purpureum (Purple cudweed)
Gnaphalium uliginosum (Low cudweed)
Gratiola neglecta (Hedge hyssop)
Hackelia virginiana (Beggar's-lice)
Hedeoma pulegioides (American pennyroyal)
Hypericum canadense (Canadian St.John's-wort)
Hypericum dissimulatum (St. John's-wort)
Hypericum drummondii (Nits-and-lice)
Hypericum gentianoides (Orange-grass)
Hypericum gymnanthum (Clasping-leaved St. John's-wort)
Hypericum majus (Canadian St. John's-wort)
Ipomoea lacunosa (White morning-glory
Krigia virginica (Dwarf dandelion)
Lactuca biennis (Blue lettuce)
Lactuca biennis (Blue lettuce)
Lactuca canadensis var. latifolia (Wild lettuce)
Lactuca canadensis var. longifolia (Wild lettuce)
Lactuca canadensis var. obovata (Wild lettuce)
Lactuca floridana var. villosa (Woodland lettuce)
Lactuca hirsuta var. hirsuta (Downy lettuce)
Lactuca hirsuta var. sanguinea (Downy lettuce)
Lemna valdiviana (Pale duckweed)
Lepidium virginicum (Poor-man's-pepper)
Leptochloa fascicularis var. maritima (Sprangletop)

Limosella australis (Awl-shaped mudwort)

Linaria canadensis (Old-field toadflax)

Lindernia dubia var. anagallidea (False pimpernel)

Lindernia dubia var. dubia (False pimpernel)

Lindernia dubia var. inundata (False pimpernel)

Lipocarpha micrantha (Common hemicarpa)

Melampyrum lineare var. pectinatum (Cow-wheat)

Micranthemum micranthemoides (Nuttall's mud-flower)

Minuartia glabra (Appalachian sandwort)

Minuartia michauxii (Rock sandwort)

Minuartia patula (Sandwort)

Myosotis macrosperma (Big-seed scorpion-grass)

Myosotis verna (Spring forget-me-not)

Najas flexilis (Northern waternymph)

Najas gracillima (Slender waternymph)

Najas guadalupensis (Southern waternymph)

Najas marina (Holly-leaved naiad)

Panicum flexile (Old witchgrass)

Panicum gattingeri (Witchgrass)

Panicum philadelphicum (Panic grass)

Panicum tuckermanii (Tuckerman's panic grass)

Panicum verrucosum (Panic grass)

Parietaria pensylvanica (Pellitory)

Paronychia canadensis (Forked chickweed)

Paronychia fastigiata var. fastigiata (Whitlow-wort)

Paronychia fastigiata var. nuttallii (Whitlow-wort)

Paronychia montana (Forked chickweed)

Phacelia dubia (Scorpion-weed)

Phyllanthus caroliniensis ssp. caroliniensis (Carolina leaf-flower)

Physalis pubescens var. integrifolia (Hairy ground-cherry)

Pilea fontana (Lesser clearweed)

Pilea pumila (Clearweed)

Plantago pusilla (Dwarf plantain)

Plantago virginica (Dwarf plantain)

Pluchea odorata (Marsh fleabane)

Poinsettia dentata (Spurge)

Polygala cruciata (Cross-leaved milkwort)

Polygala curtissii (Curtis's milkwort)

Polygala incarnata (Pink milkwort)

Polygala nuttallii (Nuttall's milkwort)

Polygala polygama (Bitter milkwort)

Polygala sanguinea (Field milkwort)

Polygala verticillata var. ambigua (Whorled milkwort)

Polygala verticillata var. isocycla (Whorled milkwort)

Polygala verticillata var. verticillata (Whorled milkwort)

Polygonella articulata (Jointweed)

Polygonum achoreum (Homeless knotweed)

Polygonum buxiforme (Knotweed)

Polygonum careyi (Pinkweed)

Polygonum erectum (Erect knotweed)

Polygonum ramosissimum (Knotweed)

Polygonum tenue (Slender knotweed)

Potentilla norvegica ssp. monspeliensis (Strawberry-weed)

Potentilla paradoxa (Bushy cinquefoil)

Ranunculus allegheniensis
(Allegheny crowfoot)
Ranunculus pusillus (Low
spearwort)
Rorippa palustris ssp. fernaldiana
(Marsh watercress)
Rorippa palustris ssp. hispida
(Marsh watercress)
Rorippa palustris ssp. palustris
(Marsh watercress)
Rotala ramosior (Tooth cup)
Sagina decumbens (Pearlwort)
Sagittaria calycina (Long-lobed
arrowhead)
Sanicula canadensis (Canadian
sanicle)
Schoenoplectus purshianus
(Bulrush)
Scleria muhlenbergii (Reticulated
nut-rush)
Scleria verticillata (Whorled nut-
rush)
Silene antirrhina (Sleepy catchfly)
Solanum americanum (Black
nightshade)
Sporobolus neglectus (Small
rushgrass)

Sporobolus vaginiflorus (Poverty
grass)
Stachys tenuifolia (Creeping hedge-
nettle)
Symphyotrichum subulatum (Salt-
marsh aster)
*Trichophorum planifolium
Trichophorum planifolium*
(Blue-curls)
Trichostema setaceum (Narrow-
leaved blue-curls)
Trifolium reflexum (Buffalo clover)
Triplasis purpurea (Purple
sandgrass)
Utricularia inflata (Inflated
bladderwort)
Utricularia radiata (Floating
bladderwort)
Valerianella umbilicata (Corn-
salad)
Veronica peregrina ssp. peregrina
(Neckweed)
Veronica peregrina ssp. xalapensis
(Neckweed)

INDEX

www.ingramcontent.com/pod-product-compliance
Lightning Source LLC
LaVergne TN
LVHW051516080426
835509LV00017B/2078